To Karen

Blessings!

Father of the Man:

*A Journey Toward
Reconciliation*

Peter L. Colman

by

Peter L. Colman

Father of the Man: A Journey Toward Reconciliation
Copyright © 2008 by Peter L. Colman
ISBN: 978-1-59352-409-8
Published by Christian Services Network/CSN Books
1975 Janich Ranch Court
El Cajon, CA 92019
Toll Free: 1-866-484-6184
www.csnbooks.com

All Scripture quotations, unless otherwise indicated, are taken from the King James Version of the Bible. All rights reserved.

Very special thanks to Gunnery Sergeant Michael J. Doyle, U.S. Marine Corps, for his gracious consent to loan his 'Marine Blues' for the front cover. A special thank you to our grandson, Benjamin, who had a 'hand' in the photo as well.

The young woman whom we engaged to do the photo is Holly Peters. She is a freelance photographer from Eau Claire, Wisconsin. Her website, should you want to see her work, or need any other specific detail, is:

www.hollypetersphotography.com

Printed in the United States of America.

Dedication

To ~~be~~ my beloved wife, companion and friend,
Judith Katherine,
whose perfect love for an imperfect man
will forever mark his life,
and the lives of their children…

"A wife of noble character…
is worth far more than rubies…
Her children arise and call her blessed;
her husband also, and he praises her…"
(Proverbs 31: 10, 28)

And…

To my beloved Uncle 'Jim'
(James A. Rogers),
whose life-long love and unfailing affection
gave a young boy
the courage to embrace and receive
a father's love.

What Others Are Saying!

This is the book to own, to treasure, to read and re-read, if you (as I) have become convinced that literacy has become uncommon among today's writers. Peter Colman loves our language, but ... far more valuable to us as readers ... he has mastered its use to provoke and entertain us. We profit from his literacy. And he has heart. He gives us an extraordinary insight into his personal family history and reminiscences. In combination, woven with a remarkable narrative ability, he bestows to us the privilege of sharing his experience as he skillfully interweaves classic quotations into contemporary lifestyles.

Herschell Gordon Lewis

As a pastor and ministry leader for over twenty-five years, I have witnessed and ministered to hundreds of wounded and hurting people. With rare exception, the primary cause of the wounds was a broken and un-reconciled relationship. Whenever the broken relationship was reconciled, healing occurred. I believe the deepest and most frequent wound is the father's wound. Read this book! It is an intimate roadmap to healing the father's wound. Do this and you will become a healing agent for others.

Dr. Raleigh Washington,
President, Promise Keepers and
President/CEO, The Road To Jerusalem

Peter's writing reflects the preciseness and passion of the old masters of the English language; Peter's stirring story of reconciliation reflects a life lived with the humble application of God's Word.

Dr. Michael Wourms,
President, Christian Services Network

Table of Contents

Foreword

My heart leaps up when I behold
A rainbow in the sky:
So was it when my life began,
So is it now I am a man,
So be it when I shall grow old
Or let me die!
The child is father of the man [1]
And I could wish my days to be
Bound each to each by natural piety.

William Wordsworth

'THE CHILD is father to the man.'
How can he be? The words are wild.
Suck any sense from that who can:
'The child is father to the man.'
No; what the poet did write ran,
'The man is father to the child.'
'The child is father to the man!'
How *can* he be? The words are wild. [2]

Gerard Manley Hopkins

---

[1] William Wordsworth, in *The Golden Treasury*. Francis T. Palgrave, ed. (1824-1897). 1875
[2] Gerard Manley Hopkins (1844-1889). *Poems*. 1918.

Proem
A Poet's Prayer

Icarus I am not. Nor Narcissus.
(At least the last time I looked…)
But here I stand, poised…
Perilously perched with waxen wings
On the fragile edge of virtual anonymity.

I am not particularly fond of the
Prospect of faltering, or falling.
But I have often dreamt of flying…
Of swinging unfettered, unencumbered,
From towering treetops, (like a 'swinger of birches…') [3]

'One could do worse…'
Or traversing, Tarzan-like, the unfriendly,
But beckoning landscape of the world's
Transient, formidable forest floor.
Like an aerial acrobat above center ring.

I shall fly, then,
And beseech the sun's
Benevolent rays
To smile upon my effort
And speed my ascent.

Peter Colman

---

[3] This, and the excerpt that follows, are taken from the poem *Birches*, by Robert Frost.

Preface

*...For now we see through a glass darkly; but then
face to face; now we know in part; but then I shall
know even as I also am known.*

(Paul of Tarsus – 1 Corinthians 13:12)

I sat staring through the silent, opaque surface as the sun's early morning rays splashed and stained the weathered glass with long silver streaks. Just how many scorching summer days and freezing winter nights the frail, voiceless glass had experienced cannot be known.

I am told that the once clear, molten liquid glass of aged windowpanes is constantly moving downward, imperceptibly, with the weight of time and the sun's irrepressible rays, toward the sill, where, after perhaps a hundred years or more, it gathers to a thickness.

Imagine that within such faceless, life-like panes lay entombed, in some mysterious fashion, the invisible, unspeakable memories of countless sunrises, of the sounds of chirping birds, of a child's laughter or innocent prayer, or a muted sigh. Is it so impossible to believe that these same fragile shrouds embody, in their humble, translucent layers, generations of ignoble, 'inglorious Miltons' [4] gazing

---

4 Taken from Elegy Written in a Country Churchyard by Thomas Gray (1716-1771):
"Perhaps in this neglected spot is laid some heart once pregnant with celestial fire…"(Lines 45-46) Far from the madding crowd's ignoble strife, their sober wishes never learned to stray…(Lines 73-74)

wonderingly against the chilling echo of a nameless 'nor'easter's wintry winds, at the opaque landscape of their finite lives?

There are other equally fascinating questions to contemplate.

Are sounds and gestures forever lost?

Is the ecstasy of love awakened by the living lyre, or the piercing, speechless pain of grief forever forgotten, lost in the infinite web of human history?

In an infinite universe, all things seem possible. Is it not just as reasonable to imagine that a hummingbird's wings are capable of altering, on an infinitesimal scale, the earth's rotation, or its fragile, ineluctable course through the deafening silence of space?

Is experience just forgotten?

Is every breath, every gesture, every painful cry or spasm of unbridled joy lost in the infinite space of a purely material universe? Is it possible to conceive that every small particle of experience may be trapped, preserved in time, only to be recaptured, recycled and reintroduced into the eco-system of the human spirit, like water recycled and reused by successive generations?

There *is* a certain solidarity in human experience that defies mere similarity. There *is*, and will always be, a sense of the mythical (a sense of *sacred* history), the mysterious, and even the mystical, in an otherwise material universe in which all of human experience is inter-connected and interdependent. In a universe composed of intricate, indestructible webs of human feeling, rational thought and moral consciousness, are we not the products and progenitors of the intricate, irrepressible gossamer strands in which we find ourselves suspended?

If this were true, and the immeasurable, elusive course of human experience, in all its exquisite detail, were susceptible to the reality of recreation and *real recollection*, it would be fair and fun to engage in some real imagining. For example, it would be harmless to imagine, in a faith-friendly universe, that every newborn's breath caresses the very face of God; that every heartfelt prayer is never lost, but collected and forever cherished and remembered, reverberating somewhere in the glorious, imperishable recesses of the timelessness of a gentler, impenetrable, but infinitely more personable universe.

For now, dispensing with philosophy and playful speculation, I will look lovingly and longingly through, and beyond, that old, fallible but faithful windowpane, as if 'through a glass darkly', and strain to see the figure of a father returning home from the hunt; on the other side, view a father's smiling face, longing to see and embrace a waiting son.

From behind the aged glass, I would like to recommend a simpler journey of one New England son and his father, a journey of innocence and intrigue, of vibrant hope and scattered uncertainties lying dormant beneath the shallow soil. It is a story of immovable 'out-croppings' and underlying layers of shattered dreams. Above all, it is a story of rediscovery, reconciliation, and a personal quest, an imaginative rekindling of fires once lost, of values and feelings once cherished; it is an impassioned quest to rediscover the truth about self and one's most intimate of relationships: a simple, sobering story of a proud, prodigal father who finds love, forgiveness and hope in the arms of an only son, the 'child' who would become the 'father of the man.'

It is my story. Perhaps it is yours. I offer it to you as your own.

***

On a clear, crisp, sunlit morning in the fall of 1953, a small boy stood expectantly at the base of an aged pine, mesmerized by the sight of his father with a makeshift burlap sack attached to his belt, ascending the towering tree. Upward his father climbed, shouting back simple assurances to his spellbound son, testing each withered, weathered branch, inching perilously but resolutely toward the distant treetop to rescue a helpless kitten.

For three consecutive, sleepless nights, the confused little lad had listened impatiently to the faint, desperate, piercing cries of the frightened little creature. That morning, with bright, hopeful young eyes transfixed, the small lad followed his heroic father's lithe figure climb the brittle beanstalk and descend again with his frenzied, fury friend. There the little boy stood, rooted to the tree's base, until, from the lowest branch, still far above his head, his victorious Dad dropped the trembling sack to the ground at his feet. With unpracticed poise, and a gratitude born of desperation, the writhing fur-ball popped playfully from his burlap womb and raced to greet the day.

Over the brief years, this young boy witnessed, though at some distance, the courage and prowess (and the fearful uncertainty and endless *attente*) of his father's ascent. The boy's imperfect, innocent view has been tempered with admiration, affection and awe. He has witnessed the heroic rescue (obscured by intermittent clouds and imperfect branches), and the imperfect, perilous, life-threatening descent, somehow managing, in the process, to salvage a few small, life-transforming memories.

The boy is older now; the imposing tree has been reduced to a lifeless stump. But he stands there still, looking heavenward. A son who waits at the foot of a tree, watching and witnessing a father's heroic rescue, could hardly be expected to walk away until his father, whom he loved and admired, had completed his descent.

The Rescue

Lying in my empty room in the cold New England night,
I heard the constant, tortured cry…
For three endless days and nights
I listened to the tiny, sleep-shattering sound.

From somewhere near the old house, out in the night sky,
A muffled *'meoooow'* permeated
The silent, sullen, worn wooden walls
Of our cold, centuries-old Dunbarton house.

Somehow,
A tiny kitten had managed to make its little way
To the top-most branches of an old tree
Near the northwest corner of our clapboard castle.

And there, he/she? had remained
Perched perilously, far above the up-stairs window,
Frozen with fear, holding lonely vigil
In the withered arms of a weakened warrior…

Even now, my childish mind can still see
A small boy, standing at the foot of an old tree…
(a fat telephone pole with bark and broken branches)
and my strong Dad climbing fearlessly toward the sun.

There, at the foot of that wizened beanstalk,
Stood little 'Jack,' his wide, wondering eyes fastened to the
sky,
Watching his god-like hero, clutching a burlap bag,
Climbing a broken staircase to heaven.

And as he watched in small amazement,
His Dad, stomped and tested dry branches,
Snapping, plundering each resistant twig,
Shifting his weight and grip, sending retiring warriors to
their rest.

He continued the ascent,
Climbing ever higher, finding fearless allies,
Vanquishing the toothless behemoth
With courage and skill.

And as I watched,
Dad came deftly down, still snapping stubborn foot-
soldiers,
Until he reached the lowest limb
And dropped the boisterous, bouncing burlap bundle on its
furry feet!

Chapter One

Through a Glass Darkly

And Miles to Go Before I Sleep

(Frost)

A blind woman knows her village better than a stranger.

(Bambara proverb)

I first met Peter Colman on a flight from Chicago to Boston where my firm maintains an office in an old, restored 'high rise' near the historic Park Street Church district. Somehow, quite involuntarily, I found myself sitting next to a friendly gentleman with a disarmingly pleasant, surprisingly professional demeanor. We were in the economy section (I usually fly First Class, but the flight was overbooked). I had misgivings about having to contend with the routine distractions and annoying inconveniences awaiting me in the typically over-crowded, plebian section of the plane, with the ever-present symphony of screaming infants (the nursery section), tuning their tiny vocal instruments, amplified by the unruly cohort of university students returning to their barracks after annual 'leave.'

As we sat silently and unobtrusively during those awkward moments, I switched into my characteristic silent mode, intending to exercise my professional prerogative of utter indifference. It was then that the stout, sturdy-looking gentleman offered these simple words:

1

"Hello, I'm Peter...Peter Colman."

I nodded, but thought guardedly to myself: *Is he going to adhere to polite protocol and desist from violating the invisible private barrier that divides his 'zone' from mine?*

"Oh, excuse me," I offered involuntarily, "I'm Steve...Steve Bachelor. Nice to meet you, Mr. Colman." *Nothing could have been further from the truth! After an already long trip, I was not terribly anxious to indulge him by pretending to be friendly. It was too late.*

"Bachelor? Now that's fascinating. Are you married? Sorry. Just kidding."

Now I was sure we never should have started this conversation. *So much for practiced restraint. 'The best laid schemes...' are sure to go up in smoke*, I thought. *He'll probably never shut up. Whatever happened to professional courtesy?*

Fortunately, this kindly gentleman seemed content to respect my space; he never spoke again until we were well into the short flight. I couldn't help but notice the enticing diversity of reading materials emerging from his 'crocodile' *attaché. Probably one of those 'wannabe' small-college professors*, I mused, *bent on imposing his idiosyncratic ideals on the closest victim.* As I pretended to relax in a practiced state of disguised diffidence, something attracted me to this figure. Perhaps it was the confidence, the sense of well-being that seemed to envelop his happy countenance. *This is preposterous,* I thought. *What possible benefit could accrue from an unsolicited conversation with a total stranger?*

What grabbed my attention during those first critical moments after takeoff was the curious array of books and articles that delightfully distracted him. I managed to get a fleeting glimpse of a couple of unorthodox titles: *"Thoughts of Hampton From Days Gone By" A Poem..." William and Eunice 'Goody' Cole of Hampton"*...And one that really sparked my curiosity, *"The Annals of Witchcraft in New England."* After carefully adjusting the light away from me, he discretely unearthed a long, yellow legal pad filled with notes, corrections and marginal references (like a well-used road map), and began to write.

Why should I be interested in some stranger's nostalgic meanderings?

He was silent; *I* was the one talking to myself. Curious.

Ironically, seconds later, almost without thinking, it was I who found myself poised to break the silence. It was like passing one's favorite ice cream shop, or bookstore, or perhaps (for the eccentric minority), even an antique shop, or (God forbid) a flea market, in hopes of finding that elusive 'sleeper' that you just must possess, but really can't afford to buy.

I could resist the innocent temptation no longer.

"Excuse me; are you a *resident* of Hampton?"

"Oh, no problem. From Hampton? No. I'm a native of Manchester."

"If you don't mind the intrusion, do you *live* in Manchester?"

"Actually, no, not since high school, eons ago. My wife and I live in the northwest suburbs of Chicago."

"Please forgive all the questions, but I couldn't help noticing your reading material. You seem to be quite 'academic.' Are you an historian?"

"No, not really, though I *have* become fascinated with history in recent years. My wife and I are actually high school English teachers…"

You can't be serious, I thought, as horrible memories invaded my myth of tranquility.

"Oh, I see," I replied with some sense of disappointment now, having fully expected that he would launch a strategy to convince me of the merits of a discipline which, I was persuaded, was hopelessly arcane and irrelevant to the 'real' world, and which I had always found to be dreadfully boring.

"So, I presume that you're brushing up on your literary material and preparing for classes in the fall?"

Much to my surprise, I now found myself widening the inquiry, drifting increasingly 'off course' from my original intention.

"Actually, I am drafting a quasi-fictional, auto-biographical novel, focusing on my relationship with my father."

Did He say 'quasi'? Is that related to 'quintessential,' or just queer?

4

"I'm exploring and expanding upon our family history as a colorful backdrop to the story. Our New England roots go very deep. My Mom and Dad, though long-since divorced, still live in Manchester; most of our other surviving relations still live in the Manchester area, some in Goffstown, some in Weare…you know, the same old town from which Supreme Court Judge Souter hails, and which has recently become the focus of the 'eminent domain dispute.' There are even remnants of the Colman clan in remote parts of Maine and eastern New York State. I even have a great-Aunt, Flora, who lives in Florida – maybe that's why they call it *Florida"*

This guy's humor is incurably lame, I thought to myself. *Enough already.*

"She's a hundred and four, the sole surviving matriarch of the long, legendary Colman lineage."

You've got to be kidding! Wow…this guy's a stitch, I thought; *he thinks he's a real comedian…another one of those old-timers who makes a career out of lame humor and limp wit. And an English teacher to boot! With probable emphasis upon the 'boot'.*

"You're kidding!" Then, without thinking, I asked: "Whatever compelled you to undertake (*perhaps 'undertake' was an unfortunate choice of words*), such an *arduous* and *fastidious* task?"

I found myself becoming very intentional about my word choices; diction, I believe, is the proper term; after all, the guy actually made a career of telling people how to write and speak. *This should be good.* In my experience, English teachers are a curious, eccentric breed, always correcting someone else's grammar, or quoting some drug-induced loser from the dusty past, or throwing out worn-out clichés. Real nut-cases. These people live in the wrong century and love to revel in a conspicuous stream of words, which the rest of the population is content to live without. I, of course, am free of any kind of bias. If a person chooses to commit to a low-paying, high-maintenance, stress-filled occupation, that's his business.

"No, really, I'm quite serious," Colman continued. "The research has been incredibly revealing and invigorating."

Here we go...point of no return...as I braced my psyche for the verbal barrage.

"In truth," he continued without blinking, "I have become increasingly fascinated about our family history in recent years. Understanding my *own* story is crucial. Ultimately, it affects the way I relate to my family, and to others...my friends, my colleagues...but most importantly..."

Now there's a conundrum, I thought...my goodness, the word-game is contagious.

"...I owe it to myself, and especially to my children and grandchildren."

This guy can't be serious! "You have grandchildren?" *I pretended to care.*

"Yes, five actually. Four grandsons: Isaiah, Josiah, Benjamin, and Colman. My daughter and son-in-law actually named their son *Colman!* And one granddaughter, Johannah."

Now I was in deep. "Interesting, I replied." *I really had to be careful now. The guy's got nearly half the Bible's list of characters already...probably one of those 'born-again evangelicals' everybody's heard about. I should cut this conversation short right now...*

"How many children?" I found myself unwittingly continuing the conversation.

"Four. Two sons, Jonathan and Daniel, and two daughters, Deborah and Esther.

They're all happily married now, and own their own homes...All but Daniel. He's still in exile."

*Just as I feared. A real comedian. Probably one of those happily confused, self-appointed souls, or a religious quack who thinks he's the only one who has all the answers except the one that speaks to family planning...What do they say? 'God commanded us to multiply and replenish the earth...' Obviously, no one ever told this guy that he and his clan weren't expected to do it all by themselves! Did he just say 'Happily'? What the poor, naïve soul doesn't know won't hurt him...No one is 'happily' married...*I allowed myself a good, reassuring dose of cynicism.

"The sole of the foot teaches us all things."

"What?!"

"A west-African proverb. It means that sometimes the most inconspicuous part of one's body can also be the most important...can yield the most truth. You know. A person rarely has an occasion to look at the sole of his/her own foot. Yet, that is precisely the part of the body, which

7

bears the body's entire weight and is most susceptible to injury. In some parts of sub-Saharan Africa, where the majority of the rural population are frequently shoeless, particularly when they are children, they are in constant danger of injury from thorns, or more life-threatening critters such as scorpions and poisonous 'pencil vipers.'"

Did I ask for the anthropology lesson? This guy was beginning to bore me and amuse me at the same time. "Ever seen one?"

"What?"

"A pencil-viper."

"Pencil-vipers are prevalent in sub-Saharan West Africa. They're about the size of a Bic pen; they look something like a chubby earthworm, but deadly. My sons and I have killed a few of them, but I keep my distance for the most part."

"You mean you've *been* there?" *Is this guy for real?* I found myself unconsciously adjusting my seat and moving a few safe centimeters away from my host.

"Sure. My wife and I were missionaries for fourteen years in Burkina Faso, a former French 'colony'..." *I sensed a subtle note of prideful distain in his tone.*

"Burkina what?"

"Burkina Faso - a small, land-locked country just north of the *Côte d'Ivoire,* the Ivory Coast. The country used to be known as Upper Volta, and was colonized by the French in the late 1800s, and was part of what was formerly known as the French Sudan. It used to be part of the old kingdom of Ghana, now an English-speaking country bordering Burkina on the south-east. The name *Haute Volta* was taken from two narrow, muddy tributaries of the Niger, which traverse the country's arid dry laterite terrain..."

He mumbled some other facts of little significance...something about rainfall, malaria, and infant mortality rate...but I couldn't concentrate over the turbulence and hum of the engines; besides, a snack was being served.

"We lived there for fourteen years; raised our four children there."

"Incredible." *Heeeere we go, the whole family history. Might as well humor him. We'll be landing soon, and I'll be on my way.*

I wanted to end this involuntary conversation and return to the real world, *my* world. I resisted every attempt to be drawn further into his strange world, but my arrogance succumbed to curiosity. *I'll indulge him, for the moment. Humor him. Maybe he'll tire and take the hint. After all, I've more important things to do, but, to be honest, I couldn't think of anything in particular.*

"So," *I thought I would attempt a bit of humor just to stay on top of the conversation,* "you said that you had four children, and that you spent all those years in Africa. I'm assuming you are married to only one wife, right?" I forced an awkward smile. "Just kidding." *Two can play this game.*

"*Touché,*" he responded, smiling as he handed me a small ream of pages.

"Actually," he volunteered, "I can only afford one wife, but she has been badgering me to find a second one to help with her duties at home…"

You've got to be kidding. This guy doesn't know when to let it go. He then timidly handed me a yellow, unfinished manuscript.

"Would you care to peruse a few pages? Please keep in mind it's a very rough draft at this stage…"

"Sure, why not? *What have I done?* Nervously, I served another question across the short gaming table with every intention of distracting the competition. "By the way, if you don't mind the intrusion, did I ask what brings you to New England?"

"Sure. I've just learned my Dad is not doing well; he has cancer. He lost his wife…his second wife, that is. My Mom and Dad were divorced back in 1956 when I was eight years old…" Dad later remarried. That was forty-four years ago. Anyway, his wife died last November, after a long illness. Dad was still sick while he cared for her. He's at the Veterans Administration Medical Center in Manchester right now. One of my uncles called me. Dad doesn't know I'm coming. I want to spend as much time with him as possible before…well, I don't think he has much longer to live. It's been a long time…

We were beginning our descent.

Maybe the guy's not so boring after all…
Slowly, I sensed some of my cynicism eroding, and I allowed myself the risk of acceptance, *or was it just my run-away skepticism reigning itself in?* In any case, the

steed I had engaged for a short, harmless canter had begun to falter and rear, and shake its bridle at the unfamiliar road we were taking, much like Frost's horse... *Yes, that was it.*

Then, from the back shelf of my mind, I remembered my college American Literature class, and one of the few New England poems that had gotten my attention:

> *Whose woods these are I think I know.*
> *His house is in the village, though;*
> *He will not see me stopping here*
> *To watch his woods fill up with snow.*
> *My little horse must think it queer*
> *To stop without a farmhouse near*
> *Between the woods and frozen lake*
> *The darkest evening of the year.*
> *He gives his harness bells a shake*
> *To ask if there is some mistake...*

I couldn't seem to recall the rest of the stanza. But a few scattered phrases returned:

> *The woods are lovely, dark, and deep*
> *But I have promises to keep,*
> *And miles to go before I sleep...*

"Excuse me. Mr. *Bachelor?*" I was wrenched from my semi-conscious, nostalgic slumber. I almost stood up in the aisle to get my coat. *Was it snowing? Did the horse know that we need to stop? Is there a light in the farmhouse window?* I sat straight up, pretending to hear.

"Excuse me," he repeated, like the annoying jingle of a horse's bells. "Mr. Bachelor, I'm sorry to disturb you, but we're about to land, and I've been meaning to ask…well, you seem to be the kind of person who has an interest in literature. You were mumbling something from Frost…If I were to send you a preliminary draft of a few of the unfinished chapters of my novel, would you be interested in proofreading them and sending me your honest comments and criticism?"

"Absolutely!" I responded without thinking. *What did I just do?* His friendliness and sincerity had caught me off guard. But for some reason, I felt no regret. No resentment. *Maybe this little experiment in collegiality-at-a-distance would be invigorating. Perhaps even enjoyable.*

"I'd be honored to read your chapters…*I lied,* only if you'll promise to send me a signed copy of your book when we've…that is, when you're finished writing." I almost felt a twinge of guilt that I had actually suggested to this total stranger that his story could actually interest me, or that I would take the time to read it. How many times had I given and received business cards, or exchanged addresses and phone numbers, never bothering to call anyone? Who really cares about what someone else thinks or does? The world is moving too quickly; time is precious. My own life and schedule demands are enough as it is…

We both sat quietly in our seats, looking straight ahead. He seemed to be peacefully but strangely distracted.

"Sorry to hear about your Dad," I said.

"I'm sorry, what was that you said?" he asked.

"Your father. I'm sorry about your father. I hope he improves. I'm sure your visit will cheer him up."

12

"Thank you, Mr. Bachelor, and thanks for listening to an old, nostalgic New Englander. I have enjoyed our conversation." *Our conversation? Wasn't he doing most of the talking? And whatever happened to that short, restful interlude I had planned?*

We were ready to land. *You mean your conversation, I caught myself repeating to myself. I wondered how he could have enjoyed 'talking' so much. Then again, what I had heard so far seemed to be more interesting than anything I had done of late.*

"Have a great time with your family...I mean your family here in Manchester."

"Thank you. God bless." *How quaint, I thought, but sincere.*

"The captain has requested that all seatbelts be fastened. We have begun our descent into Manchester. We'll be landing in about five minutes. The weather in Manchester is clear and cold...there is a fresh, thin blanket of new snow..."

We exchanged addresses and emails. Seconds later, we were on the tarmac, taxiing toward the terminal. One brief good-bye, then we grabbed our carry-ons and were off. As I followed this intriguing individual up the connecting mobile corridor, I had the strange feeling that I already had become part of his fascinating, grass-roots story, a story that was no doubt yet *en train*, as the French say.

***

That is how I first met Peter Colman!

The conversation on that plane was the first of many correspondences over a period of several months. He continues to send me new chapters, and I continue to read, forwarding comments and helpful suggestions. Strangely, I have become a willing traveling companion in Mr. Colman's (*I don't know him well enough to call him 'Peter.'*) fascinating odyssey to retrieve the missing, fragmented pages of his personal story. The source and inspiration of his compelling quest, I later discovered, was to understand his own colorful history, and to seek some path of reconciliation with a father who had been effectively absent for most of his life, one he had only recently come to know during a few extraordinary days before his father's death.

When I returned home from my Boston trip, I found an envelope in my mailbox from Mr. Colman. I neglected to mention that I had actually flown into the Manchester airport on that earlier trip and driven the one hour to Boston. No one likes flying into Logan these days, especially if you actually live and work in Boston; many travelers are flying to Manchester because the airport is considerably less congested, and it's only a stone's-throw from I-93.

The envelope contained the following brief letter and account:

Dear Mr. Bachelor:

Greetings. I trust that you had a safe, productive trip to Boston. As I recall from our brief conversation on the plane, I am compelled to express how very grateful I am for your willingness to indulge an old, itinerant New Englander in search of a story. Thanks! I am also deeply appreciative of your willingness to read my manuscript. I hope you will find it enjoyable, engaging, and not too terribly tedious, as such stories customarily tend to be. I shall make every effort to make this particular story an exception.

I thought it would be helpful to fill you in on a bit of my own personal history, some too personal, I'm afraid, so that you will better understand where I'm 'coming from,' and help you understand some of my intrinsic idiosyncrasies, one of which is the tendency toward verbosity! In any case, to help prepare you for the chapters to come, I have composed a brief (?) preface to my personal account. I hope you will not find it to be unbearably boring...

Again, thank you for kindness. I look forward to receiving your impressions and critical comments.

Cordially,
Peter Colman

***

The following unrevised 'preface' is what Mr. Colman sent to me. I thought it might be helpful to include it as an appropriate introduction to his story. In some inexplicable way, his story has become my own, but with one minor qualification: as the historical data will confirm, it is *his* unique story. If one were willing, as Coleridge proposes, to allow a 'willing suspension of disbelief for the moment, which constitutes poetic faith,' [5] it could very well have been my story, or anyone else's, had he or she lived in another place, in another time.

Use your imagination. Allow yourself a willing suspension of disbelief, just for the moment.

---

[5] Samuel Taylor Coleridge (1772-1834), from chapter XIV of his autobiography, *Biographia Literaria*, 1817.

Here is the *Preface* to Mr. Colman's novel. Even as I perused its curious pages, I couldn't help but think that it was a story whose conclusion was still being written, a history, a living chronicle…in progress still. Reading the story was like meeting the man himself, a man still learning and growing, whose story, to some extent, was everyone's story.

It certainly was mine.

That one incidental encounter, that one casual conversation changed the course of my life forever, just as a slight change of course by a touch of the ship's wheel could radically alter a passenger's final destination.

As I continued to read, I began to wonder about my own past and those who have contributed to my life, those who, without knowing it, have helped make me the person I have become.

[*Preface*]

'Father of the Man'
A Journey toward Reconciliation
By Peter L. Colman

Not every young boy is privileged to have two dads. My own father, for reasons which I fear I understand too well, left home in 1956 when I was eight-years-old. Dad, Mom and I were living at 352 Manchester Street, in a fairly spacious old apartment on the second floor. The building was covered with brown tar-paper siding, had a small wooden back porch, and a steep staircase descending to a tiny patch of grass at the dead end of a paved alley below. This was my turf, where I played 'circus strongman,' (usually right after the circus had come to town) and 'Superman,' tying one of my mother's pink towels around my neck, running and jumping (sometimes from the garage), feet first, arms thrust forward, fully expecting to leave the ground.

My friends and I (one was a pretty girl named Jocelyn) caused quite a commotion in that neighborhood. But without fail, just when it seemed we were having the most fun, an elderly gentleman would manage to appear on the second story porch next door, barking threats. He terrified me...and I was Superman! Maybe he didn't see the cape.

Here, at age eight, I had my first serious fight with a 'friend' down the alley. He had come out of his house with an arrow. I had a bow and arrows of my own, so I went up those back stairs and returned with one of my better arrows (with a metal tip) and a bright shiny garbage can lid for a shield. No one was going to challenge King Arthur in his own castle! This incident sorely tested my omnipotence. The young boy's mother broke up the fight before either of us could inflict savagery upon the other. Sometime later, after we patched up our differences, I remember bolting from his back door and tripping on a nail protruding from the edge of his wooden deck, hitting the ground flat on my stomach, rolling in excruciating pain, the wind knocked out of my pre-adolescent invincibility.

The house on Manchester Street was our first city home; I spent my first seven years (the only years Mom and Dad seemed to enjoy their marriage), living in an extremely old house (built in 1822) at the junction of the Old Dunbarton Road and Morse Road (a few miles northwest of my hometown of Manchester). My Dad had been in the Marine Corps, and experienced a radical foxhole conversion to Christ at age nineteen somewhere in the Solomon Islands (New Caledonia, I believe). He and my Mom married after he returned home, a decorated war hero, and one of five brothers, all of whom fought in the war, survived, and are still alive and living in their native New England. My Dad was a police officer. His hours were such that I hardly remember him ever being home. All I recall is the day we painted the living room bright red, right over the old wallpaper. Curiously, however, the most vivid brushstrokes that survive the childhood canvas of my life are those of Dunbarton.

One of the few memories I have of Mom and Dad together was in the old Dunbarton house the day Dad climbed to the top of an old tree to rescue a kitten that had been crying for three days. My dad looked like Jack in the Beanstalk, breaking branches as he ascended, testing their strength, then carefully descending with the frightened kitten in a burlap sack. Dad dropped the sack to the ground when he reached the lower branches. The kitten was safe; Dad was my hero that day. It's sad that Mom and Dad were unable to rescue their own marriage.

The rooms upstairs in the old house were always cold. One large, black pot-bellied stove kept the downstairs warm in winter. I remember leaning too close to the stove one day; I blackened my left arm with a small charcoal smudge; which seemed to cover my 'whole' arm; I was three. On another occasion I swallowed a large, blue cat-eye marble; it looked like a small, transparent golf ball. Mom later told me that she had waited patiently, but anxiously, for several days for that marble to 'reemerge.' I vaguely recall that Mom and Dad would both wrap me tightly in an Indian blanket each night during the winter months. The window in that old room was sideward, since it was located over the garage roof. Dad once crawled out on the roof and shot a Mayonnaise jar off the head of a skunk that had been foraging in a small dump near the house; Dad was a fine marksman. Mom said the skunk ran off down the road without a scratch.

Other than the pictures that Mom saved, then passed on to me, the only other memories I have of my father during those years were of the chicken coop he built. I distinctly remember sitting at the table in the corner of the old kitchen one morning and finding a small, sharp black tack in my plate of fresh scrambled eggs. I still cannot explain the phenomenon. Skeptics assure me that it is biologically impossible for a chicken to swallow a tack, and for that tack to find its way to the chicken's reproductive system. They're certainly right. Scientifically accurate. But what about my vivid memory of that event? What about my vivid, tangible, sentient recollection of the nearly-photographic empirical evidence, long-since discarded?

Then there was the 250-pound, ten-point buck (there's not the slightest possibility of exaggeration in the *récit, bien véritable*) that Dad shot, dragged through the woods and over the stonewall, across the road from the house. I actually have a picture of that animal to corroborate the story.

I remember a huge black spider! Mom says that I was playing out on the yard, when she *saw* the large creature crawling toward me. She called my Dad, who raced outside to the rescue (Dad was always 'rescuing' me from something). All that I recall from the incident is Dad putting the ugly black behemoth in a clear canning jar on a table on the front porch. He put a twelve-inch ruler in the jar to crush the spider, and the spider started to climb toward his hand...*how could such a story be believed unless there were a reliable eye-witness!* I can still remember standing there, my eyes level with the edge of the wooden table, watching my father crush that big spider; I distinctly remember that there was a layer of milky liquid in the bottom of the jar...

We left the old house in Dunbarton and moved to Manchester. My Mom's brother, Jim Rogers, got Dad a job down on Canal Street in one of the old red-brick buildings constructed in the late 19th century for the immigrant workers in the world-famous textile mills which lined the banks of the Merrimack River. Uncle Jim had served in the U.S. Army, helping to coordinate U.S. forces in the European theatre; he was stationed in Paris, where he met his young English bride. Uncle Jim and Auntie Joyce have lived in Manchester since the end of the war, and have been married nearly 60 years; they still live in the same small, light blue bungalow on the top of the hill on Harvey Road, overlooking Grenier Field, which is now the modernized Manchester Airport. Jim and Joyce have maintained the same address and phone number all of these years.

In the ensuing years, during my grammar school and high school career (1954-1966), Dad seemed to just disappear from my young life; Uncle Jim would become my second 'Dad' and lifelong friend.

In the final analysis, I could not bring myself to ignore or neglect the father whom I had never really known. I could only recall three instances in nearly fifty years when Dad had ever showed up. Without my knowing it, he had attended my high school graduation at the new Kennedy Coliseum (bordering my old football field and cinder track at Gill Stadium) in 1966. He met me quickly outside after the ceremony; he left just as quickly, for fear, no doubt, that he would see my Mom. Then he was gone.

He showed up once for a Sunday evening service at our old home church (The Christian and Missionary Alliance Church at the corner of Merrimack and Hall streets), where Dad had served for several years as Sunday School Superintendent and song leader. That was the one evening when I had been invited to preach in the church where I had been raised and baptized. It was during our return trip, or 'furlough,' after our first five years in Africa.

The last time Dad ever ventured in our direction had been during our second furlough in1987, when we lived in Judy's hometown of Dover, Ohio. Dad hadn't been on an airplane since the end of the war (inexplicable, since he had been a paratrooper). He stayed with us for one week. He walked the children to school, and we spent hours at the kitchen table reminiscing about the Colman clan history. At that time Dad opened a large manila envelope and showed me enlarged photos of more than a century of prominent participants in the Colman family drama. He hand-wrote the names and relationship of each person. I have those photos to this day. My grandmother, Nellie (Moy) Colman Dwire, had discarded all of her photos, and these photos were the only surviving ones which Dad had managed to retrieve.

That's the broad outline of my story. I have discovered, however, in the process of researching my family history, some rather intriguing patterns. So I chose to dedicate several introductory chapters of the novel to the Colman ancestry, not particularly unique as ancestral patterns go, except that our family dates back to the founding of the New England colonies! What fascinates me even more, however, is that their story seems to have a life of its own, almost as if it is yearning to be told, to be heard. It also occurred to me that perhaps I was just the right person, at just the right time and place, to listen, to learn, and to invite others like you to join me, to come along for the ride, to take part in the same journey, the same on-going conversation.

Chapter Two

The Journey Begins

Lord, thou hast been our dwelling place
In all generations...

(Psalm 90:1)

The flight from Chicago to Manchester would take just two hours. The price for my ticket, purchased the previous night, was equivalent to a high-school teacher's weekly salary. But this mid-winter trip was urgent. Critical. My students and colleagues at Carmel Catholic were characteristically sympathetic and understanding, as was Judith, my beautiful, loving wife and companion of thirty-five years. I packed a small suitcase, my Bible, and a couple favorite books (*The Poems of C.S. Lewis*, and a leather-bound 1893 edition of *The Early Poems of John Greenleaf Whittier*, plus the latest copies of *Traditional Bow-hunter* and *Field and Stream*), and I was off to O'Hare.

The night before I had received a telephone call from Uncle Bill in my hometown of Manchester, New Hampshire, concerning my father's health. Today my destination was the Veterans' Administration Hospital – a monumental, unpresuming faded redbrick citadel of refuge on a hill near the northeast edge of a burgeoning city that was once the textile capital of the world. In this quaint, isolated corner of the world, keeping quiet company with an abandoned granite quarry and a mammoth city reservoir, sat the tired structure of the old Veterans Administration Hospital. The building, quite remarkably unadorned, seemed anchored in the granite hills. Much like the aged water tower which straddled its weathered walls, the four-story structure stood like a faithful watchman, a tireless warrior, keeping lonely but faithful vigil over the weary souls and withered bodies of a generation of forgotten heroes.

One of those faceless heroes was Robert Everett Colman. My dad. The cancer, which had begun so surreptitiously in the colon during the previous year, had extended its merciless grip to the liver and lungs. He was eighty years old, and dying.

"Peter, you had better come. Your Dad is not well."

My father, Robert Colman (friends and family called him 'Bob'), had been receiving chemo-therapy for the better part of the last year. Dad had taken care of his second wife of forty-four years, Dorothy Samara Colman, right up to her untimely death the previous year. I recall presiding at the burial service at the Pine Grove cemetery morgue that cold November day. Dad was in a wheelchair in the front row. Family members on the Colman and Moy side, some whom I hadn't seen since my childhood, had gathered for the brief, but very emotional ceremony. There was a very small, wooden table and a simple piece of white cloth for the tiny white container of ashes. There were few, if any, chairs. But the Colmans are very resourceful. Uncle Bill and Uncle Frank and I pilfered a couple visitors' benches in the adjoining corridor, and borrowed a few bouquets of artificial flowers nearby. After a few brief words of tribute, a couple of passages from Scripture, and a few of Dottie's favorite hymns, we all proceeded to Uncle Arthur's home for a sumptuous turkey brunch, complete with Uncle Artie's homemade lemon squares, and a photo of the five Colman sons and grandsons.

That was in November, 2004. Dad returned to the tiny brick apartment near Canal and Merrimack where he and Dottie had lived their last years together, a stone's throw from my Mom's apartment on the seventh floor of the old Carpenter Hotel. I remember the day that Dad and Dottie had to vacate their apartment on north Elm in the dead of winter, and my Mom, unaware that Dad had moved so close to her own place, had begun to receive Bob Colman's mail in her own mailbox downstairs.

Dad lived in that same empty apartment for the next three months, continuing to survive by carrying a chemical bag attached to the side of his abdomen. The hallway from the kitchen to the back bedroom was too narrow to allow Dad to pass, and the strongest chemicals available had been unable to arrest the cancer that had begun in his colon.

It was the middle of February. The winter night in Chicago was typically clear and crisp. A bright blue blanket of fresh snow covered the frozen ground as the plane's powerful engines routinely propelled its fragile occupants into the forgiving emptiness of a cold sable sky. When the plane reached cruising altitude, and relaxed its gray metallic wings, passengers succumbed to the soft light and quiet flow of air. I reflected upon ageless passages from a couple of my (and my father's) favorite Psalms: [6]

Lord, you have been our dwelling place throughout all generations...You turn men back to dust, saying, return to dust, O sons of men...He who dwells in the shelter of the Most High will

---

[6] Psalms 90:1, 3; 91: 1, 9-11.

rest in the shadow of the Almighty...If you make
the Most High your dwelling –Even the Lord who
is my refuge –Then no harm will befall you...

And then, the verse, which I always read and whispered in prayer during takeoff:

For he will command his angels concerning you to
guard you in all your ways; they will lift you up in
their hands...

I remember taking particular consolation that night in the small, surprising detail that angels were described as having *hands*!

***

As we climbed into the soft sable sky, veering east-northeast across the Great Lakes toward New England, a brilliant, yet subdued chorus of lights from the breathless Chicago skyline seemed to raise its collective voice to wish me strength and a safe return.

Moments later (or so it seemed), we were beginning our quiet, unceremonious descent to Manchester's revital-ized airport facility. Given the legendary congestion in and around Logan, it was rumored that people who lived and worked in Boston now preferred to fly to Manchester and drive south...just to save time and trouble. But Manchester 'natives,' among whom I was one of its least conspicuous and uncelebrated sons, remember when old Grenier Field was a lackluster military base with a hodgepodge of scattered barracks hidden among it ubiquitous pines. No one knew that better than my Uncle, Jim Rogers – a man who, for the past fifty years, had been closer to me than my own father, the father whose unexpected demise had occasioned the present visit.

As our plane approached the surrounding hills and dropped silently over the Derry line toward the cold white asphalt runway, I peered instinctively away from the busy terminal toward the northeastern airport boundary to the familiar profile of trees skirting the old tower and red intermittent signal light – the same light that has been burning, uninterrupted, since before World War II. There, snuggled at the warm base of a solitary stand of majestic pines, still sat the same miniature white cottage with blue shutters where Uncle Jim and Auntie Joyce (their sixtieth year in the same house) huddled in the same blue-board breakfast nook sharing cheese and crackers and steaming chowder in a buttery white seasoned sauce packed with fresh sweet clams.

I closed my eyes briefly for the final descent. Strangely, I could sense the fast-reverse of decades – old Pine Island Park and its penny arcade, the old gray, rickety roller-coaster towering over fat metallic airplanes suspended from thick steel cables, and the red and silver-stained bus that carried us from Elm Street in the center of town, south past the Pine Grove Cemetery, to Brown Avenue and up the steep hill to the parking lot. The trip cost twenty-five cents per person, including the transfer for the return home. At the base of old Harvey Road, near the west entrance of the airport and hidden from view on the road above, was a sandy incline descending to the clean, shallow brackish waters of the Cohas Brook. It was there that Jim and 'Shirl,' the Dickey and Colman clans would retreat on a hot day with our swimsuits and smiles, bologna and mustard sandwiches, and a cooler of crushed ice packed with dozens of fresh seven-ounce, sea-green bottles of Coke!

As we dipped to the runway, I strained to see a tall, solitary pine with a small makeshift perch made of scrap boards in the up-most branches. My cousin aîné, Jimmy Dickey (my Aunt Shirley's son), and I used to climb that pine behemoth just to sit and watch the distant runway.

Just then, the small unsteady platform seemed to lurch. I grabbed a thin board and the nearest dry branch and held on for dear life. The soft screech of tires and the rush of afterburners interrupted my reverie. I shot one last desperate look toward the darkened hill. The luminous red, broken glare of the beacon, comforted by the soft complexion of the aging tree line and juxtaposed against the crisp white winter night, seemed like the amiable nod of recognition from a childhood friend after a lifetime of separation.

"Uncle Jim, I'm here. Can you pick me up?"

"Where are you?"

"I'm here in Manchester, Jim."

"Already? Good. Stay put. I'll be there in seven minutes. Wait for me outside the far right entrance. You know the place. I'll drive around and pick you up. That way, I won't have to pay for parking. Be there, or the police will make me drive all the way around again. You know the routine. I don't know why, they just don't let us pick somebody up without having to make us move."

"Thanks, Uncle Jim."

"Good. Glad you had a safe trip. I'll be right there."

Fifteen minutes later, Uncle Jim's car came crawling along the curb from the far *left* entrance, until he finally reached the spot where I stood.

"Hi, Jim."

"Jeez, where the heck you been? I've been circling, looking for you for at least fifteen minutes! Well, whatever, glad you had a safe trip. Wish you had more time. I suppose you'll be spending most of your time with your father."

"He's dying, Uncle Jim."

***

It was getting late. I settled in at Uncle Jim and Aunt Joyce's. The cottage had three small rooms and a tiny kitchen with the eternal nook in the corner (which also served as mailroom, study and deli). I slept on the couch, which opened into a spacious bed, filling up the entire living room. Mom's apartment at the old Carpenter Hotel on Elm and Merrimack was 'scenic' and comfortable, but terribly small.

After greetings, I borrowed the old van, made the familiar trip down Harvey Road to South Willow to the Queen City Bridge intersection at south Elm, and north on the infamous drag-strip to the center of town. Mum had given me a card for the automatic security door (which anyone could use if they simply waited for someone to enter), and a key to Apartment 709 – seventh floor. Mum had her assorted plastic bags and other memorabilia (and the customary small Zip-Lock bag of quarters for Chicago tolls (God knows, she needed those quarters much more than I). I kissed Mum, had a quick cup of 'fresh' coffee, petted the cat, and started off for the V.A. Hospital. My

Uncle Frank (one of my Dad's four brothers, all of whom had served in and survived World War II) had been the one to call me and advise me of the seriousness and urgency of my father's condition.

I climbed the Hanover Hill (the same route my friends and I had used for winter track practice back in '65), and turned up Calef Road pass the Manchester Country Club (my high school friend, Dick Fosburg's Dad used to have a membership here; we used to sneak in to rake golf balls), and on up the hill pass the old farmhouse to the Veterans Administration parking lot. The ground was frozen; all of life seemed in lifeless suspension. The lights that lit the backside of the hospital entrance were a dim yellow, the reminder, perhaps, of the slow demise of a brighter day.

The first-floor corridor was warm but stale. There were vending machines inside the front entrance, and a small carousel filled with assorted used paperbacks. The person at the desk seemed occupied and unaware of my presence. I politely identified myself and inquired as to the location of my Dad's room: "My name is Peter Colman. Robert Colman is my Dad."

"Oh, welcome. Bob's room is just over there, the first room on the right."

I walked slowly toward the entrance, fully expecting to see his smiling, two hundred and twenty-five-pound frame sitting up in bed (the same kind of exuberant reception I had witnessed when Dad made his first and last visit to his grandchildren during our furlough in Ohio nearly ten years earlier). When I entered, he seemed not to be there. Looking down the length of his bed, I could see his form and the familiar girth of his upper body. Then I

30

saw his head, turned in my direction, smaller and wizened. His hair was sparse and disheveled, his teeth a sickly brown.

"Dad?"

"Peter? Is that you, son?"

"Yes, Dad, it's me, your son, Peter. Are you alright?"

"I'm good," he replied, raising his weakened frame. We kissed. I embraced this husk of one of the strongest men I had ever known. And I cried. How could such a man, with such a history of strength and pride, of tenacity and industry, of humor and a zest for life, of spiritual zeal and vibrant faith…come to this? Why have I come so far only to see a father, lost to me for the better part of forty-four years, in such a pathetic (by 'pathetic' I mean that which evokes strong feeling, or *pathos*) and debilitating condition? Is there some kind of strange pattern here? If the skein of our lives, as Thomas Colman's Gaelic forefathers believed, is pre-woven, and its hues and colors carefully chosen and irrevocably interlaced, then how am I to understand how to decipher the nature and texture of the tapestry of my own experience, my sojourn, and that of my children and grandchildren (the Colman clan continues to expand and explore) through tenuous, twisting, but colorful corridors of my small world? Have the 'fathers eaten sour grapes… (and) the children's teeth been set on edge.'? [7]

My mind couldn't help but recall a familiar 19th-century New England writer, Edith Wharton, who, in early

---

[7] Biblical proverb – reference to the suffering and hardship experienced by ancient Israel as a consequence of their chronic disobedience against Yahweh's commands – compare Jeremiah 31:29 and Ezekiel 18:2.

descriptions of the protagonists of her 1911 novel *Ethan Fromme*, commented, "They were, in truth, these figures, my *granite outcroppings*; but half-emerged from the soil, and scarcely more articulate." Had I ever really known my father? Were there hidden recesses and reserves of truth, hidden colors and hues (or ugly stains and flaws) that would need to be exposed? Should I even care? Should anyone?

Dad had fallen asleep. It was after visiting hours, but the staff had been more than accommodating. One of Dad's nurses had come in wearing little green lighted antennas bouncing playfully above each ear. Saint Patrick's Day was approaching. "We love your Dad," she offered. "We aren't accustomed to allowing ourselves to get too close to our patients, but your Dad's an exception. He's in pretty tough shape, but he never fails to brighten the day for everyone else around here. We're thinking about moving him soon to a new facility on the second floor...but. Well, will you be up in the morning?"

"Yes, I'll be here as early as I can."

"Don't come too early. He needs his rest. He's had some pretty serious bleeding lately."

"Yes, I know, but he keeps telling me that he's OK, that he's getting better. We've been praying together and reading some of his favorite Psalms."

"I know. We all know. We've been listening. Your Dad's had one of us roll him down to the cafeteria every evening to talk with his war buddies. A couple of them don't have too long. He and one of the older guys have a cup of coffee together every day, and trade stories."

I prayed with Dad and kissed him goodnight. "See you in the morning Dad. I love you."

"I love you, too, Peter. Glad you came. Hey, we'll have dinner together tomorrow."

"Night Dad."

As I left the V.A., the cold night embraced me, but the soft, reassuring light on the frozen snow led me gently to Uncle Jim's black van. I made a quick call to inform him that I would be *home* shortly.

"Where'd you go? What took you so long? We thought you just went to see your Mom."

"I've been with Dad, Jim."

"Oh, well, whatever. I guess you had to. You're sure treating him better than he ever treated you. I suppose you'll go back up tomorrow. We won't make any plans. Too bad it's such a short visit, but that's the way it is nowadays. We never have enough time for everything... Well, see you in a few minutes. Don't hurry, and be careful. Joyce made the bed for you."

"Thanks, Uncle Jim."

"How *is* your Dad? You know, I'm the one who got him a job at Granite State Optical when he came home from the war..."

"I know, Uncle Jim. Thanks. I'll be there in just a few minutes. Oh, please tell Auntie Joyce 'good night' for me, and that I'll see her in the morning."

"OK, *dear*. Just lock the latch when you come in."

'Dear' was an affectionate term Uncle Jim used on rare occasions. Jim is the kindest, most generous, unpretentious man I know. He is a 'died-in-the-wool', no-nonsense New Englander who puts little stock in superficial talk or excessive emotion. 'Think'n ain't do'n is his favorite riposte. He has little time for hypocrisy, or for mundane distractions that seem to fuel modernity. He has a chronic but honorable disdain for laziness, waste, and excessive charges for services rendered, especially by the medical profession. Perhaps it has something to do with two eye surgeries, two open-heart interventions (one was a new procedure, through the ribcage, which caused irreparable nerve damage, and for which the presiding surgeon admitted no responsibility), plus three hip and knee replacements in recent years. To those medical challenges, add the blatant theft, by a close neighbor, of cherished, vintage rifles belonging to his Dad, a small quantity of coins, and forty cases of antique bottles from an unlocked trailer. Jim and Joyce never had to lock their home, or car, or anything else, in nearly sixty years of marriage. All the thefts occurred in his eighty-forth year! Did I mention he's also had more than half-dozen brushes with death and near-fatal accidents?

***

I forgive Uncle Jim for his disdain for my Dad; he didn't hate him, he just couldn't bring himself to respect him. Dad had experienced a very dramatic conversion to Jesus Christ on the island of *Moiseul*, as a Marine serving with the First Marine Division in the Pacific theatre during World War II. When Dad returned home to Manchester after the war, his new-found zeal for the Christian faith flew in the face of most who knew him. He had stopped cursing and smoking cigars. His own mother, Nellie (Moy)

Colman (Dwire), didn't even want to greet or kiss her own son. "I want the old Bob back," she said, when he greeted her in full uniform at the door. For Uncle Jim, all this talk about Jesus, heaven and hell, and 'being saved' was best left for church. He and Mom and all the Rogers clan had all been raised in the Baptist Church and were well acquainted with the story; they had all been baptized, had frequented Sunday school and periodic 'revival meetings,' and the like. The Bible, God and Jesus…these were things you just accepted; it wasn't necessary to talk about God personally…unless someone died.

Uncle Jim was like a second Dad. In truth, he was more like what a 'first' Dad should have been. He and Auntie Joyce never were able to have any children of their own, though they had (some thirty years earlier) adopted a beautiful, brilliant son with blond hair, my cousin Jay. When Dad disappeared in 1956, a few years after our move from Dunbarton to Manchester, Uncle Jim started a regular routine of taking me fishing, boating and skiing, visiting Mammy and Pappy and Uncle Ray and Aunt Phyl in Weare, or just spending an exciting day at Sears, or repairing the white 69' Ford Galaxy at Johnny's garage in Pinnardville. It didn't matter where we went.

When Uncle Jim called, I would wait in my bedroom window in the back corner of our third-floor apartment, watching for the familiar white-curved front fender of Uncle Jim's car. I was out the door and cascading down the old wooden staircase, nearly jumping the entire flight, before Jim hit the horn.

"Bye, Mum, I'll be back later!"

A lot later. Uncle Jim always had places to go, and didn't particularly care how long it took to get there, or how long it was before we decided to leave. We would stop for soft chocolate ice-cream at Dairy-Queen on the way home. I don't recall ever stopping for lunch or dinner; Uncle Jim didn't have time to eat. Auntie Joyce would always fix a 'little' ten-course snack when we returned at night.

Chapter Three

Wrathful Elements

The sole of the foot teaches us all things.
(Bambara proverb)

Be strong and courageous…for the Lord your God will be with you wherever you go…[8]

Like the sturdy oaks and elms that had kept a quiet, strong vigil over the storm-ridden coastal paradise of New England, Thomas Colman,[9] rugged patriarch and progenitor of the Colman clan, was not one to boast of spiritual strength. He would have been in good company in his thinking, and may have very well shared a similar view of the world, with the likes of the infamous Romanticist and mystical poet-painter-engraver, William Blake, who penned in *The Four Zoas*, "It is an easy thing to laugh at wrathful elements…To see a god on every wind and a blessing on every blast…"

Like Blake, Thomas was not inclined to laugh at adversity. Neither could he afford the simple luxury of languishing in some transient state of religious ecstasy. He

---

[8] Joshua 1:9 – New International Version of the Bible
[9] The *History of Ould Newbury* writes of "… [o]ne Thomas Coleman, who had been employed by the projectors of the stock-raising company to provide food for the cattle and take care of them for a specified term of years…" had also…"becoming dissatisfied, declined to carry out his part of the contract, and the General Court finally ordered a division of the grain that had been imported, and instructed each owner to take care of his own cattle." (p 12).

was a wiser man than that. If the religious upheavals in Europe had splintered and sifted a hundred thousand pilgrim souls, and broken the heavy chains of ecclesiastical bondage and repression, and were sufficient to fuel a biblical exodus to the New World, then he, at least, would guard whatever fiber of fervor and faith he possessed safely preserved in the bowels of his heart. He would need the rugged, realistic edge of pragmatism to survive in this new, precarious wilderness of promise and prosperity. He was not a man to quibble or speculate about his prospect for success. Neither did he believe that he could just relax in the hope of Canaan and the promises of the God of Abraham, Moses and Joshua. He had left the relative luxury of the 'leeks and onions' in his native land, and had crossed Jordan. But there would be mountains to conquer and dark valleys to traverse before the proverbial 'promised land' would become a home, a safe haven. There were strange and unfamiliar acres to plow, and enemies to subdue. Little did the itinerant patriarch know that there would be obstacles to surmount, even among his own circle of friends and pilgrim companions.

***

Thomas Colman was a strong, simple man, a husbandman, a caretaker of cattle and sheep. He had sold his modest holdings in his native Marlborough, Wiltshire, England, garnered whatever meager resources he possessed: tools, clothing, a few books – including a recent English translation of the 1611 Bible, published at the bequest of King James - a few simple cooking utensils, one favorite clay pipe, a flint-lock musket with a small supply of shot and powder, assorted bottles of lineament, cough and kidney cures, a few hundred feet of good rope, a keg of nails, leather harnesses, a small box containing scissors, knives, quills, two crude circular 'black-glass' ink wells, and one stoneware master ink. All kegs and containers were sealed with cork and beeswax to prevent seepage and mold; other items were confined to sealed wooden cases.

Thomas was a practical, soft-spoken man, but beneath the seemingly innocuous outcropping of a calm demeanor lay an indomitable Scottish [10] core of rock-hard resilience and a fierce, unyielding temperament. As he stood upon the weathered deck of the "James," one of two three-hundred-ton Dutch mercantile vessels which had left the shores of Southampton, England, nearly two months earlier, on April 15, 1635, he thought deeply and reverently about the lonely but exhilarating up-rooting he had endured. Any misgivings were carried away by the sweet sea breeze caressing his tired brow. The winds had been favorable during the treacherous crossing, the seas uncharacteristically docile as the small, fragile vessel had sought, like so many others of that generation, to traverse the dark, sinister wilderness of the North Atlantic.

***

As the sheep and horses tossed restlessly in the ship's fragile hold, Thomas surveyed the rugged, emerald coastline. His compatriots and companions were now beginning to congregate upon the deck, adorned in crude woolen breeches, cotton shirts and swaths of sun-drenched calico to protect their fragile, weakened frames from the relentless blasts of the Arctic Sea, and the penetrating volleys of icy salt-sea sprays. The next morning, just before dawn, the "James," with its tired, grateful cargo, tasted the warm, confluent currents of the Parker River.

---

[10] The Colman (e) s of Wiltshire, and elsewhere, are the descendants of Colomba (sometimes rendered Columba – b. A.D. 521), the celebrated seventh-century Scottish Christian Bishop (and missionary to the Scots). According to the *Directory of the Ancestral Heads of New England Families: 1620-1700*, the Colman name is rendered variously *Colman, Coleman,* or *Coultman*. In German, the same name is spelled Kulmann, or Cullman. The Gaelic meaning of the name is translated 'dove,' as is the French word *colombe*.

Here on these virgin shores, with this fledgling settlement of tailors, tanners, mercers, weavers, coopers and carpenters – laborers and husbandmen – the corner stones and massive oak beams would be planted – and the community of Newbury (Boston) erected.

Thomas surveyed the shore and took stock of his meager, but hearty resources. He would need to find suitable land before the coming winter to house and feed his small family of sheep and cattle. He would build a small, efficient dwelling. He was yet unmarried, which would simplify his task (at least for the present). He retired below deck for a few hours of needed warmth and rest. The morning's landing and off-loading would be grueling. He must be strong. In minutes, his tired frame fell into a peaceful sleep. It was June 3, 1635.

Thomas had good reason to be hopeful. Inasmuch as he could prevent it, he was determined not to become a victim to that which countless others of his generation had allowed themselves to succumb, namely, overly-ambitious investments. He would allow no one to 'mock his useful toil.' He was not poor; nor did he tolerate excess. But neither did he enjoy the wealth of some, or the cushion of support that many shared from the sale of spacious family estates back in England. He had always managed a modest income, and knew his trade well.

He was a *husbandman*. In the old English language, the term *husband* was originally a verb; it implied taking responsible care. A century later, when Daniel Defoe created the first full-length English novel, *Robinson Crusoe*, [11] he included the curious detail in the

---

[11] Daniel Defoe (1660-1731) wrote the first English novel, *Robinson Crusoe* (1719), when he was fifty-nine years of age. The original work, entitled *The Life and Strange*

40

account of Crusoe's discovery of cases of assorted *liqueurs* and 'cordials.' The text states that Crusoe found it necessary and prudent to '*husband*' his rum, *viz.*, to ration and carefully dispense his limited supply.

The Colman, or Coleman, patriarch would have been no stranger to the prudent necessity and practical industry of such notions. Nor would he have been unfamiliar with another vulgar term (which, in the English language, has drifted considerably from its philological moorings), namely the elusive designate *promiscuous*.[12] No one would dare to suggest that the word 'promiscuous' featured prominently, or irreverently in Thomas's mind. But it may be safely assumed that a select, or unselect, few among his contemporaries, quite in spite of the strict, intolerant Calvinist climate in which they customarily conducted their personal and private lives, were not altogether strangers to the tendency to squander or indiscriminately dispense with what limited resources they had at their disposal in order enhance their material prospects. It goes without saying that Thomas would hardly allow himself (given the costly sacrifice and condition of his displacement) to fall prey to economic philandering, or any unwise, or potentially elicit financial affair.

Surprising Adventures of Robinson Crusoe, is believed to have been based upon the factual account of the shipwreck and survival of the Scottish seaman Alexander Selkirk.
[12] Curiously, the term *promiscuous* was not uncommon in English literature, one of the more prominent usages of which features, for example, the small, but significant mention by Daniel Defoe, in his description of the infamous London Plague (*Journal of the Plague Year* – In Longman's English Classics, 1895 Edition) of the pitiful bodies of victims being indiscriminately dumped into a mass grave a local church cemetery: "...but no sooner was the cart turned around, and the bodies shot into the pit, *promiscuously*, which was a surprise to him (*an anonymous witness whose wife and children were reported to be among the dead*), for he at least expected they would have been decently laid in..." (p 60)

***

The historical account provides sufficient insight into both Thomas's disposition and early business practices so as to allay unwarranted speculation. Though there *is*, perhaps, as the reader will shortly surmise, some reason to question Thomas's better judgment, there appears to be little cause to serve notice on his integrity. The following excerpts from the *History of Newbury 1635-1902* appear to sufficiently document this critical phase in Thomas' pilgrim journey toward his (and his descendants') historic homestead and future resting place:

June 3, 1635, two Dutch ships, loaded with horses, and sheep.

Arrived at Boston: and the same day the ship "James," three hundred tons burthen, arrived at the same place with cattle and passengers. The last-named vessel sailed from Southampton, England, about the fifth of April, 1635, and is said to have delivered here cargo in good order and condition. Amoung her passengers were:

Name	Place of Origin	Occupation
Thomas Browne	of Malford	weaver
Hercules Woodman	" " "	mercer
Thomas Colman	of Marlborough	husbandman
Anthony Morse	" " "	shoemaker
William Morse	" " "	" " "
Nicholas Batt	of Devers	linen weaver
John Knight	of Romsey	taylor
Richard Knight	" " "	" " "
Nicholas Holt	" " "	tanner
John Emery	" " "	carpenter
Anthony Emery	" " "	" " "
John Pike	of Langford	laborer

John Musselwhite   ""   ""
Anthony Thetcher   of Sarm (Salisbury)   taylor

Most of the persons named in the above list came to Newbury soon after their arrival at Boston; and, July 8, 1635, the General Court ordered: "that there shall be a convenient quantity of land set out by Mr. Dumer and Mr. Bartholemewe, within the bound of Newbury, for the keeping of the sheepe and cattell that came over in the Dutch shipps this yere, and to belong to the owners of said cattell."

Thomas Colman, one of the prominent passengers who figures in the above list, could hardly have been opposed to such a benign and potentially constructive agreement. In fact, it was subsequently further recorded in a chapter from the same document entitled "THE LANDING AT PARKER RIVER," that:

> Governor Winthrop, in his History of New England, under date of June 3, 1635, records the arrival of two ships with Dutch cattle; and the same day the ship "James" arrived from Southampton, bringing, among other passengers, John Pike, father of the famous Robert Pike, of Salisbury, and one Thomas Coleman, who had been employed by the projectors of the stock-raising company to provide food for the cattle and take care of them for a specified term of years....

After citing the previous entry in the Massachusetts Colony Records regarding the distribution of lands for the purpose of raising and caring for the livestock, the account adds this enlightening, but disconcerting detail:

Evidently, those who were engaged in this new enterprise intended to utilize the vacant lands and at the same time establish a safe and profitable business for themselves; *But Coleman, becoming dissatisfied, declined to carry out his part of the contract*, and the General Court finally ordered a division of the grain that had been imported, and instructed each owner to take care of his own cattle.

This would be a curious detail, and could have very well escaped the general attention of the population, not to mention the attention of Thomas's descendants, were the same record not found to contain the seemingly *nonchalant*, but conspicuously succinct addition:

This joint stock-raising enterprise met with many discouragements, and after a few months' trial was reluctantly abandoned.

November 3, 1635, the General Court passed the following order:

Whereas Thomas Coleman hath contracted with Sir Richard Saltonstall & dyvers other gentlemen in England & here for the keeping of certaine horses, bulls & sheepe in a gen'all stocke, for the space of three yeares, & nowe, since his comeing hither, hath been exceeding negligent in discharging the trust committed to him, absenting himselfe for a longe tyme, From the said cattell, as also neglecting to provide howseing for them, by reason whereof many of said cattell are dead already, & more damage like dayly to accrue to the said Gentlem, it is therefore ordered, that it shal be lawfull for the said gentlemen to devide the oats & hay provided for the said cattell amongst themselves & soe euery one to take care of their owne cattell for the winter.

Such a detail could be construed (by a casual perusal) to be sufficiently deleterious as to cause no slight pang of collective shame for the Colman clan. It cannot be ignored that the arrangement described in the above record had not been the result of some kind of impulse or impetuous action on the part of Thomas and his compatriots. Quite the contrary. Planning and provision for the success of the fledgling enterprise had been undertaken long before departure. Nor can the reader assume that Thomas's documented 'neglect' can be directly attributed to some form of insobriety, or fit of inexplicable incognizance. Nor should one assume that Thomas was indifferent to the considerable loss of both revenue (and his own reputation), which such neglect would have inevitably provoked. We cannot know, nor are there any records to confirm, that Thomas had been able or inclined to contribute the lawful fifty English pounds to the 'common stock', which would have thereby granted him the promised two hundred acres of virgin soil in the 'first division of land' among these early New England settlers. We *do* know that he (and others transported to New England "at *their* own expense') would have been entitled to fifty acres of land. His lack of cooperation, for whatever reason, could not, then, have been a total loss, notwithstanding the unfortunate loss of numerous livestock which had been committed to his charge, and the apparent disgraceful disintegration of his character.

There are a few surviving signs, a few oxygen-bearing details, a few fresh 'leaves' among the scattered remains of silent documents, which may serve to nurture a tiny specimen of hope to nourish the humble legacy of the Colman family. Thomas was not one to lie down. What one can only assume to be a precocious, dissident determination compelled him to seek greener pastures and freer air. Indeed, one small paragraph of the specious, yet spurious account of Thomas's activities in the *Genealogical Dictionary of First Settlers of New England* unceremoniously records: "Thomas…was b. in Marlboro, Wiltshire, England in 1602, and three years after settling at Parker River he joined the Rev. Stephen Bachiler in establishing a settlement in "Winicowett" that was later called Hampton. He lived in Hampton less than twenty year."

An astounding series of information has also recently come to the writer's attention. It is a matter of historical record, in *The Annals of Witchcraft in New England*, by Samuel G. Drake, 1869, that a certain notorious, nefarious member of the rural, indigenous population of Hampton had been found suspicious of practicing witchcraft, and soon after was tried and sentenced to spend the rest of her miserable life in a Boston prison, in spite of her husband's tireless efforts to secure her release and salvage a remnant of the meager material possessions entailed in her modest estate. As the record goes, the two individuals who registered depositions to ascertain her guilt and to secure an indictment were none other than a certain, heretofore relatively anonymous co-founder of the village of 'Winnacunnet,' Thomas Colman, and his associate, Abraham Drake:

So far as is known, the following depositions are the first acts in the tragedy of *Eunice Cole*. Thomas Colman or Coleman, *on whose account an action was commenced*, settled in Hampton before 1650. He came there from Newbury, in which place he is found as early as 1635. His children, born in Hampton, were Benjamin, 1640, Joseph, 1642; and Isaac, 1647. Abraham Drake was son of Robert, at whose house the meeting of the "celekte" Men was held, as mentioned in the deposition. Robert Drake and his family came from Colchester, in Essex, England. Coleman, is the same mentioned in the *Founders of New England*, came from Marlborough in Wiltshire, in 1635.

This later account does not take into consideration three other children born to Thomas: a son, John, who was born in 1644, and a daughter, Joanna, both of whom were born to Thomas and his first wife, Susanna, who died in 1650. After Susanna's death, Thomas married Mary, known as 'widow Johnson,' widow of Edmund Johnson. Mary died in 1663. Thomas then took a third wife (in succession, of course), Margery, 'daughter of Philip Fowler and widow of Thomas Rowell of Andover. Margery had two children of her own from a previous marriage (to Christopher Osgood, also of Andover); Thomas and Margery had one son, Thomas's 'eldest child,' in 1638.

The infamous, cryptic document gives the Colman patriarch the dubious distinction of being a prime mover in the historic scandal and suspenseful drama of the notorious Eunice ('Goody') Cole of Hampton. Thomas was a contemporary of Nathaniel Hawthorne's great-grandfather, John Hawthorne, who presided as one of the judges at the legendary Salem witch trials, Hawthorne also being a fellow native of Boston. Given Thomas' sullied reputation as a husbandman in his native Newbury, and his association with the reputable miscreant and 'unforgiven Puritan' [13] the Reverend Stephen Bachiler, it is not surprising that Colman choose to relocate 'lock, stock and barrel' to a friendlier climate.

---

[13] The expression 'An Unforgiven Puritan' may be found in the records of the New Hampshire Historical Society, in an article of the same title by Victor C. Sanborn, from Concord, NH, 1917.

In subsequent years, while still pastor of the Hampton church, Rev. Bachiler was accused of having, or wanting to have an illicit affair with his neighbor's wife. The irony of the potentially sizzling, but scandalous affair is that Rev. Bachiler had vehemently denied his ravenous intentions until, according to the account, during the 'serving of the Lord's Supper' he confessed to the truth of his intent:

> "Mr. Stephen Batchellor, the pastor of the church at Hampton, who had suffered much at the hands of the Bishops *and having a lusty comely woman to his wife*, did solicit the chastity of his neighbor's wife, who acquainted her husband therewith; whereupon he was dealt with, but denied it, as he had told the woman he would do, and complained to the magistrates against the woman and her husband for slandering him. The church likewise dealing with him, he stiffly denied it, but soon after when the Lord's Supper was to be administered he did voluntarily confess the attempt, and that he did intend to defile her if she had consented...."

Curiously, not every account of the notable Reverend's illustrious itinerary in early New England includes the details of his conflict with church leadership and his tendency to exercise his professional ministry skills in favor of the female segment of the population. In his *New Hampshire History* (Concord, 1922), H.H. Metcalf simply comments that "In 1638 two other settlements were made – one at Hampton and one at Exeter, the former headed by Rev. Stephen *Bachilor*, the latter by Rev. John Wheelock, both noted religious leaders of their day, and the settlements largely made up of their devoted followers." (p 13). His closest 'follower' and companion, according to the

Genealogical Dictionary of the First Settlers of New England (1986) was none other than the patriarch Thomas Coleman.

One final 'claim to fame' which may be attributed to Colman, and which also should serve to excite and inspire his prodigious offspring to a modest measure of pride, comes from the genealogical record [14] of Eliza Starbuck Barney:

Thomas Coleman
M. b. 1602, d. 1682, # 7699

* Attributes "Thomas Coleman was *the first of Nantucket,* came here in 1660 with his family..." "He arrived in Boston June 3, 1635..."
* Immigration. He immigrated in 1660. "*The first of Nantucket*, came herein 1660 with his family. Death. He died in 1682."

According to a certain professor, popular mid-western educator and *anthropologue*, and quite contrary to popular opinion, "history does not repeat itself; rather, history is cyclical." It is certainly valid to suggest that human beings are inevitably marked by the generational chemistry, or crucible of events and circumstances in which their predecessors were principal participants, and whose character traits and tendencies they may have, to some indefinable extent, imbibed, or quite involuntarily or unknowingly inherited as part of their own experience. Such a supposition seems to make sense.

---

[14] In the Nantucket Historical Association's Research Library and Archives.

My own inclination is to conclude that there is an undeniable solidarity, a unanimity among the human specie that remains essentially unchanged, regardless of the superficial 'ebb and flow' of diverse cultures and the progressive (or regressive) manipulation of the environment, man's intellectual prowess and so-called 'progress' notwithstanding. But this seems to be entirely too philosophical. One mustn't lose sight of the real world. After all, "...there is nothing new under the sun." [15]

A number of significant questions emerge from this brief purview of events in the continuing, unfolding drama of the Colman legacy (if such a term is appropriate). Can it be understood to be entirely coincidental that nearly three hundred years after these early twists, turns and nascent kickings in the womb of one of New England's founding families, one surviving descendant, one surviving son, should live and play in relative proximity to Hampton? Or more dramatically *encore*, that generations of the same son's ancestors (the patriarch Thomas's progeny) should live in intimate proximity to the once-productive, thriving rural borough of Auburn, where the Colman clan would eventually put down permanent roots, spreading their inauspicious influence for another two hundred years? Coincidence or Providence? Let the reader decide. However history may judge the unpretentious patriarch of the Colman family, it is a matter of record that he and his first wife, Susanna, and their three sons, Benjamin, Joseph and John, left the turbulent confines of Newbury and removed to the farthest northern-most boundaries of the colony. Rumor has it that Thomas was unable, or unwilling, to endure the strictures of Calvinistic teaching and the moral restraints that were freely imposed by the ecclesiastical leadership, and accepted by the general

---

[15] Ecclesiastes 1: 9b.

population. Or it could be that the proud patriarch of the clan was simply defiant, refusing to be told how to govern his personal life and affairs.

He was not entirely free of a dissident past. One could hardly blame him for relocating to a friendlier, freer environment where his restless roots would have received a warmer and happier reception. He did have at least one sympathizer in the person of his companion.

Chapter Four

Remembrance

All the rivers run into the sea; yet the sea is not full; Unto the place from whence the rivers come, thither they return again.

(Ecclesiastes 1:7)

All species bear their own offspring, but the spoken word bears its own mother.

(Bambara proverb)

On a recent trip to Chicago's Field Museum, I was treated to a close inspection of the priceless artifacts taken from the tomb of the renowned Egyptian boy-pharaoh, Tutankhamen. I was even more delighted, after an elementary but meticulous review of the hieroglyphs of the famous king's *cartouche* and name, to be able to finally read the characters. I had met an Egyptologist a few years ago working in the ancient history section of a Borders bookstore who had given me a signed copy of a small handbook he had written and published on hieroglyphs (with basic instructions in reading the Egyptian alphabet). "A little learning is a dangerous thing." [16]

Archeologists and other purveyors of historical artifacts and buried data tell us how fascinating it is to

---

[16] "A little learning is a dangerous thing; drink deep, or taste not the Pierian spring: there shallow draughts intoxicate the brain, and drinking largely sobers us again." From *An Essay on Criticism* (1709), by the English poet Alexander Pope (1688-1744).

discover that ancient relics are strangely familiar, almost predictably recognizable. I found this to be true as I scrutinized the articles found in King Tut's and his family's tombs. The engravings were beautiful and intricate, but crude. Some seemed to resemble childlike drawings. The metalwork was ornate, but reflected the simple signature of a common craftsman.

The more we study the past, the closer we begin to see the present more clearly. Perhaps our roots are not as far removed from the trunk and the branches, or even the buds and the new leaves and seasonal fruit, as we may believe. As I delve deeper into the leaves and layers of the Colman family archives, I find the old dry lifeless pages beginning to reabsorb light and texture. Like Ezekiel's experience in the valley of dry bones, [17] old records and buried memories begin to take on a new life of their own. Forgotten faces and suppressed secrets, lost conversations, victories and shameful defeats, are unearthed and exposed to the rejuvenating influence of light, insight and *re*flection. My own journey into the past is not unlike Hawthorne's description in *The Scarlet Letter* (1840 c.) of the author's discovery of a dry, yellowed, forgotten parchment scroll, and the infamous remnant of the scarlet letter "A" with finely embroidered edges, which contained the cold embers of a once white-hot scandalous affair concerning a certain Hester Prynne (*Synne + Pryde=Prynne*). It is, indeed, a matter of historical fact that one of Hawthorne's own ancestral Quaker stock, a certain John Hawthorne, was one of the judges presiding over the witch trials in Old Salem two centuries earlier in 1692. Curiously, one of the celebrated New England fireside poets, himself a Quaker, John Greenleaf Whittier, was also a contemporary of Hawthorne and resident of Boston (and later Danvers).

---

[17] Ezekiel, Chapter 37.

54

Coincidentally or not, he also wrote copious volumes of poetry describing his forays into the New Hampshire wilderness, including the Lakes Region, the region of Merrimack and the Amoskeag Falls (of my native home of Manchester), and regions east, to his beloved Hampton, where he also lived, and in honor of which he dedicated a significant portion of his verse. Could this be simple coincidence? *Is* it also mere coincidence that a few short years ago, on a brief flea market expedition in the old town of Hudson, I happened upon a framed and forgotten hand-written page of stationery with inked, cursive stanzas from the poem entitled *Hazel blossoms* (1874), an excerpt which had been penned in loving memory of Whittier's sister, Elizabeth H. Whittier? The page, adorned with a pastel watercolor of yellow Witch Hazel flowers and verdant stems, and imprinted with the inscription "Danvers, Mass.," is also signed "John G Whittier," and dated, "4th Mo 26 1882."

Such disjointed minutia may only have a superficial bearing on the present story, but one can hardly ignore the juxtaposition of colorful detail, and what would appear to be the providential overlapping of interconnecting elements of an ever-unfolding series of events. In any case, Thomas Colman, resident of Newbury, and later, Hampton, could scarcely have predicted the direction of his uncelebrated progeny, the Colman clan of Auburn, New Hampshire, which, after a long and relatively sedentary succession of farmers and craftsmen (and women), would eventually sink their simple, resilient roots into the rich, rocky soil of the hills overlooking Massebesic Lake.

Nor could the patriarch Colman have foreseen the birth of five strong sons in a small schoolhouse in the same village of Auburn. One of those sons, whose mother (Nellie Chase Moy), was also one of five beautiful sisters (her story is left for another day), was my father, Robert Everett Colman, the father I never knew. No one else will ever have cause to tell his story, so this is a story I must tell in order to understand my own, a grassroots story others may wish to enjoy as well, or may be inclined to examine to better understand their own fragile, and sometimes fractured journey through history.

Several years ago, at an advanced stage in his own journey, my Dad happened to salvage an envelope of black and white family photos which his Mom, my grandmother, whom we affectionately called 'Nellie,' had inexplicably and without much thought or emotion, discarded in the kitchen trash bin. Dad had taken the liberty of retrieving these photos and proceeded to have them all enlarged. Thereafter, during a rare visit (which I will describe later in greater detail), Dad took great pains to identify all of the members of the Colman family, as far back as the late nineteenth century!

Nellie (Moy) Colman was one of five Moy sisters (Mable, Gladys, Alice, Nellie and Blanche – known as Aunt 'Bunny), also of Auburn, New Hampshire. Nellie's first husband was Sumner Chase Colman; Sumner was a pipe-fitter at the Portsmouth Naval Shipyard during and after World War II. Nellie had an illicit affair with a young man, Bernie Dwire, whom she had met while attending a neighborhood dance, presumably during Sumner's absence from home on one of those long working stints in Portsmouth. Nellie and Sumner divorced, a sad development, since they had five healthy sons and not-too-few happy years together on the Auburn farm. Whether they did, indeed, enjoy a measure of marital bliss cannot be easily ascertained. The only one other thing that New England folk are traditionally and typically disinclined to discuss in public other than matters of religion is the issue of sexual intimacy. More than one child has had occasion to wonder how, since sexual intercourse was such a secret, suspicious topic, their parents had managed to bear any children at all.

Several years later, Nellie and Bernie married and lived the remainder of their lives in Manchester. Grammy 'Nellie' was my last surviving grandparent. At the time of her death, she was ninety-three. She had been a woman of stunning beauty, a stinging wit, and a playful, but typically no-nonsense demeanor. She loved to play 'bino' (bingo). She kept a sacred candy-tin of nickels to fuel her habit. However, she did have one major obstacle, one 'fly in the ointment,' to overcome during her days at the Hanover Street high-rise for the elderly: according to Nellie's account, a kindly gentleman across the hall was always trying to get close to her and hug her in the narrow space between the opposite apartment doors (Nellie was well-endowed, even in her old age). Nellie repeatedly refused the daily onslaught of his passionate advances, and apparently fired a shot over his bow on one occasion, smacking him (gently, of course), warning him that there would be dire consequences to his aging ship's tackle if he continued his uninvited attempts to board her vessel! Grammy may not have been a paradigm of moral virtue, but she was a hard-working, generous woman, who knew how to beat off a stray dog. Unfortunately (though the Colman and Moy families are no exception to the universal rule, to be sure), the proclivity toward infidelity and insidious, but nearly imperceptible forms of corruption in the otherwise sturdy trunk of the Colman family tree had begun much earlier, and had spread to other branches.

Nellie's Dad, William James Moy, had also had a reputation as a 'tomcat,' a womanizer. My great-grandmother, Blanche (Callahan) Moy, had uncovered his infidelity, and had banished him from the old Auburn farmstead for six entire months. As the story goes, 'Grandpa Moy' finally came to his senses and crawled back to the Auburn farm. 'Grandma Moy' threatened him, and warned him that if he ever dared to dip his wick elsewhere again, she'd throw him away for good! Grandpa Moy had gone perilously close to the abyss, had cheated on Grandma, and had nearly lost his happy earthly home, as well as his hope of salvation.

The last time I saw Grandpa Moy was during the summer of my freshman year in college (1967). Grandpa was living at the old County Farm in Goffstown, just across the road from the Old Hillsborough County Hospital where I was born. As I stepped up to the battered porch where he was sitting statuesque in an old rocking chair, I greeted him and extended my hand. Whether he recognized me, I will never know. If I accurately recall the moment, I believe that I had had every intention to read a few encouraging words from 'the Good Book,' but before I had gotten too far, he started reciting the twenty-third Psalm from memory. It is doubtful that he ever really understood that his great grandson was even present. That's all that I remember. No, doubt, he was a more sober, smarter man in his final days. Perhaps he was still chaffing and smarting from his frequent foray into infidelity. Grandma Moy had 'given him hell,' and he was longing for heaven.

After the war, my own parents, Robert Everett Colman and Doris ('Dotty') Rogers Colman (discussed in depth in a later chapter), found themselves regrettably incompatible, and divorced in 1956. This unfortunate event occurred in spite of my father's extraordinary zeal and commitment to the Christian faith, and to the local church, leaving an only son without a Dad at home.

Though I have never been compelled, with respect to my parents' divorce and irreconcilable rupture, to probe the question of infidelity in any great detail (water, and debris, are better left under the bridge), I did learn in recent years of several disconcerting details, only one of which I feel free to relate.

One of my father's brothers (presently residing in Goffstown, NH), Uncle Bill (who, to my knowledge, has never made any profession or pretension with respect to the Christian faith), revealed to me in the days just prior to my father's death that just after Dad's combat experience at Guadalcanal, and his return to Camp Pendleton for his remaining two years of duty with the Marine Corps, Dad did have a one-night fling. According to Uncle Bill, Dad had regretted this act of passion and moral failure deeply; he had found a quiet place alone on a hill one night overlooking the beaches of San Diego and wept bitter tears of repentance. Dad had never chosen to share this moment of weakness and shame with me during his lifetime, not even in the intimate, dramatic moments before his death. To this day, however, in spite this and other weaknesses and failures, I have no reason to doubt the genuineness of his spiritual conversion. While I may be able to understand the tendency of other family members to condemn his failures as a father to an only son, I have also become keenly aware that no one, including myself, is entirely without sin. After all, both Dad and I, growing up as we did in a traditionally pietistic, conservatively 'evangelical' religious tradition, have always believed that a prerequisite to genuine faith is a real recognition of personal sinfulness. Did not Dad frequently preach and remind others, in an attempt to urge them to a place of repentance and faith, that 'all have sinned,' and that 'if any man is in Christ, he is a new creation'? Yes, frequently, and with a sense of sincerity, though tainted, I suspect, with what I can only describe as unconscious vestiges of self-righteousness. Perhaps there is a simple explanation, which Dad may have never understood, and which I have only come to understand in recent years. The popular text in Romans 3:23, which so-called 'believers' are accustomed to quoting to convince the 'unbeliever' of his/her spiritual need, was, in fact, written as a sober reminder to the *Christian* community in the church of Rome. The sober reminder was addressed to Christians who had been forgiven, but who still (and for the remainder of their earthly lives) would have to contend with their own sinfulness. 'One beggar, telling another beggar where he found bread,' as the saying goes. Infidelity has not been the only discernible stain or unfortunate imperfection in the Colman family tapestry. The Colman and Moy clans of Auburn and Manchester have also had, in the course of their relatively non-descript, modest New England sojourn, the unfortunate tendency to lose their children to tragedy. Of course, this is not uncommon. The annals of our forefathers are replete with accounts of the unfortunate, untimely deaths of children. But recent Colman family records document the very sad, and what appears to be repetitious loss of daughters.

In the mid eighteenth-century, Thomas and Phoebe Colman of Newbury, Massachusetts had a daughter, Dorcas, who only lived one day. A century later, Sumner Chase Colman and Nellie Moy Colman had an only daughter, Marion, who lived less than one year. Robert E. Colman, my father, and his first wife, my mother, Doris A. (Rogers) Colman, would have had a daughter, whom my parents intended to name Naomi-Ruth, was 'still-born;' the baby girl had been dead in the womb some time before the birth of the fetus; of course, the daughter is not listed in the family genealogies.

The most recent patriarch of the Colman clan of Auburn was none other than 'Grandpa' Frank Thomas Colman. Like many of his rustic peers in the late nineteenth century, he did not enjoy the *dis*advantage of a formal education; his was a 'privatized' farm-style education - slopping hogs, harnessing horses for the fields, and splitting and stacking kin'dlin' and firewood for the long cold winter. He also invested time in raising a large family, working night and day to assure that the children stayed healthy, learned to appreciate hard work, and eventually married and earned a respectable living. New Englanders had little time for the superficialities and impractical, costly distractions which seem to preoccupy successive generations. Grandpa Colman did allow himself one innocent distraction, and that was holding his grandson, little Bob, and posing for pictures, though grandpa was rarely known to smile, and never smiled for the camera. The Colmans and the Moys of old Chester and Auburn were a sturdy breed, and sired a stubborn, resilient, raucous, but fun-loving litter of sons and daughters. But the die had been cast...bitter-sweet days lie ahead.

The intervening years of my father's childhood are sketchy. Times were hard. During the depression, my great, great grandfather, Frank Colman, his wife, M. Fannie Eastman, and their five surviving children: Flora, Waldo, Horace, Joseph and Sumner Chase (my grandfather), apparently moved temporarily from Auburn (at that time an extension of the old town of Chester) to Troy, in western New York State. Years later, some members of the family returned to the district of Brattleboro and Wardsboro, presently in the county of Windham in south-eastern Vermont, not far from the New Hampshire state line. Generations earlier, another Thomas Colman (b. 1771), and his wife, Abigail, had moved to Auburn, NH, and settled on a hill there, which to this day bears the name 'The Colman

Estate.' It was here that my great-grandfather, Frank Thomas (mentioned earlier) resided with his wife, M. Fannie Eastman. Frank and Fannie sired several children during their life-long sojourn at the old clapboard, one-story dwelling; among them: my grandfather, Sumner Chase (b. 1897) and his brother, my great-uncle, Horace. The ancestral core of the Colman clan is currently resting peacefully in the old Auburn Village Cemetery. Horace Colman, though the record has yet to be confirmed, settled in a small village called 'Newfane Hill,' adjacent to Wardsboro. Horace was a blacksmith in Newfane for most of his earthly life, and an avid *connoisseur* and collector of Native American artifacts.

This brief resume of the salubrious historic 'outcroppings' of the Colman family history in New England could easily be dismissed, ignored or judged to be unbearably provincial and irrelevant to the current scheme of events which carry men and women, and their unmoored offspring, through the rugged, unchartered wilderness which the twenty-first century calls modernity. But sometimes the opaque windows of the past, which hide the shadows and reverberate with the friendly sounds of a former generation's often unbearable, often hilarious collective past, constitute perhaps the only legitimate lens through which we (as readers and critics) are able to make sense of the obscurity and complexity of our own frantic, fragmented lives.

If anthropologists (one of the more prominent and revered among whom is Edward T. Hall) are correct when they tell us that 'the advantage of studying so-called *foreign* (or, one might add, *older* cultures), is that such inquiry enables the inquirer to better understand his or her own culture,' then we would do well to eagerly and earnestly probe the complex, but incomparably colorful threads of our individual past. Do we not still hold the fragile, disparate threads of the living, evolving tapestry of our histories, and that of our children, in our own hands? Is this not enough reason to engage a creative, exploratory excursion into the pages of our not-so-distant past while the ink is still relatively wet and while the sounds and signature impressions are yet discernible?

I solicit the reader's indulgence as I attempt to reconstruct one last, tiny bridge which will conduct us to a more recent history affecting a father and his son. One quick, final glance back to old Auburn.

Chapter Five

The Measure of a Man

*...Created half to rise, and half to fall; Great Lord
of all things, yet a prey to all...*

(Pope's *Essay on Man*)

Fools rush in where angels fear to tread.

(Pope's *Essay on Criticism*)

*One never runs head-long into a darkened room,
unless he knows where the supporting beams are
located.*

(Bambara proverb)

If, indeed, the *fore*fathers had eaten sour grapes,
'Bob' Colman seemed to be one of the sweeter exceptions.
The handsome little lad who enjoyed visiting and posing
with his ruddy, genial grandpa at the old Auburn farm, was
the same young man whom his Manchester neighbors and
classmates admired and loved. His 1942 edition high
school yearbook, the 'Oracle,' pictures a handsome, boyish
Adonis with white shirt and suit jacket, and the ubiquitous
candy-striped tie in a tight Windsor knot. The image, like
so many others of a previous era, is not unlike the familiar
picture-perfect Hollywood images of Rudy Valley or Errol
Flynn.

The reason that such an image, preserved in virtual
anonymity from the consciousness of the modern world, is

that sixty years and countless lost opportunities later, his son would choose to rescue the memory and focus upon his father's mute, isolated image.   Only the memory and ambiguity of intervening decades could give sense and substance to an otherwise benign, isolated expression - one which betrays a fragile strength:

ROBERT EVERETT COLMAN
'Bob'
Technical Course.　　Art Club, 4.　　Rifle Club, 4.

The yearbook contains one hundred and thirty-two hand-written, inked signatures of classmates. No personal notes or expressions of best wishes. Like that small, black and white passport-sized photo, and a million others just like it that have passed slowly and without complaint or unwanted notoriety into oblivion, each signature bears the indelible imprint of one of countless indispensable souls. There *is* something in a name.

***

Dad often spoke about the family having lived in western New York State, but up until recently, no one seemed to know exactly where or when that was…until just the other evening when I had called and left a message for my Dad's brother, Uncle Artie. One of my great-uncles had lived in Troy, New York; they didn't know which one; neither could they remember the name of the cemetery. But they had visited the area once, and remembered the name of the street where the cemetery was located – it was Hoosick Street! My uncle seemed to recall that whichever uncle it was, his wife's name had been Helen. Not much to go on, but every little piece of the puzzle counts.

With respect to my great uncle Horace E. Colman, I had speculated that he had spent his early childhood with the rest of the Colman clan – the infamous 'Chase brothers' in Auburn (old Chester), Rockingham County, and had somehow migrated west to the Brattleborough/Wadsboro area of Windham County, Vermont, sometime in the early nineteen-hundreds. But I couldn't be certain. I *did* know with some degree of stubborn certainty that he had lived in the old village of Newfane (in the same county). Some years ago, Dad had taken me and my oldest son, Jonathan, who was then a teenager just back from spending his young life in Africa, to visit the old museum in Newfane. Dad had also given me a photocopy of an old, hand-drawn map of the 'Stone Markers' at old 'Newfane Hill,' the original settlement, along with a very old conventional county map of Wardsboro. As we discovered during our brief visit, the museum had quite a large collection of Native American artifacts; which had been donated after Horace's death. The following factual account will also confirm, to my curiosity, that Horace did reside and work in Newfane for a period of time as a blacksmith. There is even reason to believe that he is buried in the same town.

We entered the old town of Newfane early in the morning when traces of fresh dew were still visible. The landscape was hilly and thick with trees. It seemed as though we were just winding through the woods without any reasonable destination until the narrow, pock-marked pavement yielded a small rise in the terrain. We found ourselves on a small hill at the entrance to the town. We slowed to a near halt to savor the view when I happened to see an elderly gentleman seated on a makeshift stool in front of an old clapboard shack. He had a long white beard, and was pealing potatoes; he never looked up. We stopped the car, and the three of us slowly approached the quiet old man.

"Good morning," we intoned.

"Morn'n," he replied, without changing his expression or position, or his preoccupation with the potatoes. *I couldn't help but think of the familiar New England story of the city-slicker who happened by the home of a similar old gentleman – "Heh, how's it go'in," inquired the young man. "Howdy," responded the kindly gentleman. "Have you lived here all your life?" After which followed an extended pause. "Not yet,' was his response.* End of conversation.

Somehow, that morning, I found myself taking the lead. After all, my Dad had been gracious enough to chauffeur us to the spot. The least I could do was volunteer as virtual tour guide. I smiled and extended my hand in greeting:

"My name is Peter Colman. This is my Dad, Robert Colman, and this is my son, Jonathan, three generations," I beamed. "Would you be kind enough to help us with some information? We're looking for Horace Colman." For some strange reason, which I only now think of as I write, I assumed that Horace was still alive. There was a long, guarded silence, and then the gentleman asked rather nonchalantly, and with just a pinch of justifiable suspicion:

"Why do you want to see Horace?"

"He is my Dad's uncle and my great-uncle, my grandfather, Sumner Chase's brother." There was a longer, but innocuous silence.

"Well," he slowly allowed, "Horace was a blacksmith. He and I worked together in that old barn;" as he nonchalantly, but with a certain pride, pointed to a small, rust-colored weathered barn just across the road from where we had parked the car. "If you're looking for Horace, he's in the old cemetery just up the road toward town."

He resumed peeling his potatoes. I wondered if he just kept those same potatoes in the pot and pretended to peel them every day until someone had the curiosity to stop and ask him what he was doing. But, I had no real reason to doubt the old man's story, or the integrity of the potatoes for that matter. What really made the day complete was my son's comment once we reached the car: "Dad, I can't believe it! I really *didn't* believe all those stories you told us, at least not until today, about all those ancient New Englanders who never seemed to travel too far from their homes. He's just like the guy in your story!"

***

My grandparents on my father's side, Sumner Chase and Nellie 'Blanche' Moy Colman, spent the first and happiest years of their brief marriage at the old 'Moy Farm' farmhouse in Auburn, New Hampshire (in those years part of old the village of Chester). They raised five sons in that small house, which also doubled as a schoolhouse. Nellie used to brag that she had nursed all of her sons, and that she had had plenty of milk to spare. She had a wonderful, but characteristically-crude sense of humor. During one of her more feisty moments, she shared with me that she used to squirt Sumner with a well-aimed blast of breast milk from across the room whenever he came in the door! Nellie was shy.

Dad spent a brief portion of his early childhood at the old 'Colman Estate' at the foot of a hill on a seven-tenths-of-a-mile stretch in old Auburn, New Hampshire. I have only seen the old one-story clapboard 'mansion' twice. There had been and old gristmill somewhere out in the swamp behind the house, but no one seemed to remember the exact location. The day that Dad showed me the house, he simply, but proudly explained, in passing, that it had been there, in the same house, that he had lived as a boy. Maybe it was just a repressed memory; maybe it was the only simple, surviving memory had had to cherish. How could he have known that his parents' rudimentary, but blissful relationship would end in divorce and another fractured chapter in the Colman odyssey? Did the eventual disappointment of infidelity irreparably damage his innocence, contaminating his capacity for enduring love? Or did the rude, unforeseeable turn of events affecting his young life just render him wiser and more conscious of his own frailty, his own vulnerability, and his own flawed morality? The answer cannot be known.

We continued on soberly to the Auburn Cemetery where most of the patriarchs and matriarchs of the Colman-Moy clan have been laid to rest beneath a proud row of limestone and granite headstones on a prominent brow of the nearest hill. Dad seemed to possess a sense of pride as we perused the silent, stolid monuments, the only tangible vestiges of our humble Auburn history.   'Inglorious Miltons' perhaps?

I really don't know whether those were happy days for my father. Folks worked pretty hard from dawn to dusk in those days, without many distractions. There were no trains nor trolleys servicing the Colman Hill, and it was a good half day's buggy or wagon ride to the city. There was too much to do on the farm to waste time spending one's hard-earned money on frivolous activities. Oh, once in a while there was a county dance at the Grange Hall. Nearly everybody who could walk would go to the dance, except a small group of local 'Friends' (Quakers), or other such straight-laced religious folk whose strict Protestant traditions against attending 'worldly' functions prevented them from enjoying such potentially corrupting intercourse (an old, but equally functional English word for conversation...).

Before returning home that day, and at my request, Dad took me to the outskirts of Manchester, on the old Goffstown Road (in the direction of Glen Lake). Just at the fork in the road which led northwest toward the town of Goffstown and Weare, the old Dunbarton Road headed due north to the right, parallel to the Merrimack River.

The original township of Dunbarton and Weare, settled during the day of General John and Molly Stark, went all the way to the river. On the morning of the same day, we spent several hours revisiting and exploring the old homestead (the ancient 'Eliot or Morse' house – built in 1822 - at the junction of Morse and Montalona) in Dunbarton. An early picture of the Dunbarton house features three crude chimneys and two towering, but leafless pines standing like tired sentinels with bare, thinned arms ready to defend the lonely, feeble fortress at all cost against no one in particular.

There is a strange similarity between my father's and my high school, with some minor exceptions, which requires little speculation or imagination to appreciate. To some extent, it amounts to a repetition of history. Can it be construed as mere coincidence that both Dad and I attended the same high school? Not really. No mystery there. It is intriguing, nonetheless, to consider that my father, who grew up in Manchester, would shuttle off to the Pacific theater as a teenager, only to return, move to a remote area of Dunbarton, and gravitate back to Manchester, his only son in tow, and that his son would later wander the same streets (within a matter of block), only to retrace his father's steps to the same old yellow-brick edifice a few years later.

The squat, red-brick, factory-like building, adjacent to the high school campus, was where Dad had taken up 'wood-working,' or 'shop,' as they use to call it. I still have the small table and shoe-shine box that he made as a freshman student there.

"That's the Technical Building," Dad gestured, as we passed the immortal Central High School campus. "That's where I took shop. Built my first table there. A lot of the young guys used to study and work there. Many of them went off to the war, like me. Most of them never came back home."

Ironically, during my own 'shop' experience in the eighth grade at the Wilson School, I had made a small sign with the words 'Colman' painted in red. I later gave that sign to my father. Nearly five decades later, I happened to notice the same wooden sign, its red paint still bright, nailed to the door of his back-alley brick apartment. It was the last item I took from that hidden, lonely ground-floor apartment, just off the back alley across the street from my Mom, after Dad's death. No one, I suspect, even knew what it was, or where it had come from. I suppose that someone would have noticed it sooner or later, and eventually just discarded it, along with the memory of a small boy and his disenfranchised father, both of whom were suspended in time, separated forever.

As I exited that apartment, a little over a year ago, I tossed the wooden sign in the cardboard box with Dad's effects, and headed to Mom's place across the street. It reminded me of the green and white New Hampshire license plate bearing the COLMAN name (I salvaged that metallic memory from Dad's garage some years ago). All I ever managed to salvage from our relationship, it seemed, were priceless, but equally useless mementoes: cheap canvas military belts, a Limited Edition 200th Anniversary United States Commemorative belt buckle, a bonafide 'Bear Creek Tool Stone,' with a small handmade wooden case, and a realistic replica of a 'rare' silver dollar, which I first believed to be an original; it was not. I did manage to salvage a few of Dad's paintings. My father had a passion for Native American themes and artifacts, as did his second wife, Dorothy, who, throughout her entire, sheltered life, enjoyed anything 'Indian' (almost as an obsession). I, too, have shared that passion from the time I was just a small boy. Most of Dad's paintings displayed early American pioneers and log cabins, or peaceful pastoral scenes. But his favorites featured the sea. One large oil-painting, which he entitled "The Rising Storm," actually won a pink ribbon.

There are several distinguished artists and painters on both sides of the family, including another great, great-uncle in Barnstead, New Hampshire whose nearly photographic, life-size portraits are on display at the firehouse where he worked nearly 'all his life.' My great aunt, on my mother's side, is also a prominent artist. She paints the faces of her husband's hand-made grandfather clocks, as well as beautiful floral designs on glassware. To this day, she and her husband occupy the tiny depot of the old "Blueberry Express" train station in Barnstead, which they have entirely remodeled. One of the bedrooms is the original waiting-room and ticket counter, opening into the living room. They also managed to salvage one of the old train's original cabooses which they have transformed into a small quest house.

New Englanders seem to have an interest in collecting and preserving just about everything in the line of artifacts. Their culture is all they have, and they are bound by an unspoken oath to preserve the last vestiges of their cherished ways. They make it their business and life-calling to know and preserve the memory of those who make up their community, and with whom they share a common existence, usually to the happy and willing exclusion of outsiders. I have a dear aunt, now widowed, in Weare, New Hampshire, who has lived in the same old farmhouse since the end of World War II.

My Uncle Ray, now deceased, served in the Army in Paris during the German invasion. Aunt Phyllis was a nurse who has spent the better part of her life raising two fine sons and serving the aged and ill in her community. But in recent days, her historic and relatively peaceful paradise has suffered the unwanted invasion of 'land-grabbers' from a neighboring state. I once made the mistake of inquiring as to her new, uninvited neighbors:

"Have you met any of your new neighbors, Aunt Phyl?" Her immediate response: "I didn't ask them to come here. They can go to hell for all I care!"

Aunt Phyl always had a way with words. Hypocrisy was never her problem. She has never made a habit of going to church, and pretty much figured that anything worth believing should just be kept to oneself. A person should just try to be a good neighbor, provided that they live in Weare. In recent days, she does crossword puzzles all day, plays scrabble alone each night, with Uncle Ray sitting invisibly across the table (she vows that she never cheats), and listens to old Christian records, which is rather remarkable considering she avoids discussing religion 'like the plague'. Aunt Phyl once boasted that the only time she bothered to attend church was for funerals. On one such occasion a few years ago, she attended a funeral at the old historic Weare Church. She was most uncomfortable, by her own confession, and admitted to me in a rather humorous correspondence that during the pastor's sermon she had felt a twinge of jealousy and regret as she had reflected upon the poor soul lying unaffected in the open coffin.

"I started to envy the poor fellow," she volunteered; "I wished I were in his place. He was better off than I was. At least he wouldn't have to listen to the sermon!"

I must confess, apart from some of these items which still had some practical value, the only thing that makes them irreplaceable is that they belonged to my father; they were important to him. I also inherited an old granite 'Billy-club' with a hard wooden handle. This ruthless relic had belonged to Dorothy Samara Colman's father, who had been a policeman back in Europe at the turn of the last century. Something like that could come in handy when one has to survive without a father.

A lot of young men took 'Commercial' and 'Technical' courses in those days, including Dad. Many others were active in school sports and assorted electives such as the 'Rifle Club' or the 'Archery Club.' Curiously, one picture in the 1942 *Oracle* yearbook shows four of the more adventurous students (two young men and two young woman) holding small wooden bows (they couldn't have been more than twenty pounds in strength) with a brace of arrows in the foreground. Call it unsophisticated or simplistic, if you must, but simple things meant much more in those days. People enjoyed 'down-home' distractions and took pleasure in what was basic, a common, unembellished pragmatism of sorts. They even dressed the same way; there didn't seem to be a need to impress anyone.

***

At this point, I feel it is only fair to the reader that I peel back my writer's psyche just a bit and reveal a glimpse of where I am coming from. Twenty years ago I wouldn't have bothered. But I have learned a lot about myself in recent years, and enjoyed a wealth of experience (some as an intercultural sojourner). Teaching has become not just a profession, but a passion. As has learning. Much of the motivation for writing the present story derives from a deep desire to understand my own brief, colorful journey better, and to invite others to explore and savor their own.

As a self-proclaimed student and home-spun scholar, I have become acquainted in recent years with the concept in education of what the professionals refer to as the method of 'self-discovery.' The concept is not entirely new in the social sciences. In my own academic pilgrimage, I have become acquainted with the more technical term, 'heuristic.' The term 'heuristic' denotes the idea of 'self-discovery,' or 'problem-solving.' It is an 'experimental' approach to learning. In my own research on the function and cultural value of proverbial forms of speech, I have discovered (thanks to the insights of many notable linguists and social anthropologists, including the noted French social scientist, Claude Levi-Strauss) that the use of language, stories and mythical accounts can, in fact, yield *new* meaning. The word 'meaning' derives from an old Middle English word *menen*, which relates to what a person may have 'in mind,' that is, it speaks of *intention*. Meaning, to be recognized, usually has to do with what is familiar. But it is also possible, in the course of human conversation and interaction, to discover *new* meaning that may quite exceed and expand the conventional categories of understanding.

But what does this have to do with writing a story? Simply put, in the present attempt to explore the twists, turns and grass-roots tendencies of the lives of the actors in my own family history, I am inclined to believe the real potential of creating new meaning and understanding not only for me, but also for others who may wish to savor and evaluate their own story in light of my own. Renowned anthropologist, Edward T. Hall, has commented that the real benefit of attempting to navigate and understand the complexity and rich diversity of other cultures, is that, in the final analysis, and as a result of that endeavor, the inquirer is ultimately able to better understand his or her own culture. It's a bit like examining the sole of your own foot, the foot that has born the weight of your existence, but has gone relatively unnoticed, until now.

My second son, Daniel, and I visited the old Colman homestead in Dunbarton some years ago. We walked up to the old shed door of the house and knocked. A kindly, elderly couple opened the door.

"Good morning. My name is Peter Colman. This is my son, Daniel. We've been out of the country for several years, but I lived in this house as a child, and wondered if we could, well, just take a glance...a short tour. The couple left their bowls of hot homemade soup at the small table and proceeded to invite us in.

"I noticed the old latch on the shed door," I quipped. "That's the same latch that was there when I was a child. My Dad had built a chicken coop over there...I had breakfast one morning right there in that corner. I found a tack..." *I caught myself.* The soup was getting cold, as they led us on to the dining room and the same immortal staircase leading to the upstairs bedrooms. *Somehow, I found myself directing the unscheduled tour.*

"Now, correct me if I'm wrong," I continued, "but at the top of the stairs, to the right, there's a room with a slanted window on the far wall. That was *my* bedroom. Every night when Mom and Dad put me to bed, Dad would wrap me...well. One morning we heard a noise. A skunk had been foraging in the dump...there, over there in the flowerbed. That used to be an old dump...right next to the stone fireplace Dad build for the church picnic...The skunk had gotten its head stuck in a mayonnaise jar and was coming up the dirt road flopping the empty jar back and forth...Dad got the '22 and shot the jar right off its head. It ran away mad but unscathed!"

"Yes," they nodded incredulously, "you're right. The window is still there. That was our son's room, too."

"I swallowed a big marble one day, right here at the top of the stairs...."

After a brief visit, Daniel and I thanked the couple and left. Mom and I returned to the house another day, when no one was home, to explore the perimeter. There had been some changes, but the numbers on the ornate trim over the front entrance (now nearly invisible through the high hedges) read *1822*. Some things *never* change.

Chapter Six

Boot-Camp

Surely he shall deliver thee from the snare of the fowler, and from the noisome pestilence...

(Psalm 91:3)

Even a knife with a sharp blade cannot shape its own handle.

(Bambara proverb)

After migrating from the farm in Auburn with their parents, Bob Colman and his brothers moved to Manchester. Sumner and Nellie and the boys lived behind the A&P Store (formerly known as the 'American Tea Company') where Dad worked; that's where he met my Mom. According to her account, she had known Dad from high school. Everyone knew Dad. All the girls had liked him because he was 'a good guy.' But Dad liked Barbara Jewett. *While in high school, I had a few female 'friends,' too, and went on first dates with several. My first true love was a beautiful young girl by the name of Linda Kouri, but that's another story...*Anyway, the day that Mom and Dad really *met* (I have the strong suspicion that Mom's chance encounter with 'Bob' was anything but incidental), Dad was outside the store washing his boss's Beach Wagon.

Some months later, before any kind of romance could blossom, Dad enlisted for the Marine Corps. His four brothers went into the Navy and all served their

79

respective tours of duty aboard ships in the Pacific. Dad did his basic training at 'Camp Joseph H. Pendleton,' billed as the 'World's Largest U.S. Marine Corps Training Center,' at Oceanside, California. This legendary military camp was dedicated in September, 1942 by Franklin Delano Roosevelt. General Pendleton's widow, affectionately known in the Corps as 'Aunt Mary,' was by the President's side.

Bob Colman was nineteen years of age when he enlisted right after graduation in 1942. Since the attack on Pearl Harbor on December 7, 1941, Japan, having allied its forces with Germany, had been expanding its reign in China and Indochina, and had begun a campaign to wrest control of several Pacific island chains colonized by Britain.

According to *The Old Breed,* [18] the legendary 'First Marine Division' had been created on February 1, 1941. Its predecessor, the 'First Brigade,' quartered at Quantico, had already been to the Pacific theatre in the fall of 1940 to secure Guadalcanal. When the First Brigade returned for additional training in May of that year, they joined other forces at Parris Island. By August, the Joint Force exercises of the Corps would swell to 16,000 men. By December 7, 1941, the ragtag group of 'regulars and reserves' could only boast 518 officers and 6,871 enlisted men. In March, 1942 a small division was sent to Apia, Western Samoa. On the other side of the U.S. Continent, an elite group of Marine trainees of the 'Amphibious Force, Atlantic Fleet,' were ordered to the *Solomon Islands,* in Chesapeake Bay, off Maryland! But by June of that year, orders had come down from the Joint Chiefs of Staff to

---

[18] *The Old Breed. A History of the First Marine Division in World War II,* by George McMillan, Washington: Infantry Journal Press, First Edition, 1949.

Vice Admiral Ghormley, Commander of the South Pacific Area. His orders were precise:

"Occupy and defend Tulagi and adjacent positions (Guadalcanal and Florida Islands and the Santa Cruz Islands) in order to deny these areas to the enemy and to provide United States bases in preparation for further offensive action." When asked exactly *who* was to be expected to occupy and defend these islands, he responded:

"The First Marine Division!"

That was my Dad's Division; he had been trained as a paratrooper, and was a proud member of the 'First Marine Parachute Division.' He made two trips to the Pacific combat zone. The first trip, lasting from 1942-1944, departed San Diego and brought the First Marine Division past the Cook Islands to the south, on to New Caledonia, and eventually to Guadalcanal at the southern tip of the Solomons, where Dad's unit dug in, set up shop, built airstrips, and fought and served for two years.

Dad shipped out a second time for action in 1945, but this time he went by way of the Hawaiian island of Oahu and past the Marshall Islands to Guam, south of Saipan and the Iwo-Jima chain. Dad made eight jumps under fire during his service as a Marine, and was decorated twice for bravery. Once, he carried a twelve-man tent while being strafed by Japanese migs. Another time, under the same conditions, he had put his hand into the gapping wound of a fellow corpsman and carried him under fire to a makeshift underground 'hospital' on the beach. But those actions would not prove to be the most decisive in Bob Colman's life, or in mine. For what happened to my Dad personally during those short months would change the rest of his life. And, as I would later discover, what happened to one of Dad's *boots* was to shape the entire chronicle of the Colman history, at least as far as my side of the family was concerned.

***

There is no official military record of what really transpired in my father's young life during his first year of combat duty in the U.S. Marine Corps. While it was not uncommon for military chaplains and leaders of other religious faiths to hold regular services for the corpsmen, both before and during combat, Dad's experience did not conform to any prescheduled religious exercise. According to his own testimony, somewhere in a remote, undisclosed spot in the New Caledonia/Solomon Island chain, there lays hidden, in the long-forgotten soil or undergrowth, the remnant of a foxhole that bears the memory of his personal religious conversion to Jesus Christ. In the heat of battle, and with bullets from 50-caliber machine guns splintering the air over his head, Dad prayed to God for forgiveness and found peace. He would never be the same. He soon shed some of his old habits like smoking and cursing, and in the years to follow, tried to live a clean, godly life.

Dad was baptized with a large group of 'new converts' in a fresh-water stream on the island of *Moiseul* (roughly translated from the French as 'me alone'), a fitting name for a singularly decisive event in anyone's life. Dad later shared that all those who 'went down into the waters' that day had done so in the buff, without a trace of shame or regret. No one seemed to care; there was scant chance of offending neighbors or the church family. It was an appropriate way to make a clean start. Paradise revisited.

A small typed copy of Dad's 'baptismal certificate' reads:

82

"TO WHOM IT MAY CONCERN:
This is to certify that I baptized (By emersion)
Robert Everett COLMAN on November 11, 1943.
Ralph E. Tupper

Chaplain Ralph E. Tupper

As mentioned earlier, Dad was susceptible to temptation like anyone else, but there was no question in his heart and mind, or in the minds of any of his family members, that when he returned home from the war in late November or early December, 1945, after a decisive Allied victory over Germany and Japan, Bob Colman was a different man. Perhaps too different for some.

Throughout most of my adult life, when I did have occasion to talk with my father about the war, he only briefly shared that the atrocities he had witnessed during combat could not be described, and were better forgotten. All he seemed interested in remembering was the experience that changed the entire course of his life. I never felt the need to question him further about his war experience, though I always kept a small photograph of a proud, smiling handsome Bob Colman in full Marine uniform.

Finally, there was the incident involving the *boot*.

Just prior to his death, Dad shared an intriguing detail during a casual conversation about the war. For nearly fifty years, he had been remiss to even talk about the war, but for some reason, perhaps the fact that death was imminent, he was talking now, 'man to man,' with his son.

"We had jumped near the shoreline in Jap-infested territory in the middle of the night, and were ordered to dig in until dawn. We knew the Japs were somewhere just beyond the jungles in the hills, maybe just beyond the line of palm trees and foliage beyond the beach, but everything was dead-quiet. We couldn't see them. We couldn't see anything but the reflection of our own faces in the moonlight and the whitecaps pounding the shore. The silence was sickening. A division of Marines had hit the beach just minutes before we had landed, just before dawn. A hint of light and a soft sea breeze began to awaken the soft carpet of the sea, and stir the silent palms. They seemed friendly enough, and beautiful, but we knew that they hid danger and death.

The first Marine division had begun just before light to organize their platoon and ready supplies and weapons...and then all hell broke loose! Without a whisper of warning, the Japs opened up from the dense foliage with dozens of 50-caliber guns, raking the beaches. I saw about three hundred men cut down in seconds. Three hundred! It took quite some time for the remaining men to work their way around the Jap division and flush out those machinegun nests, but they cleaned them out fast with flame-throwers. They threw all they had at those positions.

There had been total confusion and chaos. We had underestimated their strength and cunning. We had dug shallow trenches in the beach sand in the dark, right where our feet had hit the sand, but we were sitting ducks when the migs arrived in the early morning hours, seconds after the first barrage of fire, and started strafing the beaches. Our division, the First Parachute Division, had no choice but to run for better cover, and join the other landing division to strengthen our positions. It was then that a very curious thing happened.

Many of my company had removed their boots after the jump to clean out the sand, before trying to settle down in the dark for a little shut-eye. For some reason, which I don't recall, I had my boots on when the Japs attacked, but I had forgotten to lace one of them. It was too late to bother, so I grabbed my rifle and gear and just ran for dear life, along with everybody else, for better shelter. The harder I ran, the harder it became, and then something snapped in my foot...the loose boot! In my effort to run full tilt in the sand with a loose boot, something had broken. I had managed to find better cover in the sand, but I couldn't move.

That was it. End of story. We did manage to take the beach. The Marines called in the big sixteen-inch guns from the battleships off-shore, and they blasted the Jap positions until the jungles were cleared and we were able to secure the island for a larger landing force. But that was the end of the war for me. I was shipped back to Pendleton."

"But what happened after that, Dad?"

"I became a cook for the next two years. The camp was still pretty active. Thousands of guys were enlisting by then. The marine divisions at Guadalcanal were being replenished all the time. Now I was working with a large crew of cooks helping the Marine Corps to feed these guys and finish the job."

"Wow, Dad, you never told me about that."

"Do you understand?" he continued. "If I had tied my *boot*, I may have never made it home alive, and you would not have been here! This is the grace of God. All those years and those jumps...all those casualties and bullets flying over our heads, the bombing, tracers and strafing…and I survived without a scratch. And at the last moment, I was sent home because I forgot to tie my *boot*! Oh, one last thing…soon after that campaign, just after I was sent back to Pendleton, the rest of the First Marine Parachute Division, my group, were all sent to Iwo-Jima. The rest of them were either killed or wounded there."

There is a New Hampshire boy helping to raise the American flag of Victory on a hill at Iwo-Jima. That boy's name could have been Bob Colman. Or not. But he was every bit a part of that victory. Even though he would become the father I never really knew, I was proud.

The war was over for Dad, at least the war he had fought in the trenches at Guadalcanal. In some sense, like all those who witness the horror of combat and killing, the war is never really over. The memories, the sounds, the smells, the weeping, the spasmodic malarial fevers and fits of sadness, loneliness and homesickness…none of this ever entirely leaves, but clings to the human psyche like a stubborn, festering wound. That was certainly the case with Dad, though he never talked about his struggles and feverish nightmares. Mom told me once that during their first years of marriage, Dad used to get up in the night and move around the bedroom to the second-story window, screaming in a cold sweat, pretending to fire a machine gun, pointing its muzzle into the predawn darkness of the quiet tree line across Morse Road.

But another life had just begun for Dad, too. He had a new purpose in life, a radically new orientation. His desire was to live for God and to share his experience with the world. He had come back from the brink, had stared death in the face, and survived to tell the story. His experience in that foxhole, his personal conversion, would now dictate the pulse and pace of the remainder of his earthly life.

At least this was the plan.

***

Regardless of one's religious or secular worldview, the significance of small details and inexplicable, unpredictable occurrences such as an untied boot can hardly be dismissed. It could be argued that much of history is made of such elusive and apparently insignificant details. If 'the devil is in the details,' then it could be argued that God is too. There was certainly no question in my father's post-conversion mind as to the providential nature of these events. Nor is there any doubt or the slightest trace of equivocation in my understanding of as to the reality of divine intervention as it relates to the succeeding series of events leading to my own life. Others, thousands of others, were not as *fortunate*. What is important here is not cold objectivity or a proper theology, but rather a simple recognition of events; the gracious acceptance of such events should never give the actor, or actors, a license for arrogance, pride, or unwanted and unwarranted forms of religious self-righteousness. If anything, historical details such as these, particularly when they impact one's life, should create a genuine and implacable sense of gratitude and humility. The kind of attitude one ought to live with is something akin to what William Blake describes in his sobering lines from *Songs of Innocence/Songs of Experience*:

...Then the groan and the dolor are quite forgotten, and the slave grinding at the mill and the captive in chains, and the poor in the prison, *and the soldier in the field when the shatter'd bone hath laid him groaning among the happier dead...*

87

Chapter Seven

Bitter-Sweet Grapes

A chicken drinks water a little bit at a time.
(Bambara proverb)

The rooster crows from the time it leaves the egg.
(French proverb)

During his two-year stint at Camp Pendleton, Dad kept his new-found faith alive by attending services at the 'off-campus' First Baptist church. According to a brief article entitled 'Churches In Oceanside,' in the 1944 *Souvenir Edition* of the activities at Camp Joseph H. Pendleton the previous year, the various religious groups lent 'character and spiritual leadership' to the military community. In addition to weekly services, other 'church societies' were available both to married and single service personnel. Extra-curricular activities such as "…Missionary study, aid work and sacred study," were intended to help people of religious faith maintain a vital commitment to God and to goodness in the face of very stressful wartime conditions.

When Dad was discharged in 1945, he was ready to 'hit the beaches' of his own native New England, and assault the forces of paganism, leading a one-man attack against a deeply entrenched, indifferent secular terrain. The most demanding and discouraging campaign, to be sure, would be against his own family members and friends. 'A prophet is not without honor...except in his own country.'

Dad's unflappable religious zeal would be deeply resented by his own mother and brothers who had remembered another person than the one who had returned from the Marine Corps waving the Christian flag. His mother didn't even want to greet him when he returned home a handsome, decorated hero. "I don't know you," she had said, "I want the old Bob!" The adjustment wasn't easy. If his own family didn't want to hear his religious rants, others didn't want to get near him at all. My Uncle Jim Rogers would later confide that Dad didn't know when to quit: "He was always trying to shove religion down someone's throat," he would allege. Given Dad's record for courage under fire, his record for religious zeal was probably not exaggerated. I would still prefer to believe that he simply felt very strongly about life and death issues - issues of eternity; he just wasn't terribly tactful about dealing with the present.

At this point in the Colman chronology, I wasn't even in the blueprint. It's always easier and less painful to try to put the pieces together, and to make sense of the present, in retrospect. But only the broad outlines are barely visible. So what's the use? Why recreate the story? Why recycle the past? If Santayana was correct, and studying the past is perhaps the only way to avoid repeating its pitfalls, then it follows that understanding one's personal history can be a positive, practical means of shaping the present, and perhaps even transforming congenital moral defects. Isn't the effort part and parcel to 'seeing that bigger picture,' of restructuring the present from the scattered remnants of the past? I would like to believe so, but there is a fine line. There is always the danger of a self-fulfilling prophecy. In exploring one's past, there is always the danger of exposing oneself to the realities which lay behind the buried accounts, the raw historical data, akin to exhuming a corpse. But I would prefer to think more positively, and perhaps more realistically. There is no real advantage to ignoring those realities and dwelling in a veil of naïveté or relative ignorance with respect to one's collective history.

But there is a caveat to such a quest, a principle to be observed which is critical to those in the fields of archaeology or paleontology. For example, the context within which something of historical value is found is as important as, if not more important than, the item itself. In the routine search for ancient artifacts, such as coins, mere treasure-hunting becomes an immoral and irresponsible endeavor. For one simple, sensible reason. The environment within which an artifact is found is indispensable, yielding specific, irrefutable scientific data relative to the artifact itself. The *material context* within which such an artifact is found is critical in the understanding of the specific circumstances and conditions in which the item existed.

The analogy is self evident. For an individual to fully understand his or her inherent value, or purpose, or place in the wider scheme of things, then *understanding* the unique contextual soil from which that person has emerged, and to which the same individual is ever related, can only be beneficial. The anthropologist Clifford Geertz calls the search for such critical historical minutia, or mythical data, *thick description.* Such a meticulous approach to the past yields a richer, more fact-laden account of what actually transpired. I am not recommending a nostalgic return to the past, and certainly not a preoccupation with one's past, but simply a passionate, rigorous search for truth, and an earnest excavation of emotion. A search for the *imago Dei* in man - in the common man - in one's particular history, in one's personal story. Such an earnest quest may disclose common threads, and unearth perennial roots capable of generating new growth. Roots begging to be unearthed, explored, and embraced.

***

Mom had been pretty wild in her youth, "giving the guys permission to date her," she was fond of saying. The very pretty, sedate picture of Doris ('Dotty') Arlene Rogers in the 1944 Manchester Central High School *Oracle* Yearbook betrays an underlying restlessness and thirst for adventure. She was beautiful, and extremely athletic. By her own admission, she was also extremely shy, but she was fearless.

The old granite 'McGregor' quarry near the reservoir overlooking Manchester had been abandoned in the thirties. It had flooded, leaving both workers and hundreds of tons of equipment at the bottom; its depths were a murky green. But, it was a great place to swim and to experiment with disaster. There were rocks to jump from, one about twenty feet up. This was a popular height for novices. Mom once lost the top of her two-piece suit there, 'the white one with the blue trim,' and had to 'surface-dive' while the guys watched from above in order to retrieve it. But there was one sheer, steep rock face that caused more than one foolish jumper to lose either bladder control, or a swimsuit, or both. The rock face was nearly sixty feet from the edge to the hard, cold surface below. *I stood near the edge of that legendary 'Ledge' a few years ago on a return trip from Africa…just for old times' sake, and I had to withdraw for fear of being involuntarily drawn too close.*

"Do you see the painting of the gymnasts up there on the ledge?" Mom asked during one of those early swims, "Dr Frank 'O.' Warren, Jr. painted that." The year had to have been about 1941 or 1942, just before the boys went off to war. Strangely enough, Dr. Warren had also been our school doctor; he had treated my first ankle injury in football, and was the team doctor.

"How did he do *that*?"

"He and some of the guys stretched ropes from those trees on either side of the cliff, and tied them to a wooden platform."

For years, I thought that Mom had actually helped the guys paint that design, which is still visible today. That was part of the myth I entertained in my own mind about Mom's teen escapades. I asked her about it, hoping for confirmation.

"No. I didn't do that," she said, "But I did swim there all the time. I used to always go ice-skating at the Derryfield Park rink, too," she added. "I used to roller-skate and swim. You know, that's about all we had to do in those days. There was another quarry up on Mammoth Road. I used to swim there a lot, too."

Mom is still a good swimmer; to this day she still has no aversion to cold water, fresh or salt, and has a beautiful, smooth stroke. She turned eighty this past May (2007). I would still like to believe that she helped the guys paint that picture of the three gymnasts. I'm sure that she would have been up there with them as a young girl if she could have swung it.

Back to the subject of the ledge. I asked Uncle Jim once about Mom's legendary feats at the old quarry. Was it true that she actually made the big jump as a teenage girl?

"Yeah, that was Dot. She did that, and more. She was always testing the guys' courage. That ledge was high! A lot of us jumped it. Most of the guys wore sneakers to break their fall. It was like hitting blacktop. God forbid that anyone should lose control and land on their back or face. But it happened...sometimes."

"Did Mom ever jump?" *Stupid question, I thought.*

"Did she ever *jump*? Sure, once in a while, but she usually *dove*!"

"She dove?"

"You bet. Come to think of it, she was one of the only ones who ever dared to dive..."

When I asked Mom about this, she admitted happily to it.

"Yes, I dove. I did it often. There was one other girl who did it too. I'm not sure if 'the twins' did or not. Sometimes people landed on their belly..."

***

In a recent conversation with 'Mum,' (years later I started using the British designation) and with the utmost discretion, of course, I asked her about what I had believed to be her 'reputation' as a 'Tom-boy.' I was surprised by her response. Nothing is what it seems. Or so it seems.

"I was very shy."

I was shocked.

"Sure, I was really very quiet and shy, at first. That's why I looked so quiet in the picture. That's the way I was. The reason I did all those things was because my mother didn't trust us at all. She didn't trust me or Shirl at all!" *'Shirl' was Aunt Shirley, Mum's sister, and about four years her elder.* Did I ever tell about the time Shirl and I went out? First, we always had to be home by ten o'clock. Mum didn't trust us beyond ten o'clock."

"Where did you go?" I probed.

"Oh, we went to the movies most of the time, and then out for hot dogs. Yeah, we really ate a lot of hot dogs in those days."

"So what happened?"

"Well, I had been out a bit too late. It was when we lived at the house on 404 Concord Street, the one on the hill; it was a six-room cottage. Rent was twenty dollars a month. *I had seen the old residence just once. It was a small, gray building with short steps leading to a porch with decorative posts. Pretty typical in those days.* I had gotten home late. The key was under the mat. What a stupid place for a key! Anyway, when I reached the house, I crept quietly to the door, got the key, took off my shoes, and put them under my left arm…I gently grasped the doorknob and turned it, very slowly, opening the door very carefully…When I did, Mum was standing there stone-cold just inside the door. She had heard me and had been waiting for me! She had this way of looking at us…"

"Kind of venomous, right?

"Exactly! V*enomous*. She never said anything, but you had the feeling she was judging you, condemning you. And I hadn't done a lousy thing! She just didn't trust us at all. Neither of us, and Shirl didn't go out half as much as I did. Well, after that I just decided that if she didn't trust us when we hadn't done anything, I may as well give her a good reason. So I started going out with guys and staying out late. Eventually, I just moved out and got my own apartment at 88 Manchester Street; it had just one room; the rent was four dollars a week."

Mom worked in town at the Employers' Group. She did typing, idiophone and Dictaphone for the manager. Mom was always an excellent typist, and to this day her word and grammatical skills are exceptional.

"Did you continue to see guys then," I queried. *Now I felt that I was getting into dangerous territory.*

"Sure, in fact, there was this one guy that I really liked...but there were complications...You know. Actually, he was an usher at the local church we attended. He was going through a divorce and had a daughter...I really shouldn't have been seeing him. I was only about seventeen at the time. Maybe eighteen. Anyway, I went to see him at his place one night, thinking that we would be alone. When I walked into the living room, my Mom and Dad were both sitting there waiting for me!"

I couldn't help but laugh to help cope with the mild shock.

"They were there in his apartment waiting for you, huh?"

"Yup. They were there just waiting and sitting quietly. No expression, except my mother's piercing glare. I was mortified. They never trusted me. That was the problem. That's why I did it."

It was 1945. That's when my Mom saw Bob Colman again. It was the first time she had seen him since his return from the war. She remembered how he had been 'well-liked' by just about everyone during their high school years; she liked him, too, secretly. But so did all the other girls. And she had been shy. Things had changed for both of them, but neither of them knew it. Fortunately, perhaps. That was the day she had been strolling up Hanover Street past the A&P grocery store. That was the day she happened to see a handsome young Marine hero washing his boss's Beach Wagon.

"Hi Bob!"

Dad had loved Barbara Jewett, but she didn't hold a candle to Dotty Rogers, which is no small feat, because the sun was shining that morning. Mom was never afraid of taking that perilous leap while others watched. But this time the results would be different. She had no way of knowing just how happily different they would be.

"Hi Dotty."

Bob was young, and glad to have his feet on solid ground. The foot had healed. The infamous boot had long since been discarded, along with some of the memories. There were still scars, but he was ready to settle down, ready for love and companionship. Sure, he had sown some wild oats like everyone else, but now he had a new lease on the old farm, so to speak. Things would be different. He wouldn't make the same mistakes again. One only has one life to invest, one heart to give. He was determined to make a sure investment.

Mom and Dad would soon wed, but it hadn't happened quickly or without conditions. It took all of three weeks.

Some time after that first meeting in front of the A&P store, Mom had been sitting alone during a meeting at the First Baptist church when Bob and his younger brother, Richie, came in. After the service, Bob approached Dotty.

"Mom makes a great dinner. Would you like to come up to dinner?"

By her own admission, Dotty was characteristically shy, but she quickly agreed to the invitation. According to Mom's account, Dad agreed to the visit, but upon one condition: "You'll have to take the lipstick off if you want to kiss," Bob told her. *One has to wonder which would be the most provocative, the lipstick or the kiss?*

Mom was more than willing to forego the little luxury of lipstick. It would be a small sacrifice, a small price to pay, she thought. She never wore lipstick in public again (and certainly not in church) the entire time they were married. Dad apparently believed that lipstick and make-up, along with most forms of amusement like movie-going and the carnival, were 'worldly.' He believed them to be inconsistent with personal faith in God, and everything God stood for, such as purity and personal righteousness (the old term would be 'holiness'). The problem with any such form of legalism is that if taken to its logical conclusion, the individual is progressively required to abstain from virtually everything, or to disassociate from everyone else (since nearly everything and everyone is tainted with sin).

Finally, unless the forces are restrained and reigned in, the individual is even brought to the very lonely, destructive place of self-loathing self-deprecation, which, ironically, is quite contrary to the example and teaching of Christ. Herein lies the dilemma.

Some time later, Dotty invited Bob to her apartment. He was reluctant. She respected that. In fact, her landlord had stipulated that she could rent the apartment provided that she never had boys in her room. She had agreed. Then along came Bob Colman. *Here*'s a man who could be trusted, a Marine hero, a gentleman with a sterling Christian character. She had to have known that her chances were better than average, so she spoke with her landlord and explained her situation. He agreed to allow Bob to visit.

Something quite unexpected happened during Mom and Dad's 'first date,' if the report is to be taken at face value. In the course of a very casual conversation, Dad had shared his conversion experience with Mom. Dad told her he was 'saved,' and that she was just a 'church-goer.' She needed to repent and to seek God's forgiveness. According to Mom's story, she and Dad knelt together by a twin bed; Dad led Mom in 'the sinner's prayer.' Mom prayed to receive forgiveness and to give her heart to God. No one at church had ever told her that faith had to be personal, that it required more than just church attendance. She had been attending Sunday school and services for years. She had even been baptized at the age of twelve; Shirl had been sixteen. But no one ever talked to her about faith. Or about sex.

The marriage took place three weeks later, on Friday evening, January 18, 1946, at eight o'clock. The ceremony was conducted by Reverend Lynn Levinworth, in the parsonage of the Merrimack Street Baptist Church at 112 Oak Street, Manchester, New Hampshire. There was a good deal of snow and slush that night. My uncle, Ray Rogers, who had served with his brother, Jim, in the U.S. Army in Paris during the war, drove the newlyweds to the bus station. Mom and Dad spent a three-day honeymoon at the Hotel Terrain in Boston. There was a lot of new territory to explore in their new life together, and some stubborn soil to till before they would enjoy a simple, meager measure of happiness. They had few earthly possessions, and even fewer examples of marital stability and fidelity on either side of the family, but they were ready to forge their own kind of love.

Chapter Eight

New England Roots

Many words may chase away the birds (from one's field), but they will never ripen one's grain.

(Bambara proverb)

The post-war years in the late 1940's were tough. Most average New England families had come from long lines of farmers and craftsmen, living simple lives, close to the earth. They lived practically. Their philosophical underpinnings were made of a strange admixture of Yankee pragmatism, patriotic zeal, rugged individualism, and a curious, but insipient blend of religious zeal (the result of the extraordinary surge of revivalist fires in the colonies under the 18th-century evangelistic preaching of George Whitfield – and his close personal friend, Benjamin Franklin – and company), spiritual skepticism, and indifference. New England was also the philosophical and religious breeding-ground for Unitarianism, Christian Science (Mary Baker Eddy) and the Transcendentalism of Emerson and Thoreau.

Neither the Colman nor the Rogers clans could boast of material wealth. Neither family could claim any distinction or advantage. Bob and Dotty Colman had few worldly possessions to call their own. Mom got a new job at Employers' Liability Assurance Corporation ('Assurance' is actually the French word for *In*surance), but quit two months after the wedding. Dad worked at the L.J.

Carlton Company at Auburn and Elm Streets, making cabinets. Eventually, they were able to hire the K. G. Moore Moving Company to transfer their miscellaneous, meager earthly possessions to a two-room upstairs 'attic' apartment on the corner of Pearl and Union Streets. They later moved to a two-room apartment above the Paul H. Kate Funeral Home, an unlikely climate to nurture a vibrant relationship. But it was quiet. They lived there for ten months. Their first car was a used 1931 Essex.

My parents were very active in the life of the small Baptist church. On one occasion, Dad met a Greek gentleman from Auburn at a revival service. (Dad had become a recognized church leader by then, leading periodic Bible studies. He told me once that he had always 'felt the call to preach.' He frequently carried sermon and study notes in his Bible, just in case. He was always prepared to talk with others about his faith.) The Greek gentleman owned an old house on Morse Road in Dunbarton. The old town of Dunbarton originally extended to the Merrimack River to the east, and included Goffstown and Weare. He invited Mom and Dad to his house for dinner. During that visit, he asked Dad to 'bless his car with oil.' Dad was in the habit of blessing all his vehicles like that. It was just a bit of an extension of the divine prescription for prayer for the healing of the sick from the book of James, in the New Testament. Before leaving that evening, the gentleman told Dad that he was interested in selling the house if he could find a buyer. Dad expressed an interest, applying for a G.I. loan, and was able to purchase the nineteenth-century dwelling for under three-thousand dollars. I asked Mom once why she and Dad chose to live so far out in the country in such an old house without any of the so-called modern conveniences.

"Your Dad and I both enjoyed the country. We liked the thought of being closer to nature."

They were certainly closer to nature!

There was no city water, but there *was* in-door plumbing, and even running water, as long as there was sufficient water in the spring at the base of the hill behind the house. There were also two wells on the property, from which Mom drew water by hand. The wells usually ran bone-dry in the summer. Most of the time, she had to cart water in big buckets from a neighbor's house up the road. Elise Nelson had an artesian well. Mom would pull me in a Red-Flyer wagon, and we would return with full buckets. I sat in the wagon to steady the load. She would load and off-load these heavy buckets almost daily. When I asked Mom about this, she said that she thought that the lifting may have been one of the reasons that she lost her baby girl.

We had every simple luxury imaginable. If I recall, we also put the original outhouse (or 'privy' as it was called in those days) to ample use. *One always knew where to look for the privy. You just had to close your eyes. Actually, they were always located next to the lilac bushes always planted in the vicinity.* The lilacs were a practical necessity. The house had three chimneys, but they were not in use at the time, so we had a large, black pot-bellied stove in the middle of the living room, just inside the front door.

The old mansion, affectionately known as the 'Eliot or Morse House,' had been built in the very early 1800s, and was in terrible disrepair. One of the neighbor boys had frequently used it for target practice. The siding was plastered with bullet holes. It was well ventilated. An obscure kitchen door revealed steep, winding steps leading to a dark dirt catacomb of storage shelves and pre-Civil War arched-brick foundations.

All historic New England homes had a utility cellar with a dirt floor where canned goods and vegetables were stored for the long winter months. My grandparents in Weare had a small, two-room cottage with a tiny dirt basement. The original hole had been dug, and the foundation laid in the late eighteenth century. Mammy had kept dozens of fruit and canning jars there on shelves; she canned all the fresh produce she and Pappy had raised in an acre of gardens, all that they had been unable to sell in their roadside stand. The small yield of red and white potatoes was stored in separate woven baskets. The green tomatoes were wrapped in newspaper until they slowly ripened. Pappy worked at the Kennedy Butter and Egg Store in Manchester, so he was able to keep a modest, but regular fresh supply of eggs, blue cheese (his favorite), Chase and Sanborn coffee, yellow one-pound bars of fresh butter, and brass tubs of peanut butter.

My parents' and my grandparents' homes were very similar: They were centuries old, and quaint; they had character. But they were different too. The history of the small cottage was shrouded in mystery. The only evidence of its previous occupants was a hidden cluster of tiny, worn family limestone grave markers huddled in anonymity under an old pine in a hollow near the bog. I discovered them as a child while playing nearby. When I returned thirty years later, they had disappeared, buried forever under a blanket of green moss. The old country kitchen and the dining room in the old Morse Place were combined on one half of the ground floor, with one doorway leading to an unused living room area and a staircase at the foot of the main entrance leading to the bedrooms upstairs. The house had been occupied off and on for over one hundred and twenty-five years before Mom and Dad had purchased it. Its first occupants would have had parents and grandparents who had lived through the American Revolution, or even earlier. The floorboards in the family room, or *parlor*, were nearly a foot in width, and looked liked they had been cut from the bow of an old ship. They had been hewn from solid oak. Had there been a flood, the old house probably would have stayed a float like Noah's ark. It was nearly as old, and boasted nearly as many critters.

The fragments of childhood memories and scattered black-and-white glossy pictures reveal a pleasant, robust existence. Mom and Dad had the blood of New England pioneers, rural farmers and rugged woodsmen running through their veins. Dad had been a marksman in the Corps. Food was scarce in the country, as was money, so Dad routinely hunted in the Dunbarton woodlands. As a child, I can still recall the thrill of watching from the kitchen window as my Dad returned from the hunt, in the dead of winter, gripping the rugged rack of a huge buck, dragging its carcass over the stonewall across the road. One time, Pappy joined Dad, and they posed with their 'kill' on the steps of the front porch. New England snowstorms were beautiful, but bountiful. It wasn't unusual to see three feet of snow fall in a single day. Dad was slimmer in those days. He would don a leather jacket and worn jeans, with a cheap flat shovel and a generous smile, and clear a path from the house to the road.

We had an over-abundance of assorted wildlife, including rabbits, chickens, over a dozen cats, and four or five dogs. Dad's favorite dog was a black and white spaniel which he christened 'Rocky.' Poor Rocky was killed by a passing truck; Dad never recovered. Mom killed, plucked and prepared our chickens, fresh from the henhouse to the chopping block in the shed, straight to the kitchen sink. It was not unusual for Dad to use the same sink to drown a new litter of kittens that happened to show up under the porch or on the doorstep. Somehow, I just accepted their sad fate, even as a child. We just couldn't afford to feed another family of stray cats; it would have been cruel.

Mom usually wore her long blonde hair in pigtails, a long summer cotton dress, and brown and white suede shoes, unless she was weeding in the garden or hauling water from the well. She also worked at the Godbout turkey farm just down the dirt road, to earn a few extra dollars.

After the '31 Essex gave up the ghost, Dad purchased a black 1937 Ford, followed closely behind by a vintage green, four-door Studebaker, with spacious running boards. I was then two-and-one-half years of age. I actually recall the day vividly. Mom and Dad and I were headed into Manchester on a cold, wintry day. The deep snow on the back road had been plowed high like the Lincoln Tunnel, leaving a narrow white twisting corridor extending from the lamppost to the witch's castle...*My grandfather, Sumner, had also owned a turquoise blue Studebaker with a chromed bullet snout and classy solid chrome grill. I learned some years later, when I had begun to inquire of such indispensable trivia, that the car had been named after 'Johnny Studebaker,' of western expansion fame (he was also the inventor of the wheelbarrow)!* I was standing in the front seat. *Safety seats were not required 'back in the day,' and you always got a better view.*

Without a moment's warning, a large, old black behemoth, driven by an aged couple, came creeping and sliding around the narrow turn. There was no escape, no turning back, no room to veer, no place to stop. The vehicles collided head on. Mom and Dad both threw their arms at the same moment, like the stiff tubular arms of a turnstile, to keep me from launching through the icy windshield. Dad maintained control and managed to survive the impact, but Mom's head hit the dashboard; she broke her nose in three places. I never really noticed, but her nose is slightly crooked to this day, sixty years later. I just recently got around to thanking her for the painful price she had paid for saving her infant son.

No doubt, those were serene, but equally strenuous days for the newly weds. Their time was consumed with battling the elements and scraping to survive. I suspect that one of the reasons the fragile, paradisal relationship only survived a few years, however, was the blissful tension and testing that the couple had to endure. Though I cannot, fortunately, offer an eye-witness account, I suspect that they enjoyed precious little time for the kind of intimacy which all happy marriages so desperately require. In Jewish biblical tradition, if the young husband happened to be in military service (and most were), then he was accorded exempt status for an entire year in order to have sufficient time to begin a relationship with his young bride on a solid footing. In western culture, most young couples do not enjoy that luxury, but take a short honey-moon (if there is any money left over from an unnecessarily expensive wedding) and then return to the chaos and competitive pace that society has reserved for them.

I cannot speak with any semblance of certainty as to the real nature of my parents' personal life. As discussed earlier, Dad had his own bitter, shameful taste of mortality and vulnerability back in San Diego, the details of which he never chose to share with his son. *Was this to protect him from the same fate, I have since wondered?* Mom had struggled with a chemistry involving congenital strains of inferiority and run-away surpluses of estrogen, rendering her confused and curious. As a young girl, my grandparents, in addition to nursing a pattern of distrust in the area of their offspring's sexual behavior, had also responded (when the children did inquire) that sex was something 'dirty,' pernicious, painful, and undesirable. Dad, at the same time, was a healthy male fully expecting to enjoy a normal, wholesome relationship. Of course, it didn't help that he was still fighting the war in the middle of the night. Their mutual commitment to the Christian faith, and to the activities of the church, should have helped to cement their relationship and provide strength against the multitudinous foes aligned to derail their nascent bond of love, but in some strange, incomprehensible, unforeseeable manner, their religious commitment and sincere preoccupation with 'the Lord's work' seemed to have, over time, just the opposite effect.

I could never bring myself to discredit the sincerity and simplicity of my parents' religious commitment. They read me the Bible, and prayed with me daily during my early childhood. Mom said that I had memorized Bible verses at a very early age. They were very active in the Christian and Missionary Alliance church at Merrimack and Hall streets in Manchester, making the nine-mile trek from the country several times a week for services, prayer meetings and youth rallies. Dad became the Sunday School Superintendent, and led the singing for both morning and evening Sunday services. *He told me just before his death that as a child I used to imitate him and stand in the back pew waving my hands during the song service. Of course, Dad never stood in the back pew, not to my knowledge.* Dad even used his artistic skills and designed an ornate painted logo for the denomination, featuring the sacred symbols of the cross, the crown, a pitcher, and a laver (representing 'healing' and 'sanctification'). The Alliance had been a pioneer missionary-sending society at the end of the nineteenth century. Its founder had been a Presbyterian pastor from Toronto, the Rev. Albert Benjamin Simpson.

The Alliance church at the corner of Merrimack and Hall Streets was my church home away from home. I attended Sunday school there as a child, sitting on tiny, multi-colored chairs in the classroom upstairs overlooking the sanctuary below. My beloved teacher was Evelyn Combs, a tall woman with a big smile and a penchant for sweetness and laughter. She was pure love. Her husband, Rev. William Combs, had been the former pastor of the church. He, too, was always smiling. He had been a former track star in high school, which gave me just another reason to admire and respect this vibrant man of God.

My own pastor was Rev. Leslie Burns, a sweet, quiet man who never shouted or raised his voice. When he preached, he kept a white man's handkerchief discretely available. His sermons often led him to the point of unpretentious tears. He prayed often, and without fanfare, with his parishioners at an open altar after the service. People came forward frequently in those days, expecting to hear words of forgiveness, assurances of the possibility of reconciliation and healing. Rev. Burns baptized me at the age of twelve. *I was the one who was twelve...*

My own personal conversion experience came at a young age, thanks to my parents' faithfulness and commitment to God. It is one of the only memories I have of seeing my parents actually being together in close physical proximity. Of course, I was young and always occupied with my pets and other childish preoccupations. I took my parents' presence for granted, I suppose. Of course, Dad was always absent from the home during the day, either hunting, or going on church retreats, or working. I *do* remember his rolling me up in that red 'Indian blanket' and tucking me into bed each night in the frigid empty bedroom at the top of the stairs, the room with the slanted window.

Mom and Dad had taken me to a 'camp-meeting' at old Camp Hebron in Massachusetts. There was another famous Christian camp in northern New Hampshire, Camp Rumney, which is still going strong today, but Camp Hebron was an old-fashioned favorite for the evangelistic type. It was certainly 'good news' for a young boy of five. All I recall is one evening service in the old gray chapel. There were long rows of wooden benches, and a platform and pulpit up front, dead center overlooking the center 'sawdust' aisle. I don't remember who was preaching, nor do I recall any content of the message, but I do remember distinctly that when the service was over and the invitation to 'give' your heart to Jesus Christ' was extended, I felt a strange compunction to go forward. I remember looking back toward Mom and Dad who were standing there side-by side in the pew. They both smiled and nodded their approval. So a little lad made his way out into the aisle and to the front. I knelt there and prayed *I know not what.* Whoever the preacher was that night knelt there with a little boy and prayed for him. That was it. That was my first intentional move in God's direction. *'Unless you become like a little child...'*

Some years later, as young teen, I returned to old Camp Hebron during the summers for a week or so at a time. There was the same schedule of services, but they were different, as I recall. There was much more music and many more kids my age. And there was an incredible little camp commissary that doubled as an ice cream shop, with sliding screened windows, where kids could squander their fat little pockets bulging with Eisenhower dimes and Buffalo nickels on seven-ounce Cokes, Bazooka bubble gum (with little cartoon wrappers), candy bars and colored paper tubes filled with sour Kool-aid. I bought a treat every afternoon, until my small supply of cash was depleted. Fortunately, Mom had put several packages of green Dentyne gum in my suitcase, just for emergency use. I had countless emergencies every day.

We stayed in sparse wooden cabins on the fringe of the campground, near the woods. No frills, but all the conveniences of camp life, including running water. One of our activities was to cut and tie branches for the construction of 'lean-tos.' We all had roommates, two boys per room. My roommate was much bigger than most, and nearly twice my size, which meant that he was about average height. Everyone I knew was either taller or bigger, or both, for as long as I can remember. One afternoon, my roommate and I had a serious disagreement, a silly argument, and shoved each other a bit until it became more serious than I had planned, though I don't recall having had a particular plan at the time. I had always believed that I could beat anyone; it must have been that country-boy, off-spring-of-a-Marine bravado and attending illusion of invincibility.

A few seconds after the unfortunate whirlwind encounter had begun, the very brief mêlée was over, and my inconsiderate nemesis had thrown me into the wall, leaving a stunned, but remarkable replica of an over-exuberant young camper in what had been an innocent sheet of wallboard. I was humiliated and afraid, terribly afraid of the retribution that would be exacted for such a heinous crime. Once I extricated my frame from its plaster mold, and recovered a semblance of courage and composure, believing surely that I would be condemned to hell, or even worse, prohibited from visiting the Commissary that afternoon, I belted from the cabin. Having gained my composure, and with a visible cloud of degrading guilt hanging like Damocles's sword over my young head, I proceeded slowly, uphill toward the camp office. I was determined to confess quickly and the un-bearable weight of the clinging albatross from around my aching neck.

Before I had gotten very far, 'while still on the way,' a very tall, thin, gracious gentleman, whose name I cannot remember, stopped me with a look of compassion and concern. "What's the matter, Peter?" he inquired. *He knew my name!*

I then, sobbingly, but desperately, confessed to what had happened, as if I had pre-meditated and engineered the entire debacle. What I remember next changed my young life. The kindly counselor put his arm gently around my trembling shoulder, and said:

"It's alright, Peter. You did nothing wrong. Don't worry. We'll fix it. Don't cry." *I'm not sure...whether I want to admit that I was actually crying.*

"Come on; let's go up to the Commissary..."

That's what it was called, the 'Commissary.'

"Let's get a 'tonic.'"

In New England jargon, a 'tonic' is a 'soda,' or a 'pop.' It would have been a Hire's Root Beer, or a small seven-ounce Coke, or maybe an Orange Crush...they had an Orange Crush Bottling company in Manchester. Most of the other soft drinks (including the infamous 'Moxie,') were bottled in Needham, Massachusetts...

Well, that was the first time in my young life that I had really felt God's forgiveness, or His closeness and love, though I am sure that He had been there all the time. The prodigal had 'come to his senses' and returned home; his surrogate father had embraced him, receiving him back; he had dressed him in a new robe and sandals, and put a priceless friendship ring on his young finger. The wall would be repaired. His relationship with God had already been restored that day in 1956.

The ancient Israelites had two sacred mounts: Mount Zion at Jerusalem, and Mount Gerazim in Samaria; the latter was to become a traditional source of tension and embarrassment, where the people purported to meet with deity after the division of the kingdom under Solomon. I, too, could look back on two prominent, critical encounters with God in my early spiritual odyssey. Dad, I can only presume, continued to exert spiritual leadership in the home, and Mom was content to follow his courageous, magnetic example.

***

On May 2, 1948, a first and only child, a son, was born to Bob and Dotty Colman at the old Hillsborough County Hospital on the road to Goffstown. When he was born, he was anything but attractive. It was a difficult delivery, requiring the use of large metallic forceps, resembling the crude steel forceps used to transport blocks of ice. They left a large red birthmark on the infant's left temple, which had to be treated with dry ice and injections.

113

His mother confessed that he 'looked like a frog,' and that she didn't even want to see him or to take 'it' home.

Peter Lee seemed to be a good name. Lee was my grandfather 'Pappy's middle name. *Peter*, of course, was none other than the fisherman, the fiery, impetuous roughneck who, after having denied any acquaintance with the Man of Galilee, would become the 'rock' and chief architect of the primitive Christian community in Jerusalem. In 1956, just before Dad left for good, Mom became pregnant again. She carried her daughter almost full term, until the fetus died just weeks before the expected delivery date. Dad and Mom were devastated. They had already chosen her name, 'Naomi-Ruth,' from the biblical story of Ruth, the Moabitess who had returned to Israel as a widow only to become the great, great-grandmother of King David. Bob and Dotty's only son was to have a sister, but it was not to be.

I can only speculate as to the factors that combined to erode the fragile web of happiness and intimacy that my parents had enjoyed. There are many unanswered questions. Could not the sincerity of their faith and commitment to God have served to compensate for any personal weaknesses that may have plagued their love? Should they not have been able to find strength in each other in spite of their own insecurities, or the insidious microbes of guilt that may have contaminated an otherwise wholesome, potentially fruitful relationship.

Mom said that Dad had refused to seek counseling, which I can partially believe; he was very proud. The measure of pride, and perhaps even a modest measure of uncertified prestige that he had garnered from his visibility in the Christian community, may have prevented him from admitting that his marriage was in trouble. But marriage, and its life-span, is always a two-way street. I had always believed that it was pretty much Dad's fault, as I shall attempt to explain, but it is rarely quite so simple. I'm sure that Mom had her own little demons which she had struggled to exorcise. And I am sure that Dad had issues with Mom that he never had the courage or ability to expunge. No one can ever be certain exactly how or why such things happen, but happen they did.

It may have been 1955. We finally moved out of the old Dunbarton house back into the city, living in a small second-story apartment at 352 Manchester Street. How curious is that? My ancestors were from the borough of East Manchester, England, and immigrated to the England colonies in the early seventeenth century, only to settle on Manchester *Street*, in Manchester, New Hampshire.

It was not entirely unpredictable that Dad should become a police officer. He 'walked the beat' in Manchester for years. He would later continue his distinguished career as a law-enforcement officer back in Goffstown. He rented a tiny cottage on Glen Lake, where I used to visit him. His brother, my Uncle Bill, used to run a little makeshift 'hamburger joint' across the road from the lake. *That's where I learned the secret of eating succulent, freshly-grilled hamburgers (made from pure ground steak) with just ketchup and long, tender hand-cut fries on the side!*

I rarely ever saw my father during those early years in Manchester. We still attended the same church. Dad was still Superintendent, at least at church. Ostensibly, he was still the spiritual leader in the home, but the sanctuary seemed empty. I don't recall ever feeling that he wasn't my father. I was too busy with my friends in the neighborhood.

115

I had also started attending the Lincoln Street School, the one, like all the other elementary schools in those days, that was designed like a brick warehouse with the high ceilings and imposing cast-iron fire escapes winding to the roof. *I later learned that the design was intentional, an expression of the mentality and pragmatic philosophy of education that reigned in the early nineteen-hundreds. I believe that it was John Dewey who first conceived of the educational institution as the ideal environment where America's youth could be systematically equipped to perpetuate the framework of a prosperous democratic society.* The school was a monolith...but it was functional.

I remember the first day of kindergarten. My teacher was pleasant. It was fun, especially the finger-painting. But what I really looked forward to each day during those three years at the Lincoln Street School was seeing Seena Akland. *Trust me; I could never have come up with that name, not by myself.* I was deeply in love and made it my mission in life to look good, to wear the latest, coolest checkered shirt and the newest turquoise green 'Bob Couzy' sneakers. Only the best for her, and for me!

I spared no expense to impress this blithe, breath-taking bundle of beauty, my own Cinderella. *Mom and Dad paid the tab, of course.* I did everything I could within my puerile power to impress her, or to simply get her to look in my direction, even just once, which I'm not certain she ever really did for very long. I did manage to catch those warm, laser-blue eyes turned toward me, for just a split second, accompanied by a very shy, sweet smile. That's all I needed; it lasted an eternity. At least until high school.

Chapter Nine

Tenuous Strands

Two knife-blades cannot fit into one knife-sheath.
(Bambara proverb)

A cord of three stands is not easily broken.
(Ecclesiastes 4:12b)

When Solomon wrote those wise words, he may have been mistaken about the utility of a third 'strand.' The analogy is absolutely valid, as is the metaphor accurate, when applied to the relationship between two friends, or more intimately, between a husband and a wife. In that case, God is the third strand who gives strength and security to the other two. Such a combination of cords is virtually unbreakable, and capable of bearing considerable strain. But in this particular case, on the inverse side of the analogy, an *additional* third strand is precisely what Mom and Dad's relationship did *not* need.

Dottie Samara was Mom's closest female friend; maybe too close. She was also our neighbor. She was an orphan who lived with an elderly Christian woman. Dottie had never married, and was a very gifted soprano soloist and organist. She played the piano at the Alliance church where we attended. Dottie had dark hair, a winsome smile, and a disarmingly sweet disposition that bordered on coy. Mom called her often, and visited her frequently for lunch. But so did Dad.

During Dad's beat, and sometimes after work, he had also been paying Dottie friendly visits. Harmless, of course, or so Mom thought. But one day Mom walked in to Dottie's apartment and found Dad and Dottie 'embracing,' which is a probable euphemism for kissing. Somehow, as Mom related it, she didn't think much of it at the moment. Dottie was a good Christian friend, and the three of them would often visit and go out together. They were always together during church services and other church activities. Mom did confess that she thought it a little bit strange that Dad and Dottie would be embracing, but wasn't that just a common way of expressing Christian affection? Was it just one of those 'holy kisses'?

In truth, it is not uncommon for Christian men and women, or any other men and women, in specific cultural and/or religious contexts, to express genuine affection, without sexual intent or indiscretion. But it is probably wiser to refrain from physical contact in most cases. After all, genuine spirituality aside, one never ceases to be human, which includes the very natural need for sexual intimacy. The power of genuine intimacy (without sexual complicity) that any kind of unsolicited, sincere spirituality engenders, though pure and legitimate enough, is curiously susceptible to indiscretion of the most serious, and perhaps even sinister nature. Bright, ripe red raspberries, fresh off the vine and seemingly flawless at the picking, if left unattended, even in a proper climate, quickly and inexplicably develop a pervasive mold which renders them uneatable. In the same manner, innocence and sincerity, or perhaps even simple naiveté, if denied nurture and sufficient care, are particularly susceptible to corruption.

In my parents' case, as far as I can discern, the conditions for infidelity, even in its subtlest forms, were more than conducive. Whatever the reasons, my father developed an attraction for Dottie Samara, as far as I am aware, without my mother's knowledge. Just how long Dad courted that attraction I cannot say. Neither is it possible to understand the precise nature of their relationship. During one moment of transparency just before Dad's death, I asked him 'point blank' whether he and Dottie had had a child together (the circumstances surrounding which I will describe later). Dad's response was that Dottie had been 'a virgin' when they married. This would appear to answer the question about a 'secret pregnancy,' as well as the related question of Dad having had an elicit sexual affair with Dottie while he was still married to Mom.

Whether my mother ever indulged any similar secret affections, for anyone, is a question which she has never chosen to address, and one I am remiss to pursue. I have never probed these hidden mysteries to the very back of the cave, but there is sufficient obscurity and stale air to cause me to stay close to the entrance with the light at my face. I do not want to embolden the shadows, or obscure the light that I do have by peering too closely into the darkness. 'Nothing is hidden that shall not be revealed' states the biblical maxim. I am almost afraid of what I might discover. Some truths are better left buried, like silent corpses, awaiting the searing light of judgment. 'Let sleeping dogs lie.' We all have sufficient darkness within ourselves without inviting, however vicariously, the unbearable stigma of the sins of the fathers or mothers.

Neither am I naïve enough to believe that the failure to 'work it out,' and to find happiness in their relationship, was just the fault of one actor in the fragile drama which human culture has come to affectionately christen 'marriage.' The fault rarely, if ever, can be attributed to just one person. The old cliché is true: marriage is always a two-way street. To extend the metaphor, I just can't be certain who was driving whom, or what direction they may have been heading, at what speed, and with what, if any, degree of proficiency. It is certainly impossible to know whether either of them was taking passengers along without informing the other. As the archaic English term suggests, either party may have been equally *promiscuous* with respect to the manner in which they conducted their affairs.

In any case, according to my Mom's account, one day in 1956 the doorbell rang at 352 Manchester Street. Dad was at work; Mom was alone. I was eight-years-old. I don't know whether it was the same day, or not, but the only day of my eighth year that I distinctly recall was May 2, my birthday. I was standing alone in the back alley, waiting for my friends to come out to play. It really doesn't matter, I guess, but that was the day Dad didn't come home.

Sheriff O'Brien was on the other side of the door when the buzzer rang.

"Doris Arlene Colman?" the Sheriff inquired.

"Yes, sir? *Dotty replied.* I never did like the name Doris." *The Sheriff had a folded piece of paper in his hand...He unfolded the paper and handed it to my Mom.*

"This is a divorce decree," he said matter-of-factly, and without emotion. Mom froze.

"I don't want any divorce!" she emoted, still in a state of shock.

"Well, your husband does," he replied, and abruptly turned and left.

Mom stood there for a few minutes frozen in place, unable to speak. She went upstairs and sat for a solid two hours, crying her eyes out. She then called her best friend, Dottie Samara.

"Dottie, the Sheriff was just here at the house. He served me a piece of paper. Bob wants a divorce!" There was a dead silence on the other end of the line, and then.

"I'm sorry." That was all she had said.

Whatever may have been the reasons for the rupture in their relationship, and the insipient disdain which my father developed for my mother after the divorce, it is sad to recall that one of the only bright souvenirs I retain of my Dad before he left was the day we painted the living room wall a bright, dark red, right over the wall-paper! Was Dad painting the town red, too? I don't really believe so. Dad was not an immoral man, but he was a man, and apparently he wasn't happy in his marriage. Painting over wallpaper is ill-advised. Was Dad trying to put a fresh new coat on a shameful, unhappy surface, like a new patch on an old garment, or was he really just trying to make life in a cramped apartment brighter and more livable? I prefer to opt for the memory of fresh red paint.

Sometimes several pieces of the puzzle seem to fit in the same space. In the case of my parents' marriage, and their surrounding friendships, there were three particular pieces which all bore an uncanny resemblance. They all seemed destined to be together, to fit the same space, but none of them turned out to be the perfect fit. Some of the edges were irregular; some details didn't seem to match.

And what appeared to be a semblance of straight edges turned out to be cut at slight angles.

My mother, Doris ('Dotty') Colman had married Bob in 1946; Dad divorced Mom in 1957. About five years later, probably 1962, Dad married Dorothy ('Dottie') Samara. Some years earlier, while Mom and Dad were still married, Dorothy Samara started attending services. My Dad was Sunday School Superintendent and song-leader. Dottie Samara lived with an elderly Christian widow. She was a gifted musician, and sang soprano, as did my mother. Dottie and my mother soon became very close friends, and often sang together in church. Ironically, perhaps, they shared not only the same first name, but the same birthday as well.

***

Dorothy Samara, soon-to-become Dottie Samara Colman, had another close female friend who, along with her husband and young daughter, lived nearby. *At this point, the sequence and chronology of events becomes a little murky...*I recall visiting this sweet woman and her affable husband and daughter when I was still a very young boy. The child, who was about my age, was also named Dorothy. I recall that this gracious couple were somewhat advanced in years, but it never occurred to me to wonder how they could have had a young child my age. But somehow, despite their years, they had managed to bear an infant daughter. Little 'Dottie,' as they called the girl had big brown eyes and reddish-brown hair *like my* Dad.

I should say at this point in the narrative that I have never had any real reason to believe that this child ever belonged to anyone other than the afore-mentioned couple.

But I did often observe that Dad was always very protective of his second wife, Dottie (Samara) Colman. And I must confess, I had often wondered whether my Dad and Dottie had had a child out of wed-lock, and simply hadn't chosen to tell anyone.

Perhaps such an assumption is unfounded and unfair. Though I suspect that I shall never really know the intimate details of this seemingly innocent web of friendships, the lingering mystery tends to appear yet more complicated. I shall only indulge my curiosity but briefly here, so as not to create a spurious, and potentially fictitious scenario. *Let the reader be assured that I intend to neither cast aspersions, or lend credulity to speculation as I seek to reflect upon these childhood circumstances.*

Some time ago, when I did venture to inquire as to the veracity of these events, Mom confided to me that, indeed, for a period of several months before the divorce, she had tried to contact Dottie by telephone, as was her habit; but Dad had told Mom that Dottie had been very sick and couldn't go out. Mom could only assume that Dottie was elsewhere. *Mom later confided to me, when I nonchalantly raised the question, that she had, in fact, always wondered whether Dottie had spent those months in a local Catholic medical facility. There was such a facility in Manchester, but my mother had no information to either confirm or deny this supposition.*

When Dottie Samara's friend, the mother of the young girl mentioned earlier, died some years ago, my own mother sent me the short obituary notice from the Manchester Union Leader: Curiously, there was a conspicuous omission: There was no mention whatsoever of a surviving child. Was there an explanation for this? Had this young girl simply been entrusted by someone else to their loving care, until which time she could resume her own life? Had they given her up for adoption? But the real questions in my own mind went deeper. Was she my father's child? Was she in fact my sister? How or why did she seem to possess those same rich, dark brown eyes (like my Dad's eyes), and bear almost carbon-copy Colman features? Why did I always sense a strange affinity with this girl?

But the other questions followed. Did Dottie Samara have a daughter out of wedlock? Had my Dad fathered a child and hidden the news to protect Dottie from shame, and then convinced her best friend to care for her? Were our visits to this dear couple's home nothing more than my father's attempt to reconnect with his daughter and introduce his son to his sister?

Apparently not.

I specifically posed the critical question to my Dad just days before his death: "Dorothy Samara was a virgin when we were married," Dad had said. But the same haunting question remained. Were Dad and Dottie innocent? Do I have a sister? If I do, does she suspect that she has a brother? If she does, and she has known it all these years, why had she not felt free to tell me? And more importantly, why have I not had the courage to ask? Perhaps she, too, has never had occasion to wonder, to ponder these circumstances that seem to gently enfold our distant memories…Perhaps she, too, is blissfully ignorant of hidden undercurrents that converge beneath the opaque depths of our collective past. Perhaps there were other details Dad hadn't had the courage to tell me. Was he trying in some inexplicable way to protect me too? I will never know. Have the fathers eaten sour grapes, and a son's teeth set on edge? Perhaps entombed memories are best left buried and undisturbed.

Decades after Dad stepped out of my life, I had occasion to meet this young woman again when my wife and I and our children visited my Dad and Dottie. Again, perhaps consiciously now, I sensed the same strange affinity, the same filial attraction. I had known for some time that this same young woman, whom my Dad and Dottie affectionately called 'Dorothy,' had become something of an *adopted daughter* (to use my Dad's own words). When my wife, Judith, and I as the children visited Dad and Dottie during our first return home from Africa in 1982, this same young woman, now happily married, had been present as well. I remember looking at her and recognizing myself; Judy noticed the resemblance too. Was this an uncanny coincidence? It seemed like a family reunion!

Dad and Dottie always made it a point to explain that Dorothy was 'like their own daughter'. They had pretty much adopted her after her parents' death. Over the years, the relationship became even closer. Dorothy and her husband, a very sweet, friendly and unassuming man, I learned had purchased most of the furniture, including the television, which had been in Dad's apartment. But why should this be so unusual? Dorothy and her husband, it would seem, had lovingly adopted my Dad and Dottie as well. So it was not surprising, nor, perhaps, inappropriate (given both the spiritual and geographical proximity of the two couples) that when Dad died, the same young woman was appointed as the executrice of Dad's sparse financial resources and earthy belongings. Dad had entrusted to her his credit account; she was authorized to dispense what limited funds he would leave behind. Dad had explained to me in the days just prior to his death that Dottie and

Dorothy had become close, and that this arrangement would be easier. I never had any reason to question my Dad's judgment. Nor did I then. Nor do I now, some years after the fact. My living in Chicago would have made any other arrangement difficult. I saw no reason to disagree.

Chapter Ten

'If Gold Rusts...'

When a cow has no tail, it is God who shoos the
flies away.

(Bambara proverb)

The same is true for frogs, according to the very
practical and equally profound wisdom of the Bambara-
speaking peoples of West Africa. Frogs have no tails to
speak of, which puts them at a decided disadvantage when
compared to other species. But this seemingly unfortunate
oversight may very well be, as far as frogs go, a clear
advantage in two ways. It allows them to *be* frogs, and to
do what frogs are designed to do. Whatever the deficiency
in the design of an effective rudder system for frogs, with
respect to their ability in the water, is amply compensated
by their legs, which enable them to function extraordinarily
well (or 'swimmingly,' as our good friend Ben Franklin
was fond of saying), as far as frogs go. In either case,
whether we are talking about cows or frogs, what appears
to be a glaring deficiency actually translated to a simple
and unpretentious candidacy for divine intervention.

I have few illusions about the real disadvantage
which my father's leaving created for a young boy and only
child of eight years. And I do not recall anyone even
attempting to explain what had happened, though I am sure
my mother did her best to offer a simple, comforting
explanation when the occasion warranted it. It never

127

seemed to be an issue or serious obstacle to my development as a young child, at least not any issue of which I was aware. Neither is there any question that God would honor His commitment to keep those annoying, disease-bearing flies at a relatively safe distance in the course of my early and frequent forays from the safety and tranquility of the farm.

Dad's disappearance from my life was not terribly traumatic. I was only eight years old, and used to Dad being absent; I became very close to my mother. Over time, I just accepted that she was to be my only parent. Dad's telephone calls and periodic appearances outside in the car became a matter of routine. It never occurred to me to ask Dad why he never came home. It was as if being away was all part of his job; maybe he was a plain-clothes cop. In any case, the only time I saw my father was when he came to pick me up and take me to 'his house,' which, as I recall, was a simple little rag-tag cottage on the shores of Glen Lake in Goffstown. Dad seemed to gravitate to Goffstown. Was he unconsciously trying to rebuild or restore the past? Was he subconsciously moving closer to some semblance of happiness? Actually, he was building a stone chimney.

That is one of the few days I remember. Dad was constructing a crude, stone chimney for his cottage. He was up high using a plumb-line. There were small field stones and even smaller stones from the shore of the lake. Dad was always building something with stones, like the small fireplace he had built for the men's cookout at our Dunbarton home. Was he going to build a nice cozy fire, and invite my Mom, or was it for someone else? Dad was a police officer in Goffstown at that time. I saw his heavy black leather belt and revolver in the top dresser drawer at the cottage. He also had a short Billy-club with woven brown leather clutching a lead core. Dad was very strong; he had a large Marine Corps tattoo on his forearm, which he always regretted after his spiritual conversion. The tattoo was a reminder of his pagan past. Dad would always flex his arm and smile like a Cheshire cat facing a weaker prey, and then put my arm or elbow in a 'police hold.' He smacked his hands as if 'cuffing' an opponent. I never dared to confront, or even pretend to challenge him. After all, I was only a boy; Dad was a Marine and public protector. And he was strong. He always put my arm in a hold and pressed tightly with iron fingers just to demonstrate who was the strongest. I suppose I wish he had been able to restrain his own insecurities and apprehend his marriage.

One night Dad was policing the back roads of Goffstown, a pretty rowdy place. He stopped some teenagers near a bridge. They disarmed Dad and held him over the bridge to scare him. They let him go...that is, they released him without harming him. I guess he managed to talk his way out of it, and somehow threaten the gang. He told me that he persuaded them to promise to behave, and he would not press charges. How does a policeman negotiate with a gang while he's hanging from a bridge? Dad was a hero. He seemed to be capable of extracting himself from most difficult situations.

But Dad was not invincible. On another night, he was cruising past the Town Hall in Goffstown and noticed that the side door was open. What he didn't know was that someone had broken in. A man had a grudge against the Police Chief, Earl Dubois, and my Aunt Earlene's Father. A dark, furtive profile was stalking the Chief, waiting to pounce when he returned to his office that night. The room was dark. When my Dad stepped in to survey the situation, an angry young man jumped him from behind the door, and broke a chair over Dad's head. No one breaks anything over a Marine's head and gets away with it. During the struggle, the intruder stabbed Dad in the side, but Dad didn't realize that he had a knife in him until he had recovered from the chair, hand-cuffed the man, and taken him to the station. It was only then that one of the other officers brought it to Dad's attention that he had been stabbed.

Dad was taken to the hospital with the knife still sticking out of his side, a quarter inch from his liver. Dad had a big write-up in the local paper: "Local Hero Apprehends Intruder." There was the picture of Dad, in full uniform, with that wide Cheshire cat smile. In truth, he never stopped thanking God for saving his life. I think I thanked him too, but I wasn't really surprised that Dad managed to get the cuffs on the guy. This event became another 'open door' in a long chronicle of testimonies to God's protection and goodness.

While I have never doubted Dad's sincerity, and God's protection that day, I guess I wish that Dad would have been just strong enough to stay home. He had found himself in the grip of a failing relationship, but didn't have the strength to hold on, or to negotiate his return to solid ground. He had struggled with maleficent intruders, seeking to deprive him of his life; though he managed to survive the ordeal, he had been unable (or unwilling) to prevent deeper, life-long wounds of guilt and failure. He was always good at protecting others and policing the neighborhood, but somehow he couldn't find the strength to protect or preserve his own marriage from enemy intruders. Guilt and failure never belong to just one party. If two strands can strengthen a cord, then just one of those strands, if flawed, can cause a strong cord to weaken and snap. While Samson had his weakness, Delilah was certainly an unforeseeable, but poignant factor in his humiliating and painful demise.

When Dad was not in a police uniform, he was wearing a suit, a dress shirt with a broad print tie, a man's hat, and a broad Sunday-go-to-meet'n smile. When he wasn't working, he was working the beat at church, leading the choir and teaching a Bible class. Dad was a born leader. He never lost the edge on his genuine zeal for his relationship with God and his love for the church. But after he left me and Mom, he stopped attending the Alliance Church in Manchester. He and Dottie Samara attended church out of town at a quasi-charismatic congregation in Concord. Their favorite place of worship in the spring and summer months, however, was the "Cathedral in the Pines" in Rumney, New Hampshire. Dad brought me there often, with Dottie. Mom never went. The music was mesmerizing. There was a huge organ below ground level, where the organist sat in nestled in sacred seclusion, working the stops, keys and pedals like a cherub gunner in a camouflaged pocket buried deep in the palm trees of the Pacific. The beloved 19th-century hymns sung with full-hearted piety and passion created an aura of the Divine Presence. It was just like heaven on earth. After a day of worship and sight-seeing, Dad would take me back home and drop me off in front of the house quickly so Mom wouldn't see him in the car.

***

After Dad left, Mom and I moved several times. After Manchester Street, we moved to Harvard Street, across from the Wonder Bread bakery. I can still smell the fresh bread and pastries coming from the plain brick building. Near the corner, there was a 'day-old' store where we bought near-fresh products – white and wheat bread, English muffins and doughnuts – every few days for just pennies. We still lived in a small apartment on the second floor, with an old staircase leading to a backyard filled with debris and brown grass; a narrow, paved alley was in the back. Every few days I would wait for the slow, steady sharp muffled 'clop –clop-clopping' sound of the black, bearded rag man and his tired, withered, dirty-white horse. Old Methuselah (a fitting name) smoked an old dry pipe – I never did remember seeing or smelling any smoke coming from it – and was very friendly. As I ran to the gate to watch the procession, he would simply smile and nod in my direction. Maybe he was God, and I was the only one who knew it! Was he one of those angels in disguise of whom I was 'unaware?'

I had a happy collection of assorted friends in the neighborhood, including a very smart boy across the street. We also shared a smart collection of green plastic toy soldiers and toy canons – some of which would actually shoot small but foreboding white plastic shells. We were always digging intricate defense systems in the dirt in the empty lot between our homes. There was also a girl who lived down the street. I remember visiting her often to see if she could play; she loved playing board games; she always won, but it didn't matter. I was too busy playing superman or batman during my off-time, demonstrating my particular prowess in 'flying' (more like jumping) from the nearest garage roof, a feat that I had mastered while living at Manchester Street. We didn't pretend to have many circuses as I got older. I would have loved to have demonstrated my agility and supernatural strength as a strongman, but I had to retire his character early on for lack of an audience.

Two memorable incidents – well, three actually - are worthy of mention before moving on to another neighborhood. Keep in mind that a young boy left to his own devices has the potential for either indescribable grandeur or shameful ignominy. Parents can be helpful in both extremes, but a mother alone, in spite of the volume of affection and understanding expended, is quite incapable of exerting the strength and influence required to curb a young boy's adventurous appetites. Not that I engaged in any earth-shattering exploits or criminal activities, but I have launched more than one arrow straight in the air without thinking about when or where it might return to earth. In the case of arrows carelessly launched, the choice to either stand still or run, or even move slightly from the point of departure, is never safe and hardly ever reassuring. I only mention the following episodes to illustrate how innocence and emotion find their initial encounter awkward. Without proper guidance, there is always the potential for disaster and disappointment. In hindsight, I was spared any serious dalliance with most forms of immoral or reckless behavior to which I attribute the invisible but ubiquitous presence of the grace of God.

The only real misdemeanor at this point in my earthy pilgrimage was an artfully aimed rock-hard ice-ball. The slow-moving vehicle with the luminous chrome hubcap was irresistible. One solid throw yielded the desired result: the ice-ball struck the shiny target dead center with the force of a miniature howitzer shell, creating the sound of shattered glass and scattering sharp white icy shards in every direction. My position behind the snow-bank just a few feet down the street from my home gave me just the advantage I needed to survey the damage and to savor the effect. But then the unimaginable happened. The car slid to an abrupt halt, swerving on the snowy surface. The enemy exited the vehicle in the direction of the offending party. I froze with fear, my freezing fist dripping with guilt. I panicked and ran straight to my house and up the hallway stairs to our apartment...not the best strategy for eluding an enemy bent on retaliation and revenge. I slammed the door, thinking that would deter dark forces gathering at the door, and hid under the bed in the living room. Just then, I heard slow, steady footsteps in the stairs and an angry knock on our door. Imagine anyone having the nerve to intrude upon the sanctity and safety of someone's home and actually bang on the door! My Mom calmly answered, never revealing my position, while the enemy registered his angry complaint and withdrew. Mom never punished me; she didn't need to. I never threw another snow-ball at anything again.

The only other very uneasy, fearful emotion I ever felt at that same door was the night one of Mom's gentleman friends, a very kind man, had the nerve to kiss Mom just outside our door (what a horrible place to be kissed)! I was pretending to be asleep, watching through a small crack in the door; I felt a chocking sensation of anger and jealousy. Why would Mom let a man kiss her?

It never occurred to me at that young age, living alone with my mother, that she was entitled to affection and companionship from the opposite sex. The expression "opposite sex" was not even part of my vocabulary. I just wasn't prepared to deal with the emotions of seeing my mother kiss a strange man, someone not my father. Maybe the fact that I was having to live *without* a father had made me suspicious of other men. But how would living without a father affect *my* relationship with the opposite sex? It wouldn't be long before I found out, but the delightfully confusing emotions associated with that discovery took me quite by surprise.

I think her name was Carol; she lived next door, and was older than I was at the time (still is, as far as I know), and she was beautiful. Her teeth were just a bit irregular, in a cute sort of a way, but she had a killer smile. She just seemed to love everybody; I was convinced that she loved me above the rest. She had too. After all, she was the perfect match for the girl of my pre-adolescent dreams. I hadn't paid particular attention to her at first, since all of her friends were older than I as well. But I awoke one morning and happened to look out my bedroom window.

The weathered duplex next door to ours was not more than ten feet away. I didn't even know where Carol lived until that morning; as it turned out, her bedroom window was just across from mine, but slightly to the right. As I looked out that morning, she was standing, quite innocently and completely unaware of me, dressed in cute 'shorty' pajamas, stretching to greet the day. I was a bit embarrassed, but mesmerized. I turned away for fear of her seeing me and misunderstanding my intent. I never expected to see her there. She certainly would have been mortified to have known that I had seen her, so I never told her. But I never forgot. I suppose that was probably the second time in my young life where I had felt Cupid's arrow.

I bore that happy wound for years to come. It never occurred to me that she had ever noticed the boy next door, but several years later, when I had returned to Manchester after college and seminary, Mom said that she had asked about me! She was working in one of the local offices. Mom took me there to see her and to say hello. I wondered if she still wore shorty pajamas, but I didn't ask, nor did I divulge that I had noticed her that day. Some things are better left unsaid. But it was nice to see her and to say hello. She still had that beautiful short blond hair and the pretty smile. Oh, I remember that she was Catholic, and I remember wondering if it was alright to fall in love with a Catholic girl.

My only other cataclysmic encounter with the opposite sex would leave a permanent impression. It was the classic case of infatuation. *I believe it was Eric Frome in his book 'The Art of Loving,' who cautioned against 'falling in love.' He called it infatuation, not love. People who are inclined to allow themselves to 'fall in love,' he wrote, are equally susceptible to 'falling out of love' just as quickly. He was right.* But what would a young boy of fourteen know about such frivolous semantic distinctions? Innocence is bliss. Maybe. Sometimes it leaves incurable scars.

Her name was Lenore; God forbid that she should ever read this account. Although, if she ever survived her own wild encounters, she would probably smile.

She lived in a gray house, on a hill, on Shasta Street, just east of South Willow, and a good half-mile from my house. But distance was irrelevant. Somehow, I had been invited, along with a cart-load of other charming, cherub-like, screaming pre-adolescent vagrants to a birthday party at her house. That was the day the love-bug bit its unwitting prey. She was beautiful and blond, always smiling and running; all of the boys were in pursuit. She was also a local celebrity since she had posed in blond pigtails for Wonder Bread. She was the beautiful little blond with blue eyes who graced every single loaf of white Wonder Bread. She had thus made her way into every young heart and home in New England in the late 1950s. She may as well have been Shirley Temple or Annie Oakley, although neither of them were as beautiful as Lenore. But unlike little quiet Seena Akland, whose love and admiration I could never seem to win, Lenore came my way like a bee to honey. Though I am sure that I did not qualify as honey, I was also sure that I could never resist her fiery, flirtatious 'fly-by' advances.

Lenore was my first true love. Or so I thought. I was about fourteen years old now, and well beyond the infatuation stage. A team of wild horses, or cherubs, could not have convinced me otherwise. I was smitten. When we were a bit older (still in the volatile pre-teen phase) I recall walking to her home in the afternoon to play hide-and-seek with her and all the neighborhood kids. We always ended up hiding together. On one occasion, we found ourselves under the front porch, a spacious, well-concealed area. We hugged. I was 'translated,' like the legendary Enoch who walked so closely with God that he was just taken up one day, quite alive, and was never heard from again. I, too, was quite taken. I, too, had felt a seismic dose of joy from which I never quite recovered. And it was just a hug! I went home that night feeling like I had lost my virginity, and wasn't even sure what that was, or whether I had ever had anything of the sort in the first place. I remember having been seriously concerned. No one had ever bothered to explain anything about sexual intimacy, and I was sure that I had gotten Lenore pregnant! That was quite a hug; it would have taken quite a miracle.

The last time I went out with Lenore, we walked hand-and-hand down the Shasta Street hill on a clear winter's night and went ice-skating and dancing at the out-door rink at Shasta and South Willow. But I lost track of Lenore that night. Apparently, I wasn't the only boy in whom she was interested. On one of the last turns on the rink that night, while skating all alone and musing on my short-lived romance, someone in the crowd put out a fist and almost knocked me unconscious. The wind had been knocked out of me, along with any hope of a blissful, budding love-affair.

It was probably just as well. I attended the Manchester Central High School, as had both my Mom and

Dad before me. Lenore went to Memorial High near her home. Fate is so cruel and inconsiderate. I missed Lenore for many years to come.

Memorial High School on the upper east side of town was our arch rival. Many of my former neighborhood friends, a rough bunch, including a notorious mongrel whom I will call Mike, and his equally pernicious brother, also attended Memorial. We ended up playing football against each other. I was a small second-string running back for Central High; number forty-six, green and white. As a senior, I was on special teams. Central had one of the best teams in the state; both the quarterback and the fullback were All-American. Winning seasons went back and forth. We were beaten often, but we always respected each other.

Mike was another matter, a mystery, and a beneficent bully of sorts. He was old school – your atypical tough-guy who could either rip your head off if he didn't like you, or hug you and cry like a baby if he did. Otherwise, it was Genghis Khan meets Thumper – the epitome of raw muscle and a run-away freight-train carrying volatile chemicals. Mike was a gentle giant with his friends, but Godzilla to his self-perceived enemies. He walked like a silver-backed ape, had a big smile and a broken front tooth; he was a live grenade with the pin pulled. Fearless.

Mike and I had grown up in the same general neighborhood. His roughneck custom pick-up football team had crushed ours when we were kids. They had been cruising the area looking for victims. We were game; ripe for martyrdom. And we were soundly annihilated. After the game, Mike and his blood-thirsty brood picked us up off the ground, thanked us for the light morning workout, and left to seek their next victims. In the process, Mike and I became friends, at a distance. No one in their right mind would have been Mike's enemy. We had some of the most exciting games, and brawls, that anyone in Manchester could ever remember. The last time I saw Mike was at a motorcycle rally in Loudon, New Hampshire. He still had that big brutal toothless predatory smile, like he had just come from a kill, but he recognized me and spared me the common fate of other rivals.

"Hey, Pete!" he roared, as his big fist clenched my hand. It was like meeting a rabid male lion in the wild. *I wondered if he had eaten of late.* We shook hands, or should I say, he shook my hand while I slipped mine into the titanium teeth front end of a rotating rock-crusher.

Lenore became one of the favorite girls at Memorial; she was pretty popular with the boys. With a lot of the boys, if rumors are correct, but I would like to believe differently. I would still like to think that after our galvanizing hug under her front porch, the hug we never told our parents about, the hug that I was sure had gotten her pregnant, was the first time for both of us.

***

My most memorable teen-age 'true-love' affair came while I was still in high school. Her name was Linda. I don't remember how we met, but it must have been in class. Linda was not a high school celebrity cheerleader. She was one of the hidden gems, one of the quiet, sweet, hard-working girls from the lower east side of Manchester. She and her younger brother and baby sister lived with their parents in the Greek section of town, in an old three-story apartment building a block from the Valley Street cemetery and the Van Otis candy shop. Linda worked at a local dry-cleaner after school. I used to walk there to see her and to arrange our 'dates' consisting of my walking her home after school, or coming to her house in the evening to sit on the couch together to watch TV after her parents went to bed. Linda always greeted me at the door with a big smile, as if we were going on a big date. I didn't have a car.

Linda was a no-nonsense kind of girl. She always dressed very well, and was purposeful in everything she did. So it was not unusual that she should take my sincere advances graciously. But if the truth were known, I was clueless. I was like a boy looking in the showroom window at a hot convertible. I wanted to own it and drive it, in the most respectable way, of course, but I understood nothing about cars, and even less about driving. I was sincere, and deeply 'in love,' but I was also hopelessly naïve. I was in it for the friendship. I enjoyed being with Linda. We became very close, as close as two young adults could be, just short of intimacy. Neither of us even thought of exchanging sexual favors, at least as far as I can recall. Frankly, at that point in my life, I was blissfully unaware that I had any such as favors to exchange.

Our evolving friendship was such that Linda used to walk to the Gill Stadium practice field to watch me during football drills. She would stand inconspicuously just outside the eight-foot-high chain-link fence, her light skirt blowing gently in the breeze. She was not Athena, nor Diana, but close to it; she was a sweet, fragrant oasis in an arid sea of sand.

On one particular day, Linda was standing in her usual place just outside the fence. My football coach had installed a new, green tackling dummy a few feet from the inside of the fence. The dummy was suspended on a gruesome hook with a spring device, between two heavy wooden truncated telephone poles. It resembled a makeshift guillotine. The symbolism of malevolent intent was graphic. A faceless, grotesque canvass dummy was suspended between the poles like the hapless victim of an Assyrian siege.

There was a sand pit on the far side where both the running back and the dummy would land, if the hit were made properly. A proper hit consisted of running at the dummy full tilt, pummeling, snatching and wrenching the unwitting canvas carcass with sufficient speed and strength to tear it from its stubborn mechanical noose. If the runner were fast, strong and smart, the imbecile behemoth would release its imbecilic grip. If the brainless behemoth *and* the running-back *both* proved to be dummies, then the smarter of the two would stay on the hook, wrenching the runner awkwardly and painfully flat on his back while his grinning, disingenuous stuffed nemesis bounced and squeaked in senseless glee overhead. If and when this occurred, the back was forced to try again until *one* of the dummies prevailed.

I had my fair share of failures and successes with this legendary tackling dummy, as he had with me. But on this particular day, while I was standing in line with my teammates, and Linda was still watching from the fence, one of my old elementary school buddies saw her and made a casual. off-color comment.

"Does she go down?"

I was shocked and confused. I had a vague understanding of what the term meant, and I was offended.

"No, she doesn't. She wouldn't. *We* don't do that," I responded

My so-called friend looked surprised and confused. "We just don't do that," was my final reply.

I was next in line to hit the dummy. This was a virtual test of manhood for any dummy. The sun was low and to the back of the menacing figure. Most of we young amateur running backs had plenty of raw courage, but little experience or skill. Most of us had failed this drill repeatedly, landing hard on our youthful pride only to find ourselves staring up into the red, swollen face of our crazed grid-iron coach. It seemed as if he enjoyed watching us fail, at least on the practice field. He had come up the hard way, and was determined to make hardcore little war-machines out of the handful of players who managed to survive boot camp.

"Get the hell out of the way," he barked at his last scrawny victim writhing in pain and humiliation in the dirt. "Get to the locker room! Get out of my sight, and don't bother to come back tomorrow. This game isn't for girls," he added, his face bulging with venomous glee, white froth leaking from the corners of his gaping mouth. *Does he get some kind of a perverse rush, growling like Lucifer and shoving his filthy forked tongue in everyone's face? I wondered...*

"Who's next?! Colman! OK Colman. Colman! Don't just stand there. Hit this 'g...d...' dummy like you mean it! Show me if you want to play this game!"

"Does she go down?" was still echoing in my head and spreading through my moral fiber like a poisonous viper. It was as if a mortal enemy had breached the main gate and I was the only one standing between its dumb green, impotent form, and the future of the civilized world.

It was now or never. It was *my* life and the future of the human race that hung in the balance.

More importantly, Linda was watching. The love of my life had been violated by my coach's vile tongue and my 'friend's' brazen indiscretion. It was up to me to invade the enemy citadel, slay the foul, fire-breathing dragon, and carry my princess to safety.

With clenched fists and the brute force of a 150-milimeter plastic shell, I sped toward the imposing idiot (the dummy) and hit it square in chest, ripping it from its steel harness and slamming it to the ground, my frenzied face pressed against its mute remains.

"That's the way to hit a dummy!" screamed the coach, as if that one hit had been sufficient to justify *his* love affair with lunacy.

"That's the way it's done! Good job Colman! Keep it up and I'll make a pulling guard out of you yet..." Can *anyone* imagine a 145-pound pulling guard?

My 'friend' never asked me anything about Linda after that. In fact, though we had attended elementary school together and played on the same team, I don't remember ever having a civil conversation with him again. I never told Linda about the incident, of course. For all she knew, I was just working hard to make the team. I was working hard to win her affection, too. As if my life depended on it. At least that day.

The only other time that I remember seeing Linda at the field was one time during track practice. I had a friend who weighed less than I. I was a sprinter, ran the 440-yard dash and threw the javelin; I was also on the gymnastics team. Another good friend named Tim Voorhees, the son of a Methodist pastor from Dover, was a skilled pole-vaulter; he began to teach me the art. My speed and strength, combined with my yearning to climb and to fly, gave me a certain advantage in the sport.

The day Linda came, it was early in my training. I remember landing awkwardly in the shallow sawdust pit with my spikes under me, puncturing a few clean holes in my calf muscle. Linda was sympathetic. She was also visibly proud of her athletic beau. She was always there for me, cheering me on. I by-passed Tim in the sport my senior year and went on to tie for third place in the state meet, with a borrowed fiber-glass pole. All I had ever used was an old, reconditioned bamboo pole with a handmade carved plug, and a stiff aluminum vaulting pole that wouldn't bend for anyone. But I flew, occasionally, and was proud; she was proud.

My friendship with Linda grew over the next two years. That is, until the day we went swimming at Daniel's Pond (behind my grandparents' home in Weare, ironically). Linda was on the beach looking beautiful in her one-piece, black bathing suit, when she popped the question.

"Why don't you ever hold my hand or try to kiss me? She asked.

I was stunned, and not a little embarrassed. Frankly, as impossible as it might sound, I had never thought of this aspect of our friendship. I was not brain dead; nor was I suffering from paralysis. It had just never occurred to me to express affection or to explore sexual intimacy with Linda. She was the one who was normal. She was about as far away from promiscuity as a young woman could be, but she was normal. She craved, and

144

deserved affection. I was simply innocent and ignorant of this deficit in our relationship. I suppose having a father within reach would have been helpful. But would I have even sought his advice and counsel had it been available? What's a young man or woman to do?

As we left the beach that afternoon, Linda and I were sitting together in the backseat of her parents' old Buick. Here was my chance to initiate some sort of contact. I slid my hand across the seat and grasped hers, quite pleased that I had finally breached an insurmountable barrier in our relationship. She allowed me to take her hand, but all she said, with a descent in her tone and a slight note of sadness and sarcasm, was "Wow." What should have been a joyous, exhilarating 'first contact' was a letdown...more for Linda than for me, I'm sure. But she was not unkind. We progressed rapidly in our relationship in the weeks to follow. I had never really kissed a girl, but I learned quickly, perhaps too quickly. We used to sit on the front porch and talk and kiss. No hanky-panky.

One night, while we were sitting together alone watching television, our kissing became quite intimate. I found myself wanting to explore forbidden territory, and became very uncomfortable with myself. Linda seemed more than willing to allow me to kiss her, but I stopped rather suddenly. I had become very uncomfortable with myself, and with our relationship, as it seemed to be moving rapidly in the direction of sexual intimacy. I remember sitting up and telling Linda, much to her surprise, that we needed to break off our relationship. Immediately. That very night.

"Linda, I'm Sorry," I said. I shook with uncertainty, sadness, and just a tinge of shame. Are there different kinds of shame? What kind of shame would I have unleashed had we continued that night? Was I to be blamed for doing, or not doing, what I felt was right? Was I simply afraid? Or were there other reasons that were beyond my mortal grasp?

"We can't continue like this. I'm sorry. I should go. Forgive me."

Linda was shocked and confused, her eyes filled with tears. As I exited her apartment that night in 1966, my emotions were like a fishing line, still strong and intact, but hopelessly knotted and strained. Before I turned and left her standing inside her front door, she looked at me pleadingly and cried.

"Why, Pete?" she asked quietly and lovingly.

"I don't know, Linda. I'm sorry. I just have to go."

I turned and left her standing. We had been dating for two full years. Linda was a devout Catholic. I had been raised in a very warm, conservative 'evangelical' environment. Our church had been the product of a very long, celebrated pietistic tradition reaching as far back as the Reformation in Germany and the Methodism of John and Charles Wesley in 18th-century England. I had often shared my faith with Linda, and had sung my favorite gospel songs to her; she enjoyed them. She had been intrigued. I also attended Christmas mid-night mass with Linda and her family. But on that particular Christmas, I had sought out the priest and met with him privately to share my newfound faith with *him.* He later invited me to his home and offered me a glass of Sherry. I had never drunk alcohol, but the Sherry was great!

Linda never asked where I had gone that night. Now that I think of it, I am ashamed to have left her and her family stranded. It was inconsiderate and naïve. Religious faith can sometimes blind its adherents to the reality of others, to their humanity and commonality. But Linda was forgiving and more considerate than I that night. She had forgiven me also for a sincere, but ignorant remark I had made some months earlier.

"Linda," I had boasted, "you can be sure of one thing in our relationship; if anyone ever breaks it off, it will never be me!" No sooner had the words left my mouth than I had thought of the Apostle Peter and his declaration to Christ: "Lord, though everyone else betrays You, I will never betray You...I am ready to die for You!" "Peter," Jesus had said, with a note of pity and enduring love for this impetuous man, "before the rooster crows this night, you will betray Me three times....you will deny that you ever knew Me." The Scriptures relate that after having betrayed the man whom he loved, and to whom he had promised fidelity, Peter went out to a lonely place and wept bitterly.

Yet Linda, whom I had loved as deeply as I was capable at that stage in my young life, the same young woman to whom I had sworn love and fidelity, had been very forgiving. 'Love covers a multitude of wrongs' Solomon wrote.

I would not see Linda again until a day eleven years later, after we had both graduated and married others...the day before my wife, Judith, and I and our two sons left for language study in France. We were heading for Upper Volta, West Africa, where we would serve for fifteen years as missionary educators. By the time we had returned to the States in 1992, we had two daughters. Our four children were to spend their formative years in Africa; they would have acquired two additional languages.

On that final day in 1977, before our departure for language school in Albertville, a small medieval city in the eastern French Alps in the region of Haute Savoie, we had returned to my mother's two-story apartment, which, ironically, was just a block away from Linda's house. When we entered the living room, Linda was sitting there. I went over to her immediately, and without thinking, kissed her on the cheek!

"Who is she?!" my wife asked.

"Oh, honey, I'm sorry, this is Linda. Linda ..."

Judy had remembered my having told her about my feelings for Linda. Judy and I had few, if any, secrets in our six years of happy marriage. Judy was also very forgiving, though she admitted to having been just a little surprised. No, *shocked* would be the word. Without any protocol, Linda looked across the small room and said, "I have just come to say goodbye, and to tell you both how very proud I am. I heard that you were going to Africa as missionaries. I have also come to tell you that I was converted to Jesus Christ just ten weeks ago."

Now I was really shocked.

"Linda, that's wonderful news," I said, with my mouth still open. But before I could ask her, she continued her account:

"Do you remember always talking to me about you faith in Christ? It was all so new, so sincere, and so very personal. And you sang to me about you faith, too. Do you remember that old hymn about the 'Old Rugged Cross?' Well, I just thought you would like to know that my little sister was listening. We have been attending a small Baptist church near our home. My sister attended the Vacation Bible School. I remember you talking to me about Jesus and the Bible. My sister prayed with me just ten weeks ago; I prayed to accept Jesus as my savior. I thought you would like to know."

As Linda spoke, Judy was still struggling, but what I felt at that moment I can barely describe. Deep *elation* should do it. Elation combined with a buried feeling of lingering love, a love lost to me, on one level, but found by another, forever, on a completely different level, a much higher level. A love that embraced both of us.

After her short speech, Linda simply got up from her chair, greeted both of us for the last time, politely excused herself, and left. As she exited the back door, went down the stairs, and turned the corner toward the direction of her parents' house, I struggled to release a simple, soft "Good-bye, Linda," from over the gray painted railing. I barely got the words out, then she was gone. Judy, whom I love dearly, was standing behind me, still wondering, no doubt, how to deal with her husband's and her own mixed emotions.

"I guess I really loved her," I said, ever so softly, and with some trepidation. Judy was still trying desperately to process the whole innocent affair (no pun intended). She would later confess that she had 'felt so fat' compared to Linda who had 'looked so svelte.'

"I know," she said. "I love you too."

That was the last time I would see Linda, though I have thought about her often since that day. I used to dream about seeing her too, but I was careful to tell Judy about it every time it happened. She surprised me by telling me that she dreamt about her old boyfriends, too, from time to time. I had never thought of that. She had almost married one of those old flames. He used to ride his bicycle clear across town just to see her. I was just a bit jealous; she just smiled.

I wonder what my Dad would have done had he been in my place that night at Linda's apartment? I wonder how *I* would have behaved, and whether *I* would have been strong as a young Marine returning from a long traumatic tour of combat in the Pacific. Would I have been strong enough to resist the temptation of a dark evening with a beautiful young girl on the warm, inviting sands of the San Diego seashore? Would a strong spiritual faith have prevented me from succumbing to equally strong human passions? Can I blame my father for failing to remain strong? Can I really take pride or credit for having avoided a similar situation and the sense of shame that he must have brought?

No.

The answer to these questions lays somewhere in the mysterious vale between spiritual zeal, born of sincerity, and human passion. Between the two there is a very thin, fragile line which makes us both human and divine. As Alexander Pope, in his *'An Essay on Man'* has so brilliantly expressed:

> *A being darkly wise, and rudely great...he hangs between; in doubt to act, or rest; in doubt to deem himself a god, or a beast...created half to rise, and half to fall; great lord of all things, yet prey to all..."*

Chapter Eleven

One Shepherd

While the baby rabbit is nursing, it is always looking at its mother's ears.

(Bambara proverb)

While I was doing dissertation research on West-African proverbs in the spring of 1998, I was invited to the home of a pastor and former president of a prominent Christian church in the city of Bobo-Dioulasso, Burkina Faso. During our meal together, we had been reminiscing about my years of service in that country. In the course of a very warm conversation, the pastor mentioned our son, Daniel, who had spent his early years in that city, running and hunting with a neighborhood gang of boys his age, scouring the marketplace in search of second-hand, low-cut leather Nikes and numbered jerseys. Daniel has always been a very personable and uninhibited young man. I recall having commented to my pastor-friend and colleague that I was not as well-known in Bobo-Dioulasso as my son Daniel. People used to shout out to me on the street, *"Daniel face (fachay)!"* "Daniel's father!"

There had been an incident that I shall never forget which occurred at the Bible Institute where we lived and served. A visiting evangelist from Mali, who was also a friend and colleague, had met Daniel one afternoon at the doorway of one of the dormitories. Daniel had been looking for me, but he wasn't sure how to describe me to pastor Traoré.

"Qui cherches-tu?" ("Whom do you seek?") the visitor inquired of Daniel , knowing very well that I was his father, and that he was looking for me. Daniel was at a loss for words to describe his father, so he resorted to drama. He lifted high one side of his shorts to expose a thin, wiry white thigh.

"Il est comme ça!" ("He's like this!") He exclaimed. Neither the pastor, nor anyone else present that day, shall ever forget or underestimate Daniel's flare for the dramatic, or his extraordinary communicative skills. It was just after I had finished recounting this story about my son that Pastor Daniel looked at me and quoted the above proverb. "The baby bunny who is nursing is always looking at his mother's ears." Like father like son. I was honored and humbled, all at the same time. The apple doesn't fall far…

It was a compliment and I was touched. Everyone knew and loved Daniel. I was honored to have been compared to him and to have been known because of his positive, friendly presence throughout the city, even among the local leadership. He was, and still is, a tribute to his father. He is one who has become a father to the man.

It is equally true that while the baby bunny is watching its mother's (and undoubtedly, its father's) ears, its parents are watching as well. In my own case, I was raised primarily by my mother, quite, without the strong abiding influence of my father. But there was another father who was watching - the same one who was swatting the flies away – the One who promises to be a 'father to the fatherless.'

I would be remiss if I did not state that, regardless of what particular religious convictions or beliefs a person may profess (even if none at all), personal faith and spiritual growth are a very real, fundamental part of the story. It would be dishonest and unprofessional of me as a writer to neglect such a chapter. My own spiritual journey constitutes the very soul and substance of all that is written here. The rest is just paper, ink and creative glue.

The fear of the Lord is the beginning of knowledge...
(Proverbs 1:7a)

Trust in the Lord with all your heart and lean not n your own understanding; in all your ways acknowledge him, and he will make your paths straight.
(Proverbs 3:5-6)

I have always been fascinated with proverbs. I was exposed to the Scriptures, and to biblical proverbs in particular, at very young age. Proverbs 22:6 comes to mind. "Train up a child in the way that he should go; when he is old he will not depart from it." Although I am unashamed to state unapologetically that I am a Christian, I am equally convinced that the truths embraced by the Judeo-Christian faith are synonymous with the same kind of values that are recognized by most individuals universally, regardless of the diversity and complexity of the cultural or religious traditions which they may espouse. In other words, there is, I believe, infinitely more in terms of moral content and truth-value which Christian faith has in common with other peoples and cultures, whether avowedly 'religious,' or 'secular,' than traditional socio-religious systems, or cherished creedal forms and rituals are willing to concede.

Few religious systems, or even so-called secular traditions, would deny the intrinsic worth and indispensability of such values as kindness, fairness, loyalty, freedom, compassion, and the like, regardless of the particular label attached to them. Though some would dispute the origin and ownership of the original copyright to such values, few would dispute that such a copyright does exist.

Personally, I take great comfort in the rather ubiquitous, inoffensive and friendly nature of the simple proverb. The dispute concerning their source and authorship, at least for me, was settled long ago, but not without some measure of discomfort and concern. Truth is truth regardless of its relation to, or relative distance from the source. Some people feel uncomfortable talking about a 'source' for truth. I share no such discomfort. Roughly twenty-five kilometers outside the city of Bobo-Dioulasso is a legendary fresh-water source that was effectively tapped and harnessed by the French during its colonial period of influence in that part of the world. This virtual oasis in the middle of an otherwise arid landscape is located in a half-hidden jungle basin; which is intersected by a small river. The area has been a favorite recreation and vacation site for foreigners for nearly a century. A powerful subterranean spring in the middle of the oasis still sits under a small pumping station which channels an uninterrupted supply of clean fresh water through large underground pipes to the city. My family and missionary colleagues (and countless others) have enjoyed swimming and snorkeling in the shallow river. But upstream a couple hundred yards from the camping area, the rushing river becomes a slow shallow stream, then a series of ankle-deep pools, and virtually disappears into the thick underbrush. The area is deceptively dangerous. Rumor has it that a Catholic priest from a nearby seminary who was fond of exploring these edenic shallows went swimming one day and never returned.

Exploring sources can be dangerous work. The analogy to a source for truth in this case is perhaps valid. The real source of the water for this oasis is the Niger River located hundreds of miles to the north. Its waters are filtered by the sub-Saharan sands and flow underground, undetected, until they reemerge in the soft sands of these shallow pools. What would appear to be a multitude of separate sources is, in fact, one and the same. There are not multiple sources. Nor are there variations in the quality and purity of the water. There is just one source, visible in a multitude of forms and depths, creating an abundant and indiscriminate supply of life-giving water.

The unfortunate conflict which certain religious traditions reflect as a signature by-product, is the tendency to effectively discredit or dismiss truth in favor of a particular religious persuasion or perception, at the expense of the truth itself. Or as James Russell Lowell expressed in an 1844 pre-Civil War poem entitled *The Present Crisis,* "Truth is ever on the scaffold; falsehood ever on the throne." Such artificial and parochial distinctions only blur the truth and put it out of the reach of those of us who need it the most. The search for truth requires a certain tenacious commitment to humility and honesty. As the proverb goes, it is like 'one beggar telling another beggar where he found bread.'

Please don't misunderstand. I am not advocating a smorgasbord variety of religion, or a brand of syncretism; which just takes a particular truth when it is appealing or convenient to do so, and ignores or dismisses it categorically when acceptance becomes uncomfortable. Neither am I recommending that one accept whatever *appears* to be true without rigorous critical examination. In this respect, Chaucer's axiom may prove helpful – "Not everything that glitters is gold..." At the other end of the equation, pluralism can be just as dangerous. While it is safe to assume that some truth may be found everywhere, or in everyone, is does not follow that everything is true. In Africa it is said, "You have some of the truth, and I have some of the truth, but the truth lies between us." In the case for truth, and the ability of the proverb to effectively convey truth by and for all cultures and peoples, I respectfully call as a witness someone infinitely wiser than I, Solomon himself, and will thereafter rest my case:

> *The words of the wise are like goads, their collected sayings like firmly embedded nails – given by one shepherd...*
>
> (Ecclesiastes 12:11)

***

In 1965 I entered my junior high school English Literature class relatively unprepared and unpolished. Having been 'born and bred' within a solid biblical tradition, yet still without a theological or philosophically firm footing, I was blissfully ignorant of biblical truth, though I had sufficient critical spiritual experience to convince me of what was essential, what was worth living and dying for.

Our English teacher had a particular passion for Shakespeare. In the course of our reading and class preparation, I became enamored with the quality and depth of truth embedded in Shakespeare's writing. Some of that truth seemed to bear a striking similarity to much of what I had read and remembered from my limited, but earnest perusal of the Scriptures. The result was that in the course of that year of English study, my interest in spiritual truths was rekindled. I became the self-designated source and authority for any and all questions related to the Bible. One of my more naive friends even had the audacity to predict that I would become a missionary to Africa some day! 'Out of the mouths of babes…'

No one knew that I had been experiencing a bit of a spiritual crisis in my own soul. Revival meetings and enthusiastic evangelical services were routine in my small home church. Thankfully, trumped-up emotional hype, manufactured religious theatrics, or superficial spiritual sideshows were never part of the program. Just quality home cooking and genuine spiritual fare. On a particular Sunday evening, our pastor preached passionately, but quietly, to the point of tears, inviting the congregation to the front of the church for prayer. Many went forward. Others simply knelt in their place in the pews, but all were overwhelmed with a sense of unworthiness and a need for forgiveness.

I was no exception, but for some reason I hadn't the courage to go forward. I left the church that night before the service ended, ran a mile home and knelt in the privacy of my own room seeking God's forgiveness and guidance. One of the results of that experience was a new desire to read the Bible. And read it I did all the way through, for the first time. After all, I had to come to class prepared.

I was making excellent progress until the end of the year when I had a very painful lesson in humility. I and another young man, a classmate and very congenial sort, who was much less serious and astute than I…and who had a notorious reputation as the class clown, were chosen to debate two other students in the class, one of whom was a very soft-spoken, brilliant Jewish girl. During the final debate, she single-handedly decimated our flimsy arguments, wrapping up her treatise with a quote by Jesus from the gospels. We had been soundly and expertly thumped!

Surely you will quote this proverb to me...I mused... *'Physician, heal yourself!'*
(Jesus, in Luke 4:23)

Fortunately for me, the young woman was genuinely sweet and gracious. She knew very well that she had used my own spiritual arsenal and celebrity spiritual status effectively against me, and she came to me after class to apologize. She was sincere. I had learned a vital lesson. She actually admitted that she admired my enthusiasm and passionate commitment to the faith, but that given the nature of the debate, she had not been able to resist the angle of attack. It was a great debate; she deserved the victory; I deserved the lesson.

Wounds from a friend can be trusted, but an enemy multiplies kisses.
(Proverbs 27:6)

The experiences to which I referred earlier are too critical to omit, so I will speak to them only briefly. One such experience is the critical turning point; which I have described above, and which set me on a firm footing and in a new direction. I was convinced that I wanted to make my life purposeful, that I wanted earnestly to honor the truth; which I had come to experience in a radically new way. I had never been encouraged to consider a college education. In fact, my life had been pretty aimless to that point in the journey. But now I had the clear conviction that I should apply to a Bible college where I could study with others who shared my views and values, a place where I could effectively exploit my newfound love for God and for literature. It had never occurred to me that not everyone in my own spiritual community would share that same vision, especially with regard to the study of literature, which, in my own religious context, was considered by most devout believers to a 'secular,' fruitless, counter-productive pursuit.

The period during which I was experiencing this very unpublicized and very personal spiritual watershed was just about the same time I was reevaluating my relationship with Linda. I still cared for her deeply, and regretted our break-up on the emotional level, but on the night I left Linda for good I felt a heavy weight drop from my shoulders. Not the unbearable weight of her affection, or the genuine joy of our friendship, but rather an invisible yoke which, I believed, had been somehow keeping me from experiencing a higher purpose. I ran all the way home that night feeling as if the weight of the world had been removed. I was heart-broken and elated at the same time. Does that make any sense at all? Perhaps only to a young man who is trying to sort out his love for God and his love for a beautiful young woman.

In any case, another very dear elderly English teacher at my high school had been impressed with my English scores on a national test, and virtually ordered me to change to the college-prep curriculum. Before the end of my senior year, I only applied to one college, the only college that I had heard of, Nyack *Missionary* College in Nyack, New York. Did I neglect to mention that I had met numerous singing groups from Nyack that had visited my church on the few days that I had chosen to show up? Did I also fail to mention that after my baptism at age twelve, during a missionary service, I was one of the only young people to raise his hand in response to the invitation by the guest missionary speaker to volunteer for missionary service...somewhere, someday?

The only letter I sent to a college, and the attending response I received a few short weeks later, was a letter of acceptance at Nyack Missionary College. When I announced the news to my dear pastor and his wife, and visited the parsonage to request their prayers, they prayed joyfully and earnestly for me. But when I announced to them my intention to study literature, they quickly separated every literature anthology from their own collection of Nyack textbooks (they were both Nyack grads), advising me that literature was of no consequence, and proceeded to bequeath to me a stack of biblical commentaries and manuals to help me in my preparation for ministry. Hadn't they understood that I was going to study English? I felt no particular call to any kind of church-related ministry at the time. I was just a bit offended and confused, but grateful for their loving support and encouragement.

So I was off to Nyack Missionary College in the fall of 1967. I had no car, and just enough money to cover part of the first semester. I had worked for a fence company the summer before, ten hours a day for $1.50 an hour. When I returned home in the late afternoon, my hands blistered and aching, I mowed lawns until dark, returning home with just enough time to woof down a late supper and take a bath. I walked a mile up Hanover Hill each morning to catch the seven-o'clock bus to the Massebesic Lake traffic circle where Standard Fence Company was located. When I missed the bus, I 'thumbed.' Once I even walked the four miles. On Saturdays, I cleaned the church in preparation for Sunday services. The church gave me ten dollars a week. It was the most important work I did all week. I tithed ten percent of all my earnings.

The week before I was to leave for college, our small church family organized a special going-away celebration. I was told that I had been the very first person to be sent from our church to prepare for Christian ministry, although no one, including myself, knew exactly what that ministry would be.

Our church family was made up of common folk; many were on welfare, and others were single parents struggling to survive. I hadn't told anyone that I still lacked a few dollars to complete my first tuition payment. At the end of the informal fellowship in the church basement, someone announced my plans to leave for Nyack and passed a basket to help me along the way. It was very humbling. As the small basket passed, people (even some children) put in dollar bills and handfuls of pocket change. When the church treasurer counted the money, it was $72 and change (within pennies of the exact amount I needed). Someone had been reading my mail.

God was still in the business of swatting the flies away.

Chapter Twelve

The 'Wife of My Youth'

*Who can find a virtuous woman? For her price is
far above rubies.*

(Proverbs 5:18; 31:10)

Up to this point in my young life and spiritual
pilgrimage, my father, Robert Colman, had been
conspicuously absent, though I do confess to remembering
three separate times that he was actually present for
important events. He *did* (though rather surreptitiously)
attend my high school graduation exercise at the Kennedy
Arena in 1966. I also recall his having attended a service at
the Alliance Church at Merrimack and Hall Streets in
Manchester (the same church we had attended, and where
he had served so enthusiastically as Sunday School
Superintendent for so many years) one evening when I had
been invited as the guest speaker before leaving for
language study in France. Dad *was* very proud that I had
chosen to enter the ministry and was now on my way to the
mission field. And he did, just once, along with his wife,
Dottie Samara, and his father (my grandfather), Sumner
Chase Colman, come to visit me at the college during my
freshmen year. I had entirely forgotten about this visit
until, very recently my mother sent me a colored photo of
the three of them smiling, standing in front of old Mosley
Hall. How could I have forgotten such a rare visit?

My attending Nyack Missionary College was anything but coincidental; it was there that I pursued my study of English Literature, and where I learned to reconcile and assimilate fundamental spiritual issues and principles of personal faith with intellectual and social concerns. My experience in and outside the classroom served to provide a stable, sane personal grounding for years to come.

More importantly, Nyack College is the place where I would eventually meet the foremost and final love of my life, the 'wife of my youth' (we have been in this same *youth* phase for thirty-six years now), my beloved wife and friend, Judith Katherine (Labus) Colman.

Judy and I had much in common, including that we were both English majors. We were in all the same classes together. Judy was at a decided disadvantage, as I see it. I must confess, she had turned my styrofoam-stuffed head more than a few times. You see, she was, in truth, angelic, managing to hide her halo under long brown hair which curled in delicate, smiling rings just below each ear. She had a bright, beautiful smile, generously but discretely dispensed. She was quiet, self-restrained, gentle, discerning...everything I was not. She was every young man's dream.

I was out to lunch most of the time, blinded by the bright, loving twinkle in her soft eyes, paralyzed (when I should have been joyfully and freely mesmerized) by her luscious smile and soft lips. In short I was clueless. But I had noticed. Often. She had gotten my clueless attention without even having tried. As hard as *I* may have tried, in the blissless, listless state of naiveté in which I wandered the campus, I couldn't forget or ignore her. Her beauty was anything but superficial, though a man would have to have been blind, or stupid, or both, not to have fallen in love with such a girl *just* for the sake of her beauty. The old cliché, "Beauty is only skin deep" did not apply in her case.

Judy and I both come from 'dysfunctional' homes. To my knowledge, we are the only ones to complete college on either side of the family. In my case, very few, if any, in my family ever went beyond high school, with the possible exception of our only prominent ancestor, the 'Honorable' Dudley C. Colman, born in Newburyport, Massachusetts in 1745, who disagreed with his own party on the question of slavery and voted for the presidential candidate, Abraham Lincoln, in 1860.

Both Judy and I were raised in the same religious tradition, and grew up attending the same missionary denomination, she in Dover, Ohio, and me in Manchester. The Christian and Missionary Alliance was, and still is, predominantly a missionary-sending society. It originally started as an interfaith community with a focus on a deeper personal walk with God. It held services in an old theatre in New York City, commissioning and supporting young men and woman for missionary service in places like Japan, Korea, Indonesia, the former 'French Sudan' (West Africa), the former Belgian Congo, and beyond. It was a pioneer missionary society, and Nyack was one of the first missionary training institutes in the United States. Judy also had a very strong interest in missionary service and related Christian ministries. We had something else in common. Neither of us could afford to go to college, and neither of our respective families could afford to help us.

Judy and I both worked on campus the entire four years we were there. Judy served tables in the college dining room, and I washed dishes. Quite independently, we were both later promoted to separate positions in a very

165

small campus commissary called the 'Hub.' We also shared athletic abilities and a love of sports. Judy became the captain of Nyack's elite cheer-leading squad; I became All-Conference center-forward for Nyack's legendary soccer team. Though I can claim only fifteen goals in two seasons, one of those games in which I scored was against Barrington College. We actually lost horribly with a score of eight to one, but the game made the short column of Sports Illustrated. Barrington boasted a Russian player who was virtually unstoppable; he scored all of Barrington's goals. I scored the other one, a header into the upper left corner off a perfect corner-kick (from the left side) by a close personal friend and soccer mentor, and Nyack's best, a Dutchman whom we called Johnny.

Since Judy was the head cheerleader, she was always there to encourage and console her favorite player. In truth, there was another very godly young man, and superior athlete, in whom Judy had some potential interest, named Harold. He was one of four missionary sons, whose parents had been pioneer missionaries in Africa. Harold was a gentle giant, fearless and harmless. He loved God and every one else with a pure, sincere heart, even when he was challenged or abused by an opponent on the playing field. His refusal to return bad play but rather react in a gentlemanly manner had the power to both enrage and endear his opponents. Harold went on to become a missionary pilot, flying support and relief missions in Ethiopia in the late 1960s and early 1970s.

When I was a youth pastor in Dearborn Heights, Michigan in 1976, struggling with the decision to commit myself and my family to missionary service overseas, I sat down at the kitchen table and found a small column in a Christian journal. A certain young missionary pilot had been evacuating other missionaries to safety during a political up-rising. He managed to save his passengers, but in the process was shot in the neck and perished. He died saving those whom he loved, just like the One whom he had always loved and who had given his life for others.

Nyack Missionary College sponsored a huge missions program every year at Philharmonic Hall in the Big Apple. I was trying painfully to decide on a date. Judy was, at the same time, and quite unbeknownst to me, praying fervently about which young man she would prefer ask her. I don't know what Harold's position on the matter was, but yours truly had a strange strategy. Alone in my room one night, I wrote the names of several worthy candidates on small pieces of white paper, spread them out on my dresser top, and prayed..."Lord, help me to choose..." At that very instant, my roommate, who was engaged to be married, and unapologetic and zealous in his campaign to get me to date *anyone at all,* burst into the room, kicked my chair with his characteristic disdain for any trace of sensitivity I may have possessed on such a delicate matter, and blurted out, "Hey, Colman, why don't you ask Judy to go with you to the missions program?!" What my roommate didn't know at that moment was that I had just finished my very short prayer, literally seconds before his uninvited barrage, and had flipped over one of the small pieces of paper to read my answer: *Judy Labus.*

A few days before the event, during half-time at one of Nyack's basketball games, I took the chance of my life - I walked up to the cheerleading captain, and with the polished, irresistible charm of Don Juan himself, with a mouthful of yeast, I sputtered something resembling "Hi...Judy?...Hi...Um...would you...I mean...Are you going with any...(breath)...Would you like to go together to the missions program in the city?"

I had actually done it! She accepted. Poor Harold. He was with his team in the locker room. I not only took Judy, but we were quite unexpectedly chosen to *be* a missionary couple and to march in the big opening parade, right down the center isle of Philharmonic Hall! Little did either of us know how prophetic such an event would be.

Our four-year romance was an emotional roller-coaster ride for both of us, but it was particularly traumatic for Judy. Poor thing. I never knew how I felt, or how I was *supposed* to feel in such situations. I was afraid and terribly insecure, not to mention immature. Judy had virtually given her heart away, and I would either just walk away, or stay away for long periods of time. Not intentionally, of course. I would never have hurt her intentionally. I became extremely involved in college activities. Studies were hard enough, but there was soccer, and I also became very involved with the Brooklyn Gospel Team. I spent weekends walking the streets of Bay Ridge sharing my faith with anyone who would listen. I had some pretty hair-raising experiences, including a couple attempts on my life. Those weekends, and the people I met, made a permanent impression on my heart and life. I learned a lot about my own faith in God, and a bit about myself. But I still knew very little, if anything at all, about how to express or receive the love of a young woman. I was so committed to the Gospel Team that I missed the Senior Banquet. Judy went with some of her friends who also hadn't been asked. She said later that she had had a good time, but she went without me. My loss. I would counsel my own children to do differently, to find some kind of wholesome balance between spiritual zeal and social intercourse.

We did manage one extraordinary date which we still both talk about. This was a good one, and it broke my piggy bank. We took the bus to the city and made our way to the infamous "Bitter End" café, a brick underground birthing center for folk and rock groups in the late 1960s, groups like 'Peter, Paul and Mary,' 'Simon and Garfunkel,' and countless others. I don't remember who played that night, except that it was a very skilled guitarist with an unorthodox fingering style. His music was low-key and mesmerizing, but what really fascinated me, in addition to Judy's sweet, simple company, was the one large ice-cream Sunday, the only one they served and the only one I could afford…that came in a huge flower vase (I think the vase was green). It was filled to the brim with every imaginable flavor, and then topped with nuts, cherries, several sweet, sticky sauces, and a mountain of Chantilly lace (*chantille* is the French word for whipped cream).

I was really trying to be polite. I was also oblivious to Judy's love for ice-cream, engendered by her allegiance to the Goshen Dairy Ice-Cream Shop which she had attended religiously back home in Dover, Ohio, where she also worked each summer. She was a *connoisseur* of good ice-cream.

Well, to make the tale of a tall ice-cream Sunday short, I kept pushing the vase toward Judy, urging her to enjoy it.

"Go ahead. It's alright. Enjoy it. There's plenty. I'll get a few bites later."

Judy just took a modest spoonful and pushed it back.

"Please, take some," she insisted.

But I was determined to be a considerate date, and simply slid the vase and its shrinking contents back again in her direction, focused on the red brick wall, the guitarist, and the quiet beauty sitting next to me as she continued to discretely dispense with what appeared to be a healthy share of the creamy contents of *our* Sunday, the one I had used my last meager funds to pay for.

By the end of the first or second song, I remember taking a long, hitherto unused spoon with the intent to finally savor my investment (the ice-cream). I was just trying to be polite. But the ice-cream was gone, the cavernous container empty. All that remained of that imperial vase of ethereal, creamy delight was a little remnant of juice and a few surviving walnuts floating perilously at the bottom, like miniature survivors caught in a whirlpool.

"I'm sorry," she offered, so sweetly, as she discretely wiped chocolate sauce and whipped cream from the corners of her luscious mouth.

"It's OK," I added quickly, not wanting to offend her. "I'm glad you enjoyed it."

That was nearly forty years ago. I *still* have to watch my dessert. And I wouldn't dare infringe upon a tub of buttered popcorn. But the benefit of joy and unconditional love that I have known, and continue to enjoy, from Judy has been incomparable. Immeasurable. Incalculable. Well worth the price of that sundae and the last three dollars I spent for the return trip to Nyack that night.

I mentioned that I really hadn't understood love, nor how to recognize it when it came along, nor how to receive it when it was offered. This was sadly true. I was not an unloving person, I was simply ignorant, uninformed, uninitiated. I have no excuses, but rather every reason to be grateful for having met and married a woman of infinite patience and love who was, and still is, willing to take me by the hand and teach me how to love. Yes, she consumed virtually that whole ice-cream sundae.

There is some serious symbolism hidden in that sundae. I have since received from her more love and understanding than I could ever have known elsewhere. Maybe the young woman, the mother, is the 'father of the man,' too.

There is one final incident I feel compelled to share, a critical event in my own understanding of this journey of love and spiritual growth which began quite sporadically in my childhood, but which has somehow come to fruition in subsequent years. But before I do, I should reiterate that throughout my brief life I considered myself to have been something of an orphan, or at least an amateur, as far as understanding and receiving love is concerned. Whether this is attributable to my having survived without a father in the home, I will leave for others more competent than I to judge. A far greater man than I once said, responding to his detractors who had been in a flagrantly judgmental mode toward one whose behavior they deemed offensive, that, "...I say to you, her sins, which are many, have been forgiven, for she loved much; *but he who is forgiven little loves little."* (Jesus, in Luke 7:47)

My wife-to-be, Judith, had volunteered to spend six weeks during the summer of 1969 touring with a missions group in what was then the combined Upper-Volta/Mali field of West Africa. She was nineteen. We had been dating off and on, but our friendship had reached a more serious level. Yours truly was still struggling with his feelings, and with the issue of a commitment of love, and perhaps even *marriage*, though I had never thought seriously about the necessity or possibility of the latter.

I was working for the Standard Fence Company of New Hampshire that summer, as I would for seven consecutive summers, and had been receiving letters from Judy Labus almost daily, describing her African experience in excruciating, but delightful detail. She is a great writer; she writes from the heart. The stack of letters I received from her that summer are a vibrant chronicle of every moment, every trial, discomfort, and every bright, joyous bit of discovery and bitter disappointment that anyone could possibly capture. I lived for those letters! I even returned a few of my own.

At least one.

Working as a young man on several different veteran fence crews was anything but easy. I was innocent and naïve. I suspect that some of those men suffered as much from me as I did from them. In spite of my refusal to laugh at their off-color jokes, or react to their taunting about sexual issues, I simply whipped out the small pocket New Testament and read quietly, seated right in the middle of three other men in a three-passenger front seat. They really loved that. The taunting and teasing got so intense that I finally chose to ride in the back of the truck, on top of the sand and gravel and under one of the wheelbarrows. It made for better, uninterrupted reading. But it was freezing cold on those early morning mountain trips west to Keene or north to Jaffrey, New Hampshire.

I eventually earned everyone's respect.

My salvation was that I did not limit my activity to mouthing spiritual truisms and slaying the adversary with well-aimed rounds of verses. I worked hard, without complaining, going the extra mile and back again. I arrived early and finished late. I cleaned the trucks and organized the tools while we waited for the next job, even after a full day with the bar and digger. The summer before the year we left definitively for Africa, I returned to say my goodbyes. The owner practically restrained me physically.

"You won't go, Pete," he said. "You'll be back. I want to promote you. I'm going to make you a foreman and give you a crew of your own. The pay will be good..."

Temptation was not even an issue; the certainty and confidence of the calling that I sensed overruled every offer.

"Thanks for the offer," I replied. He insisted, repeating his dour prediction.

"Thanks again," I repeated, and left. I never turned back or returned. But I never lost those skills. I have been building fences ever since, just to help the family, my children, and about everyone else.

During that previous summer Judy had spent in West Africa, our crew spent a week on a government job. We were a crew of four; two of us were in college. My colleague was Doug. We had been teammates at Central High. Doug weighed about 160 by now, and had only weighed only about 145 pounds in high school. He ran the 100-yard dash in just over ten seconds, and routinely benched-pressed over 400 pounds. He was chiseled, and had about a twenty-eight inch waist. I was in pretty good shape myself, not as strong, but I was fast. I reveled in hard work; I have my uncle Jim to thank for that.

It was a tough week in Vermont. The ground was like cement. We did not use heavy drilling equipment. It was a circular chain-link fence, seven feet high, with six-gage galvanized wire. The holes were seven feet apart and had to be dug twelve inches in diameter, and nearly four feet deep. We dug holes all day long, by hand, using New England-style clam-diggers (no relation to the chowder), and thirty-pound, seven-foot steel bars with a point on one end and a sharp chipping blade on the other. Hand-mixing and shoveling the tons of cement required to set the posts was easy work after a week of digging. And that was just one job. Government jobs were very demanding; the fence was several hundred feet around a huge water tower.

We stayed in a cheap hotel. There was just one large table in the room, covered with a red-checkered plastic sheet. While the guys drank next door at a local strip bar, I sat contentedly alone in the room reading and rereading Judy's most recent letter from Upper Volta – or maybe this time it was from the village of Sanga, on the falaise in the region of Timbuktu, Mali – and looking at the plasticized black-and-white photo of her that I kept in my snake-skin wallet. That same photo was the only artifact that survived a mowing accident the summer after my senior year when I worked on the grounds crew at Nyack. That was also the year before I went off to seminary in South Hamilton, Mass., the year I rented an old room in the attic.

Judy and I worked together mowing lawns in the Nyack area, using an old Craftsman mower with a Briggs & Stratton engine that I had rehabilitated. We used to share peanut-butter sandwiches and a quart of cold milk on a wooden crate in my room. There was no furniture. I'm pretty sure that we were in love; at least Judy was in love. Actually, I was too, but I *still* didn't know it at the time. Mercy.

I am ashamed to say that I cannot explain *why*, after Judy's return from Africa, when she arrived back at Nyack in her Dad's van, I came out of the dorm to greet her, opened the van door, looked at her still-beautiful, but significantly emaciated self sitting in the back seat, and walked right back to my room without even so much as a 'hello.' She should have dumped me for good right then! Why she didn't I will never understand, except to say, in retrospect, that she loved me ever so much more inexplicably deeply than I loved her, or perhaps ever could. Even as I write, more than forty years after the fact, I am deeply indebted to God, to family, to friends, but especially to my darling wife. Perhaps even to my Dad. I do know that he prayed for me during those years.

After the first year at seminary, living only with guys on a lonely hilltop in a former Jesuit facility in South Hamilton, Mass., I finally came to my senses, realizing how lonely and lost I was without Judy. The love prodigal was coming home. One of the popular songs that year (1971) was *'Lonely Days, Lonely Nights...Where Would I Be Without My Woman?'* Right on. I took a bus to New York City, arriving at about three in the morning, carried my large suitcase across the George Washington Bridge, caught a ride with a city detective in a Volks-Wagon up the Palisades Parkway, and walked the last few miles uphill to the Nyack campus. Judy was working at the time as a Residents' Assistant in the women's dormitory. She had an apartment all to herself on the first floor, the same apartment where my former roommate's *new* fiancée had lived previously, and where, ironically, they had freely

175

flaunted (innocently, of course) their new-found affection (and that before *we* had even kissed)!

It was about five in the morning. I discretely knocked on Judy's window. She was shocked. Within minutes, I pulled a maroon-colored, wrinkled penny-wrapper out of my wallet and handed the wrapper to her. Out popped a gold engagement ring. Judy fell backwards into the adjoining room. I think that I remembered to ask her to marry me, but through tears of disbelief and joy she said "yes!" Almost before the words had left my stammering mouth.

I took a week off from classes early the following semester and signed up as a 'cow-hand' at a local horse farm. I fed and rode the horses, worked the fields with gargantuan green John Deere tractors, nearly got crushed by a black bull, did occasional roof repairs, and earned enough money for our wedding – right around $600. Judy left her job at the college and packed all of her earthly belongings in the used 1964 gray Ford Fairlane with the red stripe that she had purchased upon graduation. It was to become our first car, the first either of us had owned or driven.

Judy and I were married in her home church in Dover, Ohio on the fifth of June, 1971. The rest is history. The rest of Judy's story, and mine, will have to wait for the next edition.

***

This story is about relationships, and about the power of relational reconciliation. I cannot speculate as to how circumstances would have flowed and interwoven differently had my parents' marriage survived. I cannot say what kind of godly example and counsel my father would

176

have offered an only son had he been able to see things differently, stay the course, and seize that opportunity. I am in no position to blame anyone. I have no real regrets; I bear no grudges. I have been forgiven of much, and I have forgiven what I can, probably more than I even care to know. There *is* no other way. Children whose parents, or grandparents, or even whose distant ancestors have 'eaten sour grapes' cannot simply dismiss or disregard the impact such events may have had, or may still have upon one's appetite for grapes. But they also have a responsibility to cultivate such a wholesome appetite, for the sake of their own relations, as much for everyone else's. They must not allow what others have done, or neglected to do, to condition or determine the course, or quality, or outcome of their own brief existence. Even a knife with a sharp blade cannot carve its own handle.

There is another African story which tells of a hand that became very angry at the mouth, so angry that the hand in question decided to teach the mouth a lesson by refusing to give it any food. Eventually, the hand died.

Chapter Thirteen

A Father to the Fatherless

One hand cannot wash itself; two hands are required for the task...

(Bambara proverb)

This proverb about one hand washing another has particular importance in my own experience, growing up us a young man who did not have the advantage of a father's influence. I have a very dear uncle who, soon after my father left our home, became a sort of surrogate father to me. Yet he did so quite unpretentiously, without the least bit of fanfare. He is still a father and close personal friend today, fifty years later, at the robust age of eighty-five. His story must be told as well.

***

James A. Rogers is my mother's brother. He and my Mom were on the same gymnastic team at Central High. Jim and 'Auntie' Joyce have been married for sixty-one years, and have lived in the same little cottage on Harvey Road, on a hill over-looking the Manchester airport, for the same period of time. Jim met Joyce when he was stationed in England during Hitler's assault on Europe; they met at a dance. Jim was shy and not a good dancer at all, but Joyce got his attention. She did everything she could to avoid him. Jim was never one to overestimate protocol; he pursued Joyce until she finally agreed to see him. That was the beginning of a short romance which culminated in an English wedding.

Jim borrowed a suit and showed up on the steps of the church early. The parson didn't recognize him. Thinking that he was one of the guests, the parson corralled the young, unpretentious soldier to help him place hymnbooks on the pews in preparation for the ceremony. Not many grooms have that kind of privilege.

Everyone knows Jim as a good, gentle and generous man. He is all that, and much more. But Uncle Jim would be very uncomfortable about my including a chapter on him in this story. He is not the kind of man who craves admiration, or who requires any unnecessary attention, howbeit well-intended. But include him I must. The story, which is my story, focusing as it does upon the Colman side of the family, would be woefully incomplete without Uncle Jim. Where I have excluded others, I am intentionally including his full, factual name in this account. I don't expect that he would approve of that either, though I have made him fully aware of my intention to do so. But if I know Jim, he will tolerate this slight indiscretion for my sake.

Jim Rogers is the kind of extraordinary citizen, known only by his friends, who will never be a celebrity. He will never achieve national notoriety, and he wouldn't have it any other way. He is one of four children. My Mom, and her sister, Shirley, are in their eighties. Both have survived countless physical hardships and life-threatening conditions. Uncle Jim's only brother, Raymond, passed away several years ago. At Uncle Ray's funeral in Goffstown, just prior to the burial service, Jim stood silently before the open casket. His brother lay there in a bright blue suit, his favorite pipe, and a small plastic pouch of pipe-tobacco not far away. Then Jim walked quietly to the outside porch and stood alone gazing at the trees behind the funeral home.

"Uncle Jim, are you alright," I quietly asked, placing my hand on his shoulder. And then, holding back a life's worth of tears and memories, Jim responded: "He was more than just my brother. He was my friend."

Jim had been with Uncle Ray in the hospital the day before he died, but always regrets that he hadn't been at his side throughout the previous night.

"I felt so bad that I hadn't even been able to say goodbye," he confided to me. Jim is always worried about his failure to do something for someone. He complains constantly that he doesn't have enough time in the day to do all the things he wants to do. And then he spends every waking hour helping or visiting others, tending the garden, making repairs, keeping the vehicles running and the bills paid, and caring for his beloved English bride.

***

When I was in my early teens, Uncle Jim started showing up in his white Ford Galaxy to take me with him wherever he happened to be going on that particular day. Sometimes it was just a trip to the Rogers' house to visit family, or a short trip out to Weare to visit my grand-parents. More frequently, we left early and traveled north to the Lakes Region to fish for lake trout or salmon. In the winter, we went ice-fishing. Those were the days when you dug your holes with an ice-chisel and set your six-traps-per-person on the open ice. Ice-houses were over-rated, but we didn't just fish.

Uncle Jim was adventurous and fearless. When the ice was thick enough, usually close to three feet, he drove the car out onto the ice and we built a small, wood fire and cooked minute steaks on our ice-scoops. While waiting for the traps to spring, we put on our black figure skates…no sense slipping around on sheer ice when you can skate! Sometimes Uncle Jim would pull me down the length of the lake on a 100-foot rope tied to the bumper of the car. Sometimes we used a canvas tarp like a sail, caught the cold winter wind, and cruised the ice surface at top speed, turned and tacked back to our spot. I nearly froze half the time, but had great fun, the kind a son should have with his father.

My feet were usually the first to freeze. Thin, green rubber boots and one pair of wool socks don't provide real protection in sub-zero weather on the open ice. Uncle Jim was very strong and had short, leathery fingers. He *never* wore gloves, not even when he cracked and scooped the frozen ice out of the hole, which is something we always had to do. Gloves just got in his way. He loved fishing too much to worry about such a small thing like the cold.

My uncle bought me my first pair of everything, including a pair of green wooden, fiberglass-coated skis. He taught me to ski by bringing me with him to a half-mile high 'beginners' slope; which looked like Mount Everest. It was at night. It *took* me nearly the entire night to get to the bottom of the slope, snow-plowing back and forth all the miserable way. I later graduated to skiing the snow-banks on the sides of the mountain roads, while Jim pulled me along with that same rope tied to his car bumper. The abundance of snow in northern New Hampshire often required that plows not only clear the roads, but they also prepared the pile of plowed snow for the next storm. They

182

often used two plow-blades in tandem, creating a flat, ski-worthy surface on the upper edge.

Jim taught me to fly-fish at an early age, supplying me with a rod and dry flies and all of the accessories. I spent most of those early days walking the rivers, following behind his left shoulder, watching him expertly cast the shallow pools and rapids. He later taught me to tie my own dry flies, using deer-hair and hackle, in a small customized vice.

As a teen-age boy living alone in an apartment with his mother, I learned to help out with the cleaning and the laundry (we took our laundry to a Laundromat about a half-mile from home). I also painted the apartment and put plastic on the windows every winter to seal out the cold. We lived on the third floor at the northeast end of the building. We had a large back porch that needed to be cleared of snow and ice after every storm. We heated the living room with an old-fashioned, oil-burning stove, the kind requiring a five-gallon can to be tipped up-side-down in the back, allowing the oil to flow full-circle on a white wick in a narrow moat. We kept a spare oil-can nearby, meaning that every few days I had to traipse to the dark dirt basement four floors below, fill the cans with a funnel, and carry them back up icy stairs.

I learned how to work and fend for myself. But as I grew a bit older and became involved with my friends in sports activities, I started to neglect my duties, creating concern and hardship for my mother. On one occasion, Mom resorted to a simple phone call to Uncle Jim, informing him that I was not helping her. She may as well have called the police, or told God Himself. I was scared to death. Jim was the last person in the world I wanted to offend or disappoint. When I heard his footsteps on our stairs I ran, opened the door and apologized earnestly, hoping I could head off a mild scolding. Any scolding would have been unbearable.

"Your mother tells me that you haven't been helping her," was all he said. That was enough. I promised him, and my Mom, that day that I would never neglect my duties again. That was it. He left and never spoke of it again, though I'm sure that my Mom kept him up-dated on my daily progress. I was horrified to think that I had offended him; he was apparently content with my apology. He was never abusive, or even angry, just hurt and terribly disappointed. And he was forgiving. Now that I think of it, that's how I would expect God to respond. That's how a father would respond.

Throughout those early years, Jim was always there for me. When he didn't come to the house, he called. When I told him that I was planning to go off to college, it was he who offered to drive me to New York. And so he did, in a small red Volkswagen, the same one he had used to teach me to drive. When we arrived at Nyack Missionary College, Jim dropped me off in front of the massive slate dormitory steps, unloaded my few bags and suitcases, and one checkered Indian blanket…gave me a few dollars for spending money, and waved goodbye. He was not one for excessive emotion or protocol; he just always did whatever needed to be done.

Uncle Jim and Auntie Joyce would have loved to have children of their own; they tried. But Joyce miscarried at least twice early on in their marriage; later, they adopted a son, my cousin, Jay. Now he was the one who would stand in the front seat of the car between his Mom and Dad. He was the one whom they would take skating and fishing. Jay would become their first love, but our love would grow with the years. Not too many uncles can boast a nephew who behaves like a son; not too many sons can boast an uncle who behaves like a true father.

I blame Uncle Jim for most of my hobbies and interests, outside of those related to study and teaching. Thanks to him, I still have a passion for fly-fishing. Some years ago, after Jim 'retired' officially from government service, he took up the hobby of antique bottle collecting, and bottle digging…a hobby which he pursued with a passion for nearly thirty years, and managed to share that passion with me. To this day, we talk bottles, exchange new finds, share information, and sometimes even travel to far-away places to sell and trade our eclectic fare at bottle shows across the country. But we are always learning and enjoying the hobby. Today, the books on my study shelves share space with a strange cornucopia of colored varieties of bottles and fruit jars. The baby rabbit is still looking at his mother's ears, and has developed some pretty significant ears of his own.

I have probably said enough about Uncle Jim, but I cannot underestimate the impact he had, and continues to have, in my life. We have also had some disagreements, as well as some serious differences and discussions about religion, personal faith, and social events. Jim is a true New Englander. He is not quick to express how he may feel or what he believes deep down inside. He is justifiably skeptical and cautious. But talk we have, and still do, almost daily. In the past few decades, he has had many close brushes with death and misfortune. He is aware, more than most, of the fragile nature of our existence. He is not content just to talk about God, or faith, or loving one's neighbor. He's too busy getting most of those things done, and prefers to let others do the talking. So he would appreciate what James (his namesake?) had to say about the relationship between what a person believes about God, and what he does about it:

> *What good is it, my brothers, if a man claims to have faith but has no deeds? Can such a faith save him? Suppose a brother or sister is without clothes and daily food. If one of you says to him, 'Go, I wish you well; keep warm and well fed,' but does nothing about his physical needs, what good is it? In the same way, faith by itself, if it is not accompanied by action, is dead.*
>
> (James 2:14-17)

End of discussion.

When Judy and I left for language study in France, Uncle Jim took us to the airport and brought Mom home after our departure. He cared for her and checked up on her during those long years we were in Africa; he was father to the Mom. When we returned home every four years, Uncle Jim came to the airport to get us and collect our baggage; it was Jim who helped us pack twenty-two full-size suitcases, trunks and duffle-bags a year later, and haul them to the Boston airport; though he could never quite accept our leaving, or the reason for our going in the first place, and knew that he wouldn't see us for another long, lonely four years. He was always the first to brag to family members and friends about his missionary nephew and his family.

That was Uncle Jim, and is still Jim today. When I told him some months ago about my intention to write this book, he repeated his favorite cliché, "Think'n ain't do'n." When I told him recently about the progress I was making, he asked me how in the world I ever thought about so much 'stuff to write.' I had no answer. My only concern is that I may have failed to include details and events which are critical to the on-going saga.

"Should've, could've, would've..." These are the kind of words Jim says should be eliminated from one's vocabulary. Along with expressions like 'personal debt.'

***

Uncle Jim continues to 'father' our family, including his notorious nephew and his four great-nephews and one great-niece. He continues to check on my Mom, and like me, calls or visits her nearly every day. He still calls her to check up on me, too, just to be sure that I am still helping Judy at home and keeping up with my duties.

In recent years, with the exception of some minor theological issues, there has only been one area in which Uncle Jim and me have had serious disagreement, and that is with respect to my feelings toward my father. That is one area that I am remiss to discuss. Jim deeply resents my father for having spent most of his adult life away from his only son, and cannot bring himself to acknowledge any merit in the course he has chosen, or to respect him as a man. For Uncle Jim, the 'proof of the pudding is in the eating.' That my father tried desperately to convert him upon returning from the war, and has claimed to be a devout believer for all the years since, has given Jim more reasons to doubt his sincerity and integrity.

My father, and anything vaguely related to him, including discussions of Christian faith and values, has always been a sore point in our relationship. Back to those sour grapes, only this time they were in someone else's mouth as well as my own. To be fair, we are all flawed; we have all had our share of failures and disappointments, and have no doubt caused a considerable degree of the same for others. None of us are exempt; we all fall far short; we all have eaten our share of sour grapes.

My father's history, and the history of our relationship over the decades, did not help my situation when my Dad became critically ill in the late winter of 2005. I do not get to visit my relatives in New England very often, perhaps once or twice every two years. As one might imagine, when my own father became more distant and inaccessible over the decades, even with the birth of our children and grandchildren, my Uncle Jim became that much closer to us all. He called and wrote often; he remembered all of our birthdays; he sent notes and cards and gifts for every holiday. Uncle Jim was particularly generous and thoughtful at Christmas time. Our own children began responding by writing and calling, which was a great encouragement to both him and Joyce. The stage was set for a minor crisis of ill-feeling and misunderstanding when it became necessary for me to make short, unannounced trips to Manchester, and to spend most of that time visiting with my father and my father's surviving relatives, namely his four brothers.

Uncle Jim didn't have much tolerance for the infringement upon the limited time we had to spend together, and even less sympathy for my Dad, himself, even in his critical condition.

"I suppose you're going to see your father again," he would say. "I guess you'll do what you have to do," he would repeat, as if it were possible to persuade me to reconsider. "I don't know why you have to see him again; he certainly didn't do much for you over the years."

"He's my Dad, Jim. He needs me," was all I could offer in response.

"Whatever..." was his favored mantra. "I guess you'll do what you have to do."

I can't say that I blame him; nor am I in any position to judge him. That would be the last thing I would ever do. To be fair, Jim understood my position and my concern to do what I believed was right under the circumstances. He didn't like it, but he was supportive.

The irony is that during those last few months of my father's critical illness, my uncle, who had been more than a father to me for over forty years, was effectively deprived of my company, while my own father, who had effectively ignored me and my children during the same period, became the object of my attention and affection. It was going to be a wire-walk, a delicate balancing act, and a tough row to hoe. But there was no other way. I had no other choice. The words I had learned and cherished since my youth were ringing in my ears: "Honor your father...and it will go well with you in the land..."

Chapter Fourteen

The Lost Son

*...But while he was still along way off, his father
saw him and was filled with compassion for him;
he ran to his son, threw his arms around him and
kissed him.*

(Luke 15:20)

One of the last, enduring conversations I ever had
with my father was at Blake's Restaurant on Manchester's
west side. Ironically, Blake's had been one of my Mom's
favorite watering holes. I hadn't told Mom where we were
going that day; I had invited Dad out for breakfast. It
seemed that I was usually the one doing the calling, or
visiting, or inviting, but that was OK.

Moments were always tense with Dad, for as long
as I can remember, ever since those days we would sit in
his car down the street from our house, and he would
complain about the alimony, the 'blood-money,' as he
called it. The only other time he resorted to such language
was when he felt an occasional sense of weakness or
failure. Rather than admit to anything in particular, or talk
about any personal short-coming, he was fond of saying,
with a sense of religious assurance bordering on defiance,
that everything in the past was 'under the blood.' I knew
what he meant, and agreed with him in principle. But I

thought, forgiveness does not free an individual from responsibility, or from the debt of reconciliation.

I do not want to be overly critical of my father. No one ever understands everything there is to know about another person's interior life and the spiritual forces and factors which combine to make people think and behave the way they do. It's hard enough to understand oneself, and to reconcile one's own behavior, without presuming to think that we can judge another's. If there is anything which I always had a difficult time accepting about my father, it was his tendency, ever so subtly and with self-righteous confidence, to castigate me, to create a sense of guilt for my apparent failure to inform *him* of my activities and agenda. Isn't it a father's responsibility to take some initiative with respect to his own son, and his son's family, including his own grandchildren? It would seem so.

It is precisely this tendency that irked my uncle, and annoyed my own wife. It was this tendency that compelled Judy to write that infamous letter to Dad years earlier, asking him ever so lovingly, but with a righteous conviction that bordered on indignation, what possible justification he had to ignore his own grandchildren while, at the same time, scolding and shaming his own son for not calling him or communicating with him more often. That same letter compelled my Dad, at least that one time, to fall on his knees in repentance, and take a plane to Ohio to see his family. It would be the last time.

Neither do I want to paint a picture consisting of gloom and dark colors, or raging storms and horrific hues. Dad was an amateur painter. Ironically, one of the last and finest works he painted was of the ocean waves crashing against the shore. He entitled it "The Last Storm." The surface of the sea is turbulent, with a chorus of white caps visible in the foreground. But there is light and rich color in the painting as well, as there were glimpses of light and hopeful tints of hue and traces of happiness in his own tortured existence - 'tortured' because I imagine that he always had to live with the memories and disappointments of the past. More than once he had mentioned to me that our separation from one another, and my failure to keep in touch more often throughout the years, was simply part of the price he and Dottie had to pay for their own secluded and solitary existence, a 'sacrifice' they were both willing to make. Maybe he *did* suffer more than I will ever know. Did he pay an enormous spiritual and emotional price for the path he had chosen? I could not be responsible for Dad's attitude toward me, or for the reasons he advanced for his own behavior. My responsibility as a son was to be sure that *I* honored him, and that I did not allow myself to perpetuate the same error, if it was an error.

Nor do I want to imply that Dad never did anything for me or with me. The times we did spend together in recent years were enjoyable and memorable. Even as his life began to ebb, and those whom he loved began to disappear from view, the contours of his descent still reflected sufficiently pleasant memories, including the periodic visits we made to places like Dunbarton, Auburn, and Newfane/South Wadsboro, in the area of Brattleboro, Vermont –all of the areas where the Colman clan had lived and settled. Every visit and moment spent reminiscing seemed to justify and rekindle a spark of love in our relationship where only cold smoldering embers had existed before.

***

The day that we ate at Blake's Restaurant, our conversation was pleasant, but somber. In the middle of our conversation, one of us mentioned the gospel story of the prodigal son. I remember Dad looking straight at me and saying it was one of his favorite stories. I may have misjudged Dad at that moment, but in my own mind I sensed that he was sending me another subliminal message, another subtle rebuke: *"Just like you. You have been a prodigal son!"* But what possible reason could my father have for implying such a thing? I sensed that time was short, that I may not have many more opportunities to talk with Dad. I never had the courage to challenge my father in the past.   Maybe this was the right time to be courageous, lest there be any doubt in the matter; I asked him directly and without hesitation:

"Dad, is that what you think? Do you think I have been a prodigal, son?" *I couldn't believe what I had just asked.* The die is cast. Point of no return. *What would I do? What would I say if he said yes?* I didn't have to wait long for a response.

"No, Peter. *I* have been a prodigal father."

I was speechless. I don't remember what I said or did, nor do I recall having said or done anything. Everything switched to slow motion. There was a moment of truth, an eerie silence. An understanding. A cessation of hostilities, a truce, a calming of the storm, a silent exorcism of demons.

I don't remember Dad ever having admitted he was wrong, or ever having taken responsibility for any misunderstanding in our relationship.   Not that I have always been the innocent victim, but this time it was

194

different - Dad was using a different voice, the voice of humility and resignation. I could see that Dad was uncharacteristically embarrassed, like a child who had been caught with the goods. He was a proud man, a military hero, and a police officer. He was not accustomed to admitting his own weaknesses. It was the first time I had seen Dad even approach vulnerability. There would be no police holds today – no painful grips – no Cheshire cat smiles of superiority and self-satisfaction. This was the Dad I had never known, and it only lasted a moment.

We finished our conversation and returned home. Dad seemed appreciative. More relaxed. For once, I didn't sense the same kind of intimidation or heavy cloud of superiority. There were fewer intangible barriers to our friendship. But I still had the feeling that I was on the outside looking in. There was still a lot I didn't know, and probably never would. But that was OK.

I drove Dad home this time. That was a first too. Lunch had been at my invitation. I paid the tab. I had insisted. I was determined that this would be my time with Dad, no holds barred, no disadvantages or phony obstacles, and at my expense. My nickel.

That was a nickel well spent; it was a turning point in our relationship. There is a saying in Africa that if someone takes your arm, and you stiffen it, then that person will break it. But if you do not react, you will pose no threat and will remain unharmed.

Dad had loosened his long, tight, tenuous grip that day. For the first time, we were able to relax in our relationship, to actually enjoy each other's company. It is also written that "a man with a damaged or withered eye is always spilling water on his chest when he drinks..." No doubt the divorce had been painful and awkward for Dad. I had never stopped to think that maybe the failed marriage had been difficult for him, too. Maybe *that* was why every conversation and gesture had been marked with discomfort. Maybe the shame and sadness had run deeper than even *he* had cared to admit or imagine. Maybe he couldn't really help it. The damage had been done. Maybe he couldn't help spilling water on himself every time he tried to take a simple drink of water. Maybe this had been the very first time he had had the courage to show that withered eye to someone else. Maybe this had been one of those moments of transparency, one of the only times he had allowed himself to see clearly. Up to this point, the village of the blind had had no king. It had been like one blind man leading another. But now a bit of fresh, liberating light had been allowed to enter; both began to see the road ahead and to walk with a still-familiar stagger, but with a surer step toward the future. Just maybe.

***

In the summer of 2004, Judith and I and our youngest daughter, Esther, traveled to my native home-town of Manchester. We only had a few days, before returning to our classrooms for the new fall semester, to enjoy the sights and smells of New England, and to visit with my family. But therein was the rub. My delicate, tortured family triangle consisted of my Uncle Jim and Auntie Joyce, who were still maintaining vigil in their little Hansel and Gretel-like dream-cottage on Harvey Road, beneath that ubiquitous blinking light. My mother, 'Dotty' Colman, occupied a seventh-floor apartment of the old Carpenter Hotel on the corner of Merrimack and Elm Streets. My father, Robert ('Bob') Colman, and Dotty, lived together in a small brick bungalow, right across the street from my mother. Their small, hidden residence was part of a tiny cloister of reconditioned red-brick hovels that used to house immigrant textile workers a century earlier. Now *that* kind of brief description reflects the utter delicacy and simplicity of my situation.

Every trip was a challenge to our creativity; our agenda consisted of attempting to dispense equal time. My primary commitment was to my mother who has always been resilient and considerate in spite of living for years without adequate resources or male companionship. Mom, Jim and Joyce get under each other's skin on a routine basis, which makes scheduling visits and activities a bit like walking a razor tightrope barefoot. Mere contact can be hazardous. Maneuvering can be just as precarious as falling.

What complicated the situation was that both my Dad and his wife were extremely ill and increasingly immobile. Dad had been diagnosed with colon cancer months before. During the same time, Dottie had been in and out of the hospital with a host of debilitating discomforts. When we arrived she had been confined to a chair and had grown increasingly and uncomfortably overweight. She had become a very pitiful shell of her former self, and had just enough energy to smile, stutter and pretend to be on the threshold of recovery.

Dottie had never worked outside the home. In her more robust years, she had been very active in church work singing and playing the piano or organ. She had even been an amateur writer of stories, and a poet. She never came anywhere with Dad and me, always preferring to let us be together alone. I sometimes found that strange. She would never even come out to eat with us, and Dad always protected her right to stay at home. "Dottie's a real 'prayer warrior,'" Dad would always say; I am sure that she was. She was a very devout Christian and devoted wife, always very affectionate and supportive of me. Dad had pampered, protected and preserved her from criticism for as long as I could remember.

There was something else that still, to this day, is difficult to get a handle on. As recluse as she had been over the years, Dottie had a very playful, almost childish sense of humor, and was always ripe for discussion. She was a little girl on one side, and a shrewd stateswoman on the other. She seemed starved for a good intellectual debate, and often expressed pretty unorthodox views about very conservative issues. She was a very avid reader and enjoyed news and religious broadcasts on television. She had little time or tolerance for some of the religious showmanship and shenanigans which claimed to be authentically spiritual or related to genuine Christian faith. Inversely and ironically, she almost seemed like she had become a prisoner to her own cherished traditions. She boasted of personal freedom, and reveled in matters of personal faith, but it seemed at times that she was choking, that she didn't have a real life.

And now she was helplessly confined to a chair.

Dottie seemed to relish what she must have known would be our last visit with her that day. Dad, for his part, was doing the best he could. He couldn't afford any kind of professional care for Dottie, so he was taking care of her as best he knew how, which included short trips to the supermarket and pharmacy, and making meals. But Dad was extremely sick as well. By this time he was doing chemotherapy and was required to carry a plastic sac of chemicals attached to his side. He had lost all control of his bowels. When he wasn't with Dottie, he was cleaning the bathroom.

That was the situation we stepped into on the day of our visit. While Judy and Esther spent time visiting with Dottie, I prepared a breakfast of eggs, sausage, toast and fresh coffee - Dad's favorite combination. One of our favorite breakfast spots had been Parker's Restaurant and sugar house just over the New Hampshire border in Vermont. Everything there was made from scratch in an old country kitchen. The bacon and sausage were smoked with hickory and real maple sugar locally. But today Dad didn't have much of an appetite. We sat together at their small table in the kitchen corridor just under his 1964 painting "After the Storm," hanging on the crude brick wall just above our heads. Other paintings with Native American and pioneer themes were hanging nearby; some had been painted on leather.

Dad ate one egg and a bite of sausage. I finished the rest while we talked. Before we left we prayed together around Dottie's chair. I remember praying for her healing. When we had finished she did something which took me off guard. She pulled me close to her, and with her arms tightly around my neck, sobbed almost uncontrollably. She repeated my name in desperate, pitiful tones. She clung to me like she was drowning. Was this just catharsis? Did she know that she was near death? Was she purging her soul? Maybe there were buried memories, unresolved issues of repressed guilt or shame that had come to the surface one last time, clamoring to be released. I felt helpless. Maybe this was just apart of the final healing for which we had prayed. It was like a living *agonie,* as the French would say, the final painful gasps of a living soul. Whatever her emotions or thoughts at that moment, I had the very real sensation that she was somehow trying to reach out one last time, to express and receive love. I hugged her and prayed for her one last time, then we said goodbye.

That would be the last time that I would ever see Dottie Samara Colman again in this life.

Though I didn't know it at the time, that would also be the last time I would ever see my own father as I remembered him to be. Though he was still huge in his upper body, and had strength in his arms, his face had begun to pale, look drawn, and his strong white teeth had begun to discolor. His had the smile of certain death.

Dottie died in November 2004. Her struggle was over. Dad had taken her to the emergency room in the night, the plastic bag of chemicals sloshing uncomfortably under his coat. This would be the second time, maybe the first, that he would lose the love of his life. Now he was alone. He returned to the small brick apartment alone and sat in Dottie's chair and wept.

I received a call from Dad a few days later wanting to know if I would be available to handle Dottie's funeral service. She was to be cremated. Dad couldn't afford a casket and an expensive funeral. He hardly had enough in his meager savings to pay the rent.

"The funeral won't be for a week or so yet," he explained on the phone. "You're the only person I can think of who should do this," he said. "Dottie loved the Lord, and she loved you, too. She would want you to do this. I want you to be there and talk to the family about Dottie's faith in Christ. The family needs to hear. You're still a pastor, right? Can you be there?"

Well, I was still ordained as a pastor, and was serving as an elder in our local church, so I could legally preside at the funeral, but I really *did* want to do this for Dad, so I accepted.

"Thank you, Peter, I know you'll do a good job. The whole family will be there. All of your uncles, including your uncle Louie from Bedford."

Uncle Louie was the last surviving Moy. He was still living near the old Moy farm in Auburn. His brother and one of my cousins, both of whom my Dad took me to visit when I was a child, had both hung themselves from the rafters of the old barn years before. Dad's brothers would be there too. They had all survived World War II, and were still living in Manchester and Goffstown. One of those uncles, Arthur, had five children of his own, but three of them had deserted him after his divorce. He still saw one son, my favorite cousin Gerry, whom I haven't seen since we were children. One of his daughters, Marion, whom we always called Marylou, had been named after my grandmother Nellie's daughter Marion who had died shortly after birth. I was really looking forward to seeing Marylou again, but I expected her to look just as I had remembered her fifty years ago.

***

The ceremony for the committal of Dottie's ashes took place a week later at the Pine Grove Cemetery in Manchester. I had flown out from Chicago, spent a few short hours visiting with my Mom and with Uncle Jim, then stopped by to see my Uncle Arthur who informed me of the schedule. My mother, of course, would not be invited. It would not have been appropriate, though, as hard as it may be to believe, Mom would have gone had she been invited. She and Dottie had been very close. Mom told me often that she still loved her and had no ill feelings. That's something else I find difficult to understand. While I do understand the importance of forgiveness, some things cannot just be dismissed and forgotten.

201

The ceremony would be simple. My experience in Africa had prepared me to accept and adapt to almost anything. I had prepared a short eulogy and a brief homily. I had also chosen a selection of what I knew to be some of Dottie's favorite hymns. I was planning to sing a couple stanzas of one of them after the homily, and conclude with a few personal words of comfort and remembrance to the family. Everything went pretty much as planned.

I arrived early at the Pine Grove Cemetery Morgue, a plain marble structure in a back corner of the property. A glass entryway led to an empty chamber with only a small table with artificial flowers in the center. The cemetery custodian had accompanied me to unlock the front door. I inquired about a table for the ashes, which had not yet arrived. He opened a side closet in the room and came out with a tiny wooded tray-table of sorts, and used piece of off-white linen. I placed the table in the center of the room near the front. By that time, my uncles had arrived. With their help, we quickly commandeered a few folding chairs stacked in the side hallways, where the burial chambers were neatly organized and labeled in the walls. At the last moment, we slid two molded alloy two-seaters that had been placed at the doors and placed them in the middle of the room. There were now only a dozen or so seats, which we reserved for the elderly.

In a short time, the rest of the Colman remnant arrived, including Dad, who had to be transported in a wheelchair. I had seen him when I had arrived earlier in the day, and he had given me a few simple verbal instructions.

"I'm sure you'll do a good job, Peter. You always do. You have a real way with words. I am proud. Dottie would be very pleased." Then he repeated what was really on his heart. "I want you to really tell the family about Jesus. Most of them know. Your Uncle Louie has heard so many times, but seems to be holding out. He's not getting any younger you know. This is a great opportunity to share the gospel with the whole family."

I shared Dad's concern for the family, but I was also keenly aware that while I needed to honor Dottie's testimony of a deep personal faith, I also needed to try to extend comfort and strength to Dad and to those of his family who knew Dottie best. Dad was now alone and dying. Nearly every word spoken that day would be directed to him, if I could have anything to do with it. But Dad had wanted me to share a message of faith with the rest of the family too.

The funeral director arrived with a small white cardboard box just minutes before the ceremony was to begin. I took my place behind the wooden table. In the interim, I found another small flower table in the foyer, which I placed behind the smaller table. There, along with my Bible, my folded notes, and an old hymnbook, I placed a wedding picture of Dad and Dottie, which I had salvaged from Dad's apartment. Dad was sitting quietly and reflectively in his wheelchair not ten feet away to my left. His expression was serene, but tears had begun to well up in his tired eyes.

Dad and Dottie had known forty-four years of relative happiness. Now he was alone. His only son, with whom he had spent only a fraction of those days, had become a pastor, then a missionary, and was now a professional educator. Bob Colman's four grandchildren and four great-grandchildren were far away. He had barely ever seen his grandchildren, and only ever seen his great-grandchildren's pictures. He would never actually see them in this lifetime. But now his son was standing in front of him, a son who, ironically, seemed uniquely fitted to do just what was needed at this tragic time in his life; the son who now stood in front of thirty-or-so members of an estranged family; a son who wanted desperately to reach out in love, to say something that would bring hope and healing not only to their tired, fractured lives, but perhaps also to his.

Dad had made his ascent. Some of that ascent had been heroic and heart-breaking. But now he was near the end of his heroic journey, the final steps of which he would take alone. I was one of the only remaining strands in a fragile family cord that had been severely damaged and nearly completely severed years ago. The Colman clan fabric was tattered and withered. It had lost much of its original color and vibrancy. It would be my responsibility to try to breathe life into that tired remnant now.

Chapter Fifteen

The Descent

A man with a damaged eye is always spilling
water on his chest when he drinks...

(Minyanka proverb – Mali)

Eulogy and Committal Service for Dorothy
Virginia Samara Colman

"Dottie loved Jesus Christ with all her heart. She loved
my Dad. She loved others with a joyous effervescence
and a child-like glee. She was a woman of deep
spiritual faith, fortitude and reflection.

She was a gifted soprano, musician and poet.
And she was a woman of prayer, a loving wife and
faithful companion.

I, too, am a beneficiary of Dotty's love and prayers. She
prayed for me daily. Though she did not bear me, she
loved me as a son, and bore me daily before her heavenly
Father's throne…

Dad, Dottie, if she could, would want you to hear
these words of her Savior from Isaiah 40: 28-31:

Do you not know? Have you not heard? The Lord
is the everlasting God, the Creator of the ends of
the earth...

He gives strength to the weary and increases the power of the weak, even youth grow tired and weary, and young men stumble and fall; but those who hope in the Lord will renew their strength.
They will soar on wings like eagles; they will run and not grow weary, they will walk and not be faint.

I then read briefly and commented from the story of the raising of Lazarus from the dead in the Gospel of John, chapter eleven.

The Homily – Excerpts from John 11: 17-44

Jesus had not arrived in time to save his sick friend. Lazarus's sisters, Martha and Mary, were sick with grief and sorely disheartened.

"Lord," Martha had said to Jesus after his arrival at their home, "If you had been here, my brother would not have died." And, curiously, she added, "But I know that even now God will give you whatever you ask."

It is recorded that Jesus responded to her, "Your brother will rise again."

Martha was a devout Jew. She believed in the resurrection of the dead. She was a good student of Scripture and a firm believer in the God of Israel.

She answered with confidence, "I know he will rise again in the resurrection, at the last day." Martha must have been a New Englander. Let's be realistic. Dead is dead. Resurrections come later. But then she got the shock of her life, as if losing her brother wasn't enough.

Jesus said to her, "I am the resurrection and the life. *He who believes in me will live, even though he dies*; and whoever lives and believes in me will never die."

"Do you believe this?" Jesus asked Martha.

"Yes, Lord," she told him..."

The rest is a matter of record.

***

I offered a few closing comments to encourage the family to take these words to heart and to place their faith in God, even as Dottie had done. Then, before a few final words of comfort to Dad and the family, I sang a couple of stanzas of what I knew to be one of Dottie's favorite hymns. I had not informed Dad or anyone else present that I was going to do this. A professional singer I am *not*. I searched for, and found a copy of the old hymn in the *Book of Worship for United States Forces,* published under the supervision of *The Armed Forces Chaplains Board,* printed by the U.S. Government Printing Office, Washington, D.C., 1974. Trying desperately at this point in the ceremony to control my emotions, I happened to look in my Dad's direction. His eyes were large with tears, his face frozen in place, somewhere between euphoria and total collapse. I took a deep breath and somehow managed to sing most of the stanzas:

O Love that wilt not let me go, I rest my weary soul in thee; I give thee back the life I owe, that in thine ocean depths its flow may richer, fuller be.

O light that followest all my way, I yield my flickering torch to thee; my heart restores its borrowed ray, that in thy sunshine's blaze its day may brighter, fairer be.

O joy that seekest me through pain, I cannot close my heart to thee; I trace the rainbow through the rain, and feel the promise is not vain that morn shall tearless be...[19]

After a final prayer and greetings, our tiny delegation drove slowly to a nearby remote corner of the cemetery where Dottie's ashes were to be laid to rest:

"Friends, we gather here to commit to this resting place the body of our beloved sister whose spirit is already with the Lord. While this spot of earth will hold the form of one whose memory we shall always treasure, we look not here in sorrow as those who have no hope...we therefore commit her body to the ground in the renewed and fresh hope of the soon coming of Christ, at whose appearing the dead in Christ shall rise and we which are alive and remain, shall be caught up together with them to meet the Lord in the air. And thus shall we ever be with the Lord. Wherefore, we comfort one another with these words..." [20]

When I greeted Dad at the end of the committal service, his eyes were flooded with tears. The cancer, combined with the weight of grief, had caused his face to be visibly drawn. The pallor of death hung over his emaciated brow. But through the sadness and pain there was joy and a bright smile. The discoloration in his aging eyes found a burst of fresh light and hope.

"You did great, Peter."

---

[19] *O Love That Wilt Not Let Me Go,* George Matheson, 1842-1906
[20] Taken from Paul's letter to believers at Thessalonica - in I Thessalonians 4:13-18.

For some reason, I don't remember him ever calling me 'son.'

"I could feel the presence of the Holy Spirit as you spoke," he said. "Boy, they really heard the message loud and clear today. Dottie would be so pleased."

When we left the cemetery, I moved on to my Uncle 'Artie's apartment. All of Dad's brothers were there, including my Uncle Richie. I remember Richie as a handsome young man with a charming smile and soulful laugh. But Richie has never been quite right. He suffered shell-shock in the U.S. Navy. He had been standing next to a sixteen-inch gun when it fired. Uncle Bill was still the comedian with the big mouthful of teeth and the string of bad jokes. He was always flirting with the nurses, or any other females within range, but he loved Aunt Earlene dearly and she had kept him well-behaved and deeply in love with her for nearly fifty years. Uncle Frank was there too. He never seemed to age. He was big like Dad. He had been a traveling salesman for as long as I can remember. He couldn't resist doughnuts every day with his coffee. But now he had cancer too. Dad was right in the middle when we all took that last family picture. We all knew that it would be the last. Dad knew it, too, and smiled even broader.

***

There is a certain security when surrounded by one's family in a time of deep personal loss, and Dad took every advantage. He was like a child at a surprise birthday party. He concealed his sadness well. His brothers, now all in their late seventies, laughed and told harmless, lame jokes as they viewed the sumptuous down-home feast spread before them – roast turkey and hot and cold tart

209

cranberry sauce, buttery mashed potatoes with bowls of rich brown gravy, steaming white onions and fresh sweet corn, and for dessert, an assortment of homemade pies. But the real treat was the deep baking pans filled with soft yellow lemon-squares covered with sweet, golden layers of soft crust. Uncle Artie was a practiced pastry chef; his specialty was lemon squares. And then Uncle Bill arrived.

"Hey, everybody! Wait'n for me, huh? Can't start the party without *me*."

Then he did a little dance and let his false teeth drop, just for effect. He was a clown. If you didn't know him as the little boy who never grew up, the one who hid his insecurities behind a façade of boisterous and bawdy behavior, you would probably check your wallet and hold on to your children before calling the police, or letting out the dogs, or both. But Uncle Bill was harmless. He went down the line, slapping the men on the back and hugging the women a bit too long. Aunt Earlene kept him on a short leash. Poor Uncle Richie, now without teeth, dressed in an ill-fitting leisure suit, tight short slacks and used tennis shoes (all salvaged from the nearest thrift store), sat there looking homeless and forlorn, but content to be with family. Uncle Richie looked lost and nearly retarded, until he spoke.

"Nice words, Peter. You did a good job. That was a good prayer. I liked it."

"Thanks, Uncle Richie."

"Heh, Frank, get me another helping of turkey and potatoes and gravy," he said with a toothless grin.

He ate like there was no tomorrow. Dad said that in his earlier days, he had taken Uncle Richie to a camp meeting where he had wept at the altar and given his heart to Jesus.

"How's your dinner, Uncle Richie?" I asked.

"Good," was all he said, as he continued to shovel potatoes and gravy into his mouth, his jaw working like the hungry rusty steel bucket of a giant coal shovel.

It was a sad day for Dad and the family, but you wouldn't know it by the meal and the laughter. Dad was sitting right in the middle of the commotion. I'm not sure if we talked about Dottie much more during that meal. It was more like a going-away party for Dad. It was for him.

He was no longer alone.

***

I flew home to Chicago the next day to resume classes. Word had gotten around that I had to return home for an emergency, that there had been a death in the family. Someone had heard that my mother had died. During homeroom that morning, several members of the Student Council at Carmel Catholic stepped into room 603 with a big basket of lavender flowers, and on the brink of a nervous chorus of silent tears, solemnly placed the flowers on my desk.

"We're so sorry for your Mom's death, Dr. Colman. Please accept these as a token of our love on behalf of the student body."

"Thank you," I said, trying to hold back the tears, as I embraced each student. I didn't have the heart to explain the situation. Dottie may as well have been my Mom at that point in time. I accepted them joyously in my Dad's behalf. Those flowers flourished a full year before we had to finally discard them.

Not one month later, as the frigid cold held North Chicago, and much of New England, in its cruel embrace, I received a late-night call from my Uncle Bill.

"Peter, your Dad is not well. We had to move him out of his apartment. I got him a bed at the V.A. They weren't going to let him in; said they didn't have a bed available, but I went up there and threw my weight around. I told them that he was in the Marine Corps and that he was a police officer in Goffstown, and then in Manchester for many years, and that if anyone deserved a bed it was your Dad. Well, I caused quite a fuss. They called me a few hours later to tell me that they had an empty bed, right on the ground floor next to the nurses' station! Your Uncle Bill knows how to get things done, huh?!"

He hadn't told me that he had charmed a few of the nurses, too, and that they probably surrendered to his demands just to keep him from tormenting them. I suspect that was the case. Whatever. Dad had gotten a good room and was receiving excellent care. So I called him from home that night.

"Dad, this is Peter...Dad, are you OK?"

"Peter!" he answered, his voice trembling with controlled emotion. "How 'bout that!" That had been my grandfather, Sumner Chase Colman's, favorite expression, as it was Dad's. "Hey, Peter, How 'bout that!"

"Dad, are you alright," I repeated, just to keep the conversation going.

"Fine," he answered. "I'm good. They're taking good care of me. I'm a little tired, but, praise the Lord, I'm *better*!" Dad always said that he was better. It was because of his faith. He fully expected to recover. And for as long as he had breath, I expected him to recover too.

"I'm praying for you, Dad," I said. And I did. Every day. We prayed together on the phone. I prayed that God would rid his body of cancer and grant him renewed health. I was not naïve. I had witnessed cancer reduce others to skin and bones, to a slow and certain death. But I kept calling, and I kept praying, earnestly. Dad prayed for *me*, too, and for the family. Our daughter, Esther, was engaged to be married in March. Dad asked about her and her fiancé, and our other children, and the grandchildren whom he had never seen, nor ever would.

"They're all doing well, Dad. They're all praying for you to," I reassured my father. It was true. They *were* praying. I had been calling them and reporting on Dad's condition. They hadn't really known Dad well enough, but they loved me enough to be concerned. So when they prayed for me, they prayed for Dad, too, for the only grandfather whom they hadn't really ever gotten to know, and for whom they were simply unable to feel deep affection.

I requested a couple of day's absence from school that week in late December and flew back to Manchester to be with Dad. I told him that I was coming. He was glad, and talked as if I were only a block away. Some block.

213

"Dad, I'm coming to Manchester. I'm leaving school early. I'll be there sometime tomorrow evening. I love you Dad."

"OK, Peter," he had said. "That's good. Love you too. Bye dear." Dad called me *dear* on a rare occasion, as one would breathe a last desperate, but sincere sigh.

I felt a strange hollowness in the pit of my stomach, and an inexplicable surge of emotion, of compassion, for the father whom I had never really known. Though I wasn't in the frame of mind to reflect upon it at that moment, it occurs to me now that this was the same young man, the same strong Marine hero and father who had ventured into the Dunbarton woods in the cold of winter in 1952 to seek venison for his wife and child. I could see him smiling, dragging the carcass of the large buck through the dense woods and over the stone-wall. I was running to meet him. For an inexplicable instant, he was a young, lean sharpshooter poised, rifle in hand, on the shed roof just outside my slanted bedroom window, taking aim at the glass mayonnaise jar on the skunk's head. He was the man who used a twelve-inch ruler to crush a big black spider in the old canning jar on the front porch, while a little boy peered at the horrific spectacle from just below the edge of the table. He was the same man who climbed broken branches to the top of a beanstalk to rescue a tiny kitten. He was my Dad, my hero.

Now I was the one returning to *him,* the one calling out, going to the rescue. *He* was falling; alone; dying.

"I'm coming, Dad. I'll be there with you tomorrow. Sleep well, and don't worry. I'm coming. Night Dad."

"Good night, Peter," he said. "I'll see you tomorrow," his voice slowly declining. As if I were just around the corner, just in the next room.

"See you soon, Dad."

***

I parked my old Ford pickup in the farthest parking lot at O'Hare and took the monorail to Terminal Two where I thought my flight originated; I should have read the electronic ticket more carefully; I should have known. I should have seen the small additional paragraph at the bottom, the fine print. I should have taken a few more minutes to verify...but I was in a hurry, and the security procedures seemed to take forever. I didn't have that much time. I simply couldn't miss that flight. Not tonight. Not after all these years.

In a panic, I dragged my suitcase and small carry-on back to the train. As I stood alone in the narrow tunnel, the red neon dotted sign seemed a blur. It seemed to be going backwards. I lost all sense of direction. I had done this many times before on previous trips, but this time I needed to ask directions just to be sure.

"Which train goes to Terminal One?" I asked a bystander. He looked at me curiously.

"You're standing right in front of it," he replied. "That's the train coming now. It's the only one running."

"Thanks," I said, as the aluminum doors opened.

I finally stopped at the United Terminal and rushed across the bridge to the elevator and on to the ticket-counter. I was in time.

"I thought this flight originated in Terminal Two," I said, nervously fumbling with the crumpled white sheet of paper. *Why is there so much print? Can't they just simply print the flight information?* " It says right here that my flight is to be on American Airlines..."

"Oh, no," she offered. "United doesn't have a flight from Terminal Two," she assured me. She directed me to the small paragraph at the bottom of the page, bewildered to think how anyone could have misunderstood such simple instructions.

"Yes, I know now, but I thought..."

"You'd better get in line," she urged me. "Your flight is leaving momentarily. You still have time."

When I finally found my seat, my heart was racing. I was in a cold sweat. *Don't worry, Dad, you'll be alright. I'm coming. Sleep well, Dad.*

***

When we landed in Manchester less than two hours later, the terminal was packed with arriving passengers, all converged at the one conveyor belt which seemed to be functioning. Our flight must have been one of the last flights that day. I had called Uncle Jim earlier to warn him of my arrival. He was always happy to see me and eager to help, but this time I sensed a note of dissatisfaction and complacency. We had arranged to meet clear on the other side of the terminal, at the extreme end where the parking agent was least likely to terrorize drivers waiting for passengers. But tonight, the airline had sent us to the opposite side to await our luggage. For some reason that day, the baggage conveyor belt hadn't activated for over a solid half hour. I waited. In the meantime, Uncle Jim, who always likes to be early to avoid the confusion and congestion, had circled the parking lot nearly a dozen times, wondering where in the world I had gone. After all, hadn't I promised him that I would be there waiting for him right after the flight landed?

When the mechanical belt finally disgorged the string of assorted debris that had been lodged in its cavernous throat, I found my self standing empty-handed, along with several other passengers whom I recognized from my flight. I looked carefully at those around me who were still waiting, and noticed a young woman who was sitting quietly, seemingly unaffected by the delay.

"Excuse me. Are you still waiting for your bags too?" I inquired nervously, forgetting that I was a total stranger. "What's going on?"

"Oh," she said calmly, "Didn't you know? The flight was backed up just a bit. That baggage was from the previous flight. Our should be out shortly."

"Thanks," I responded, feeling conspicuously ignorant. *Be there soon, Dad!*

In the meantime, Uncle Jim was still circling the parking garage like a vulture closing in on the convulsing carcass of its helpless prey. When my bags finally appeared, I rushed to the other end of the terminal, exited the electronic doors and stepped into the unfettered solitude of the cold New England air.

Just then, I saw Uncle Jim's van patrolling the perimeter like a border agent looking for run-away strays. I waved my arms franticly from the same spot on the far side of the lot where we had agreed to rendezvous. I could see his strained expression. Won't he be glad to see *me*! It had been months since my last visit. He was always so helpful. So accommodating. So hospitable. So...

"Uncle Jim! Uncle Jim, "I shouted, relieved to finally have arrived, to finally be home. I was exhausted, but relieved. But before I could leave the curb, he screeched to a halt, popped the trunk, and exited from the hearse.

"Where the heck have you been?!"

"I..."

"You *said* you would meet me right here nearly an hour ago! What the heck have you been doing all this time?"

"But Jim," I made a feeble attempt to explain, but he wasn't listening. I suppose that he needed time to vent. '*But wait,' I thought, 'I'm the one who had to lose work, to leave school early, to drive to the airport, to drag my baggage across a country mile across the Chicago skyline...just to visit my dying father...and you're complaining because you had to circle the parking lot??'*

"Whatever. Did you have a good flight?"

"Well..."

"Glad you're here safe, I guess. Aunt Joyce made supper for you earlier, but it's late now. She's probably asleep; she made up the couch for you."

"Thanks, Uncle Jim. I'm really sorry..."

"Whatever. You're here safe. I suppose you'll have to see your father for a while tomorrow?"

"I have to see him tonight, Jim."

"*Tonight?* Already? Didn't you see him last time?"

"He's really sick, Uncle Jim. He's not well, Uncle Jim. He's dying."

"Well, you've been a good son. You've always done what was right, I suppose. More than I can say for your father. More than he ever did for you. You know, I don't want to criticize your father, but, well; *I* got him his first job you know, right after the war when he and Dot were living in that old house in Dunbarton. *I'm* the one who got him a job…"

"I know, Uncle Jim. Thanks."

"I can't figure him out. I've always tried to do what was best by people; always tried to help out. I guess there are just some things we'll never understand."

"I know, Jim. Thanks. You've been great."

"It's not that. I'm not looking…I just don't understand why you have to help him now, but I guess he's your Dad. I'm sure you'll do the right thing."

For just a split second, a strange lump arose in my adult throat. I sat still. I was speechless, too tired to argue. I was a little boy again. I felt as if I were back on the far side of the front seat of my Dad's car, on one of those days when he came to pick me up at the house, wanting to be with him, but sitting right near the door so that I could leave, and listening to him complain about Mom. He always talked about the 'blood-money,' the alimony he had to pay every month. Uncle Jim had a happy marriage, I guess. He never had to pay alimony. He couldn't understand. Some years later, while I was a student in college, someone (I think it was my Uncle Jim) counseled my mother to bring Dad to court to force him to make back payments. For some reason I pleaded earnestly with Mom on the phone not to do it. I thought that it would ruin Dad. But I was wrong. Dad wasn't helping Mom, and he wasn't helping me either. But Mom dropped the charges and reneged; she was the one who suffered. She was the one who helped me in college. Dad never had to pay. I don't think he ever knew that I had intervened. And he still complained about the 'blood-money.' I was too intimidated to challenge him. Too fearful. Why couldn't I have found the strength and courage to do what was right for Mom? She never complained. Was my Dad something less than a hero? Even worse, was I becoming like him? Needless to say, Uncle Jim was very upset and disappointed with me. Great. I had done nothing to relieve Mom's situation. I had defended Dad's unjustifiable neglect. And now I had disappointed my Uncle. Good thing I was in Bible College learning about what it means to think and live the right way, and to lead people to God. 'Physician, heal thyself.'

"We'll talk in the morning," Uncle Jim continued. "Let me know what your plans are. I'll just be fussing around the house. Got a lot to keep me busy. There's never enough time. Too bad you can't stay a little longer. Just give me a call whenever you can. By the way, your Mom called. You'd better give her a call and tell her you're here. She'll worry.

"I called Mom when I landed, Uncle Jim, just before I called you. She knows I'm here. I told her I would stop in tonight to say hello."

"Well, she'll probably worry anyway. It's getting late. You should have waited to call until you knew..." Uncle Jim hated it when people used words 'should've,' 'could've,' or 'would've.'

"You know...it only takes me seven minutes to get here from the house. If you'd have called to let me know you'd be late, I wouldn't have had to spend so much time circling the parking lot...*whatever*."

***

I dropped my things off at Jim's house on Harvey Road, borrowed his old van, and headed into town. The darkness on the hill was interrupted only by the red beacon light circling every few seconds of its lonely, interminable vigil. The lights of Manchester were bright in the distance, like small flickering candles floating on the surface of a dark sea. Somewhere in the middle of that flickering chandelier was the small table-lamp in my mother's seventh-floor apartment, a stuffy two-room apartment that used to be a deluxe *chamber* in the Carpenter Hotel, Manchester's finest. In one of those rooms, some forty-five years earlier, as an eighth-grader at the Wilson Elementary School, I had won a "Keep America Beautiful" poster contest, and received a shiny new silver dollar and a fifty-dollar U.S. Savings Bond. But the only thing new about the Carpenter Hotel now was the elevator. The old one had been out of order; the rancid smell of decades of neglect and human incontinency permeating its rusting surface.

On the way into town, I called Mom on my cell phone.

"Mom, this is me. Were you asleep? I'm sorry. Mom, I'm running late. I probably won't be able to stop in tonight. It's too late. Will you be OK? How about if I come up in the morning? We can go downstairs to the Merrimack Street Restaurant for breakfast, OK? Don't eat before I get there, OK Mum?"

"It's OK, Peter. I'm OK. You better go see your Dad before it gets much later. I know that he must be anxious to see you. How's he doing? I've been praying for him. It must be hard for him all alone there in the hospital, you know, since Dottie died. I still think of her often. I still love Bob..." Mom started to cry, but held back the tears. "You go see your Dad, Peter." Just give me a call in the morning. I always like to make an egg early with toast and coffee...but I'll wait. Call me before you come. You don't have to come too early. I know that you must be exhausted with the flight and all. If you can't make it, it's OK. I'll just have breakfast here. You can come up later when you have time. I know you'll have to see your Dad tomorrow too. Don't worry about me."

"I'll be up in the morning, Mum. Sleep well. I'm just going to see Dad for a few minutes and get back to Jim's. It's pretty late and they're in bed by now. Don't worry. I'll be OK.

"Please drive safely, Peter. You know the traffic on Mammoth Road at night. There are accidents all the time. You know how people drive at night...don't hurry. You're tired. Don't go too fast..."

"Good night, Mum. I love you."

"Bye Petah," she closed, her voice fading in a loving, but lonely tone of desperation, as if *she* were the one who was bent under the weight of guilt; as if she were the one who lay dying, wondering if she would ever see the sun rise on another day.

Chapter Sixteen

The Return Home

*I tell you the truth, unless a kernel of wheat falls to
the ground and dies, It remains only a single seed.
But if it dies, it produces many seeds.*

(Jesus, in John 12:24)

The old Veterans' Administration Hospital building
stood like a solitary sentinel in the cold night. It had
maintained its proud, lonely vigil, quietly evading fanfare
or secular urban status, for nearly eight decades. Standing
alone, at the top of a wooded hill with intrusive, but
indifferent interstate lanes passing near the base of its rocky
perch, the hospital bid quiet welcome to each of its children
and to all its war-torn, time-weary wayfarers.

It was just another forgotten, frozen New England
night, but inside her sea-weary helm, the corridors and
crevasses of this fragile ship of hope were swarming with
smiling faces and life-giving gestures. Though most of her
crew would never be called to active duty again, her tiny
frame breathed with the homely air and the indiscriminate,
unpolished warmth of a small sickbay, treating the
wounded as best it was able, releasing her tired, faceless
warriors to a final, more grateful resting place.

Dad had just come in from the front lines, from a
long, tired tour on the battlefield, a field littered with the
debris of a broken marriage and a lifetime of restless bliss.

His presence there was almost surreal, but not entirely unpredictable. He had survived Guadalcanal more than sixty years earlier; he had courageously rescued others in the heat of battle, carrying them under fire to makeshift jungle hospitals; he had miraculously evaded the horrific tragedy of Iwo Jima simply because he had forgotten to tie his boot! Now he was lying helplessly in the bowels of the last frontier he would know on earth. To a stranger, the vessel that was the Veterans' Administration Hospital had the feel of a forgotten, converted funeral frigate anchored in dark, foreboding waters just off shore.

The few tall, tired lights surrounding the building were friendly enough, as I pulled into the near-empty parking lot on the back-side of the unimposing structure. The old black van blended into the dark pavement, its worn tires settling and cooling as though returning home from a long journey. I walked nervously up the cement steps and along the curved walk to the back entrance. Someone in a wheelchair glided past the interior of the glass doors like a faceless ghost. The only signs of life came from the bright colored lights of a vending machine. As I entered quietly, I brushed by a tall, thin book carousel holding a scant supply of used paperbacks. Its fragile frame resembled something akin to a phantom dime-store mannequin with missing body parts and a sad toothless grin.

The elderly woman at the desk wore a plain green gown. She was busy at her desk when I stepped up to the low counter. She never looked up. Didn't she understand that I had traveled all day? Didn't she know who I was, and that my Dad was dying? Wasn't she expecting me? Couldn't she at least recognize who I was? People always told me that I resembled my Dad. Couldn't she see that I was his son?

"Excuse me. Hello. Good evening. I'm here to see Mr. Robert Colman. My name is Peter Colman. I'm his son. He'll be expecting me. I live in Chicago, but I'm originally from Manchester…"

"Mr. Colman is in the room on the right, just over there." She pointed in the direction of the first-floor corridor, just beyond the entrance. "He's in that room right there; he's sharing the room with another gentleman. You're his son, you say? Good. He's been expecting you. Go right in."

During the previous few weeks, Dad's cancer had advanced from his colon to his lungs and liver. I had called him almost daily. He was upbeat. He was a man of deep personal faith in God; and he was proud. Some family members and friends had been to visit. Uncle Bill had been to see Dad every day. It was no secret that Uncle Bill thought highly of Dad, though they never had agreed when it came to issues of faith. But in recent weeks, Bill came every day. When he wasn't in Dad's room with him, he was flirting with the female nurses, taking every opportunity to raise his trousers above his skinny, boyish knees to show his invisible scars from knee-replacement surgery. Uncle Bill was a stitch, a real comedian.

During our numerous phone conversations, Dad insisted that he was getting better. That was his favorite word: "Better." "I'm better today," was the way he had begun and ended each conversation. He was trying desperately, as was I, to believe God for healing and recovery from this pernicious and debilitating disease. I prayed with Dad, and for him, after each conversation, and then said good night, assuring him of my love and prayers. The situation had taken a turn for the worse. Uncle Bill had informed me that Dad was declining quickly. In recent days, he had had a lot of bleeding and could no longer control his bowels. Nurses had to take him to the bathroom frequently; all he seemed to do now was bleed. It had been my Uncle Bill who had made the final desperate call. "Peter, this is your Uncle Bill. Your Dad is failing quickly. You'd better come now. He may not make it."

***

As I rounded the corner of the first room on the right, I sensed a strange silence. I didn't know what to expect. My heart was thumping in my chest. I stepped quietly into the entrance and stopped at the foot of the closest bed. I could see a large man in the far bed. The curtain was partially drawn. He was watching television. I noticed a black-and-white framed picture on his dresser. It was a handsome young soldier in full uniform, and his new bride. The man in the bed had a large muscular frame and a broad hooked nose. But it was not Dad.

The bed closest to the door appeared empty, the covers in disarray. It was then that I realized that the bed was actually occupied. Someone unknown to me was lying there under the covers; his head was barely visible from the short distance where I was standing. The loose bed-covers hid his short legs and distended abdomen. His head seemed smaller than usual. I had been looking for the strong, broad smile and the dark wavy hair I had remembered, but all I saw was a tiny, disheveled form.

"Dad, is that you?"

Dad raised his head slightly from the pillow and looked in my direction. His hair had thinned and hadn't been combed. His face was pale and drawn, and had a yellow hue. He smiled broadly, but his teeth were stained. They matched the color of his face.

"Peter..." His voice strained, almost weeping; he propped himself up on his side slightly, and with difficulty. A nurse came in and raised his bed, fluffing and tucking the wrinkled pillow behind his wizened scalp. As she did, I stepped closer to the bed. Dad extended a skeletal limb and grasped a stainless-steel triangular bar above his bed, pulling his tortured torso a bit higher. As he pulled himself up, his glazed eyes were fixed upon mine; his Cheshire cat smile seemed to be stretched taut to his tired face. The Marine Corp tattoo, which had graced his strong forearm, was now stretched and hanging limp on his withered frame, creating an obscene expression on his skin. The pagan memento Dad had come to despise after his conversion had been his erstwhile companion, but now it seemed to sneer at him with a perverted sense of glee. I offered to help, gently grasping Dad's arm, but Dad smiled and pulled harder. Though wasted by the disease, he still had enough strength and pride to manage the maneuver. We embraced and kissed. The man I held was the withered shell of the father whose strong chest and massive arms had given more than one miscreant pause to reflect. I was in a reluctant state of shock.

"How are you, Dad?" was all I could manage. The question seemed lame.

"Better," was his quick response. "The doctor says I'm doing better, Peter."

***

During those last long days on earth, Dad had somehow acquired a small plastic replica of a rustic white country church. The little model was covered with artificial snow, and came with an interior electric light. Dad had the nurses turn the light on every day. At night, that small country church was an oasis in a dark, lonely landscape, bringing warmth and hope not only to Dad, but to a constant stream of hospital staff and friends. It seemed to light Dad up, too, rekindling within his flickering, fading spirit, new reminders of an undying faith. I must confess that I don't recall looking too closely at the church; I kept careful, constant vigil at his bedside instead, during those hours when we were together.

All of Dad's earthly belongings, at least all that he cared to take with him to the hospital, were tucked away in the two top drawers of a small wooden dresser near his bed. On the next-to-last evening before his death, the hospital was serving a special meal to celebrate Saint Patrick's Day. One of the nurses, a bright, bubbly red-head with a sweet, fiery disposition came into Dad's room that day all dressed in green with a bright little insect antennae attached with bouncy springs to her head. We laughed and ordered our meal.

"That gal is special," Dad had said. She comes in every day to see me and to say hello. I've been talking to her about the Lord. I have opportunities every day to share Christ. These people are wonderful. We have a great time. It's *beyond*..."

'Beyond' was another one of Dad's favorite words. He used it to express spiritual elation. It was a reference to heaven, but it had clear earthly connections that went far 'beyond' the routine pains and pleasures of everyday life. It was Dad's way of expressing the joyous mystery of a simple faith; of summarizing his own perception of the divine, without undue diction or reflection. The only other native expression that was prominent in Dad's conversation was one that his own father, Sumner Chase Colman, had no doubt heard from his aged clan of common Colman stock: *"How 'bout that!"*

There was another young nurse, an intern, who had taken a particular interest in Dad's physical and spiritual condition. She was a shy, but vibrant believer. She said very little herself, but became a willing audience of one as Dad freely spoke of his love for God. Dad introduced me to this young woman the day before he died.

"This one's a gem. She knows the Lord, and had been a great companion and comfort in recent days. She's attending a good church in Concord...I've been telling her about you, and your years of ministry, your family, and your teaching...She seems so interested to listen. I am so very proud of everything you've done, Peter."

When the special Saint Patrick's Day meal was delivered to 'our' room, there was a small procession of hospital staff. This time it was the cook himself, whom Dad had befriended. They had much in common. The man was much younger, but he knew all about Camp Pendleton. He took to Dad quickly. The 'janitor' also stopped by to say his daily hello. He was still referred to as a janitor; political correctness hadn't gained acceptance as yet at the V.A. Dad had met him in the hallway, and had shared with this gentle man the story of his days in the Corps, and his dramatic conversion to Christ.

I offered to pay for the meal, but Dad insisted. "No, Peter, not this time. This is my nickel. I'll pay." He reached painfully and opened the top drawer. He found his black leather wallet, found a few bills, and paid the gentleman who had delivered the meals. Guests had to pay for their own meals. We had to pay before we could eat.

The meal was exceptional, the best that the V.A. had to offer: hot roast turkey, mashed potatoes with gravy, cranberry sauce and fresh boiled carrots, pie and coffee.

Dad couldn't eat very much, but he did do a job on the turkey. It would be Dad's last good meal. The Irish nurse with the insect antennae bouncing atop her red hair, and disarming smile, led the procession; and then they were gone, leaving Dad and me to eat alone in euphoric silence. When we were finished, I read to Dad some of his favorite verses from the large black King James Bible, with the black electrical tape binding, which he kept by his bed:

> *Lord, thou hast been our dwelling place in all generations...Thou turnest man to destruction; and sayest, 'Return, ye children of men...' We spend our years as a tale that is told. The days of our years are threescore years and ten; and if by reason of strength they be fourscore years, yet is their strength labour and sorrow; for it is soon cut off, and we fly away...Make us glad according to the days wherein thou hast afflicted us, and the years wherein we have seen evil...let thy work appear unto thy servants, and thy glory unto their children. And let the beauty of the Lord our God be upon us...*
>
> (Psalm 90)

From right across the page, I added a few verses of my own which I felt were particularly appropriate for Dad, given his rather miraculous escape from an early grave as a U.S. Marine:

> *He that dwelleth in the secret place of the Most High shall abide under the shadow of the Almighty.*
> *I will say of the Lord, He is my refuge and my fortress:*
> > *My God; in Him will I trust...*
> > *A thousand shall fall at thy side,*
> > *And ten thousand at thy right hand;*

232

But it shall not come nigh thee...
Because thou hast made the Lord, which is
my refuge,
Even the most High, thy habitation;
There shall be no evil befall thee,
Neither shall any plague come near thy
dwelling...
Because he hath set his love upon me,
Therefore will I deliver him: I will set him
on high
Because he hath known my name...
He shall call upon me, and I will answer
him:
I will be with him in trouble;
I will deliver him and honor him.
With long life will I satisfy him,
And shew him my salvation."
(Psalm 91: 1-2, 7, 9-10, 14-16)

These were the words that we had read often before. We read them again, late into the evening and on into the next day. Dad closed his eyes and listened. I had the feeling that he was losing consciousness. Perhaps he was just tired. He kept drifting off. I had put his pillows and the plastic wastepaper basket behind him to help hold him upright so that he could eat his supper. Now he was tired and seemed content. He needed to sleep. We prayed. I hugged him and told him that I loved him. I had asked him questions earlier that night, questions that had been haunting me for years; he had answered them as best he knew how, as well as his courage and declining strength would allow. But I wondered whether his memory was failing. He continued to smile. He seemed happy that I was there. He kept saying, "I love you, Peter. I'm proud of you. You've been a good son."

I prayed with him one last time, kissed his pale, disfigured brow, smoothed his thinning hair, and said goodnight. Dad went to sleep that night, but his breathing was coming harder. He slept restlessly, like an exhausted swimmer struggling against the unyielding waves, straining to breathe while the air burned in his throat and his lungs filled with salt water.

The nurses came to dim the lights and adjust Dad's pillow and blanket for the long cold journey home. When I left the hospital that night, nothing moved in the gray parking lot. The black van was resting peacefully, with the patience of a proud caisson, right where I had tethered it earlier in the afternoon. The night air was clear and cold. I gripped the wheel and gave the command. Reluctantly, the van inched out of the parking lot and crept quietly down the dark hill toward home. There would be another day after all. It was the evening of March 17th, 2005.

***

As I moved slowly down Mammoth Road and over the wooded crest of the Bridge Street hill toward South Willow, the lights of the city shown like crystal candles in a sable sky. I prayed, *"Lord, grant Dad peace and rest tonight. Give me strength. Grant me the grace to bring comfort to Dad and to my family."* My own breathing came hard. Rest eluded me. I reached for my cell phone and called Mum.

"Mum? I'm sorry. Were you sleeping? It's me. I just left Dad…"

"How's Bob doing?" she asked, not seeming to mind that I hadn't called earlier or gone to see her. "I've been praying for you and for your Dad."

234

"He's not doing well, Mum. I don't know if he will survive the night. I'm exhausted. I'm going to Uncle Jim's to try to get some sleep. I'll call you in the morning. Maybe we can have breakfast together. Sorry I wasn't able to see you much today. I had a real good time with Dad. We talked a lot, and had a great supper together…"

"Did you talk about me? I miss Dottie, you know. I bear no grudge against your father. Did you tell him that I asked about him, and that I am praying for him?"

"No, I didn't, Mum, but I will be sure to mention it if Dad asks. I'm sorry, Mum. You know, he's still grieving over Dottie's death, and it's been so many years…"

"Your father and I had eight happy years together when you were a little boy…"

"I know, Mum. That's something to be thankful for isn't it? You did enjoy eight happy years."

"He was my husband. He is a good man. I have no bitterness in my heart. I still love him…"

"Yes, I know, Mum. I'll tell him that you said hello, and that you are praying for him. I think he knows that, but I'll tell him if he asks. Good night, Mum. I'll see you in the morning, but not too early. Jim and Joyce like to sleep a bit later these days."

Mom's voice started to break and rise in pitch. She was at the point of tears. She sounded like a child who had waited all year for the circus to come to town again; but on the very last day, the trip had been canceled. She had to stay home. She had always been courageous and thoughtful. She had never remarried, and had lived the last

235

fifty years without the benefit and comfort of intimate companionship. She had her share of common quirks and idiosyncrasies, but was, and still is, essentially generous and unselfish. She has enjoyed little in this life, from a material perspective; has never owned her own home or her own car, but she has a surfeit of friends, and is desperately proud of her family.

"Don't worry about me. Take all the time you need with your father. Uncle Jim will be worried about you, too. He'll want to spend some time with you. You don't get to come very often. I don't know how you and Judy manage to do all that you do, with visiting the children, and teaching, and… Well, I'll be fine. Just give me a call in the morning to let me know what your schedule is. I'll be up early. I'll wait for your call. I need to have my egg and toast and coffee…Do you want me to make you bacon and eggs? I have plenty in the fridge…"

"Wait on those eggs, Mum. I'll call when I get up. Let's go down to the corner restaurant and have breakfast there, OK?

"Breakfast is pretty reasonable there," she volunteered. "The waitress remembers you. I'll tell her you're coming. Come through the lobby when you come. There'll be some of my friends sitting there. I'll need to introduce you…"

"Good night, Mum. I love you. Sleep well."

"Good night, Petah."

Chapter Seventeen

Good Grief

*...To die: to sleep; no more; and by a sleep to
say we end the heart-ache and the thousand
natural shocks that flesh is heir to, 'tis a
consummation devoutly to be wish'd...*
(Shakespeare's Hamlet – Act III, Scene I)

*The Lord is my shepherd, I shall not be in want.
He makes me lie down in green pastures, he leads
me beside quiet waters, he restores my soul...*
(David, in the 'Shepherd' Psalm, 23:1-2)

After breakfast the next morning, I returned to the
hospital. Dad was sitting up in a chair by his bed. The
image the previous night of his bed-ridden, emaciated body
had been irrevocably fixed in my psyche. The sight of him
sitting in a prone position, and in such good spirits, came as
a bit of a pleasant shock. He smiled when I entered. He was
still talking about the previous night's visit and his daily
trips to the lounge. He had a 'drinking-buddy,' (coffee
drinkers, that is), an elderly gentleman who had also seen
action in the Pacific theatre. They sat for hours trading
stories and sharing strong black coffee. Dad really enjoyed
those daily treks to the lounge. He said that he had been
talking to his friend about his faith; the gentleman was
apparently close to death's door; Dad was trying earnestly
to help him to reach out to God, to look beyond the
threshold of this life, as it were.

Dad seemed to live for those daily meetings. Every week, local church groups organized worship services and other activities for the patients. The V.A. also organized Bingo for the beleaguered troops! I'm not certain that Dad was ever tempted to participate in the gaming aspect of his social environment, but I believe that he may have slipped away in his wheelchair to observe the proceedings. Had she known (and who's to say she didn't), his mother, Nellie, would have smiled at his having been delightfully drawn in to such a den of iniquity. Such an admission of enjoyment and harmless recreation would have, perhaps, provided some reassurance of a devout son's humanity, and restored a simple thread of credibility in matters of a higher order. For Dad's part, he had probably wished more than once to have had surreptitious access to that infamous can of nickels his mother had so jealously cherished. She would have been more than delighted to have lent him a handful, just one last time. Just for fun.

In more recent weeks, Dad had attended a special Veteran's Day celebration with his aged comrades-in-arms. They had all been given bright red Veterans of Foreign Wars caps, and had their individual pictures taken with a large American flag as backdrop. Dad gave me that picture during my last visit. The colored five-by-seven photo was in a loosely-fitting cardboard frame. There he sat in his funny red cap, festooned with Marine lapel buttons, his paratrooper wings pinned dead center just above the visor. Dad was seated right below one of the white nylon stars on the huge flag right behind his head. He had on his large reading glasses, and wore that broad Cheshire-cat smile.

Dad's body was failing, but his broad smile and the bright gleam in his eyes gave luster and life to an otherwise pathetic pose. His teeth were still terribly yellowed. His abdomen was visibly distended under a new, brown long-sleeve woolen shirt; the tiny brown buttons wound in a crooked caravan upward toward his wrinkled neck, like an aerial view of little elephants crossing the Himalayas. His big hand, sporting a large gold wedding ring, rested on the arm of the chair. This last picture of my father reveals a curious splash of personal pride and integrity, but dignity and décor were hanging by a perilous thread. The man in the picture was only a fraction of the man whose heroic and fearless ascent I had witness as a boy of three. Was this the same strong hunter who had challenged the wild and returned from the Dunbarton woods in dead of winter with so huge a trophy? The father whom I thought I knew and whom I had come to recognize had become only a semblance of his former self. A stranger.

The message to the right of the photo was classic Bob Colman, but it also betrayed small innocent *indices* of near-fatal deterioration and decline. The message embodied Dad's final attempt to reach out in love to his son and daughter-in-law, and to his grandchildren, most of whom he had never seen or, more tragically, had never embraced. For whatever reason, he had rarely, if ever, written to his grandchildren; he always complained that he had never been properly informed of their activities, though he always kept every picture and every tiny relic of information memorabilia that he had managed to salvage over the years in a family scrapbook. The note at the top of the opposite page to the left of the photo was written in long-hand with Dad's characteristically ostentatious flare:

'Merry Christmas & Happy New Year - (2004)
Your Dad & Grandfather *Too* family & Children
Love and Prayers, Dad'

The day was March 18, 2005. Dad and I spent nearly the entire morning and early afternoon together in candid conversation about the past forty years. It was during that conversation that I had finally garnered the courage to ask Dad about his 'adopted daughter.' She and her husband had been visiting Dad almost daily as well, for the past several weeks, though rarely during my periodic visits. I had asked Dad about some of the irreconcilable details surrounding Dottie's birth. And I had finally asked point blank if Dottie was my sister.

"No, Peter." Dad had responded. "Dottie (Samara) was a virgin when we married."

At the time, it seemed to be an air-tight, sincere response. If there had been other details, Dad was not saying. Neither, it occurred to me later, had he ever divulged anything that I can freely repeat concerning the circumstances of the divorce. Come to think of it, I cannot recall Dad ever having shared with me or spoken to me freely of any difficulties or weaknesses with which he may have struggled as a young man or father.

The hospital staff brought Dad a light lunch: a ham and cheese sandwich on white bread, a small carton of skimmed milk (the same kind we use to buy in grade school for three cents), a cup of black coffee, and a tiny plastic container of instant pistachio pudding, which was curiously both Dad's and my favorite flavor. Dad wasn't hungry, but he did want the pudding. He offered to share it, but I refused, opting instead for the half of ham sandwich. I hadn't eaten all day. Dad also passed on the coffee.

Not a good sign.

Dad had been put back in bed by this time. His bleeding had increased and he had weakened considerably. When the sumptuous half sandwich and copious smidgeon of pudding had arrived, I propped Dad up in bed again, using all of his pillows and the plastic waste container (clean and emptied) between the pillows and the bed-frame. I used all my strength to hold him vertically while he attempted to imbibe the pudding. I fed him one small spoonful at a time. He seemed to relish it, but he was unable to finish.

"That's it, Peter. I've had enough. It was good. Thanks. I'm OK, but I'd like to lay back down now." As he sat there in bed, I read a few more of his favorite verses from the Psalms. His eyes began to water, and he smiled.

"I love you, Dad."

"I love you, too, Peter," was all that he seemed to be able to say.

I gently removed the container, fluffed his pillows and laid him carefully back down. I prayed for him, but his breathing was becoming more irregular and he seemed to be half asleep. I didn't know it at the time, but he was slowly losing consciousness. I stroked his thinning hair and kissed him before leaving.

"I'll be back up later tonight, Dad," was the last thing I said. Dad was asleep. His breath was slow and seemed to have a rough, congested sound. His lungs were beginning to fill with body fluid. Little did I know that that would be last conversation we would ever have.

I went straight down the Bridge Street hill to Merrimack and Elm to my mother's apartment. I was exhausted. Mom had been expecting me. She had made fresh coffee in her tiny two-cup coffee-maker. She had accumulated a fridge full of assorted meats and cheeses, puddings and pastries, but I apologized and declined any supper. We sat and shared a hot cup of coffee with white sugar and half-and-half instead. She always just used milk, but kept half-and-half 'on hand,' as she always said, just for my visits. She was always doing for and thinking of others. She had piled the used cot in the small narrow kitchen with layers of quilts and assorted blankets, miscellaneous pillows and a few of her ubiquitous stuffed animals.

"You must be tired, Petah. Why don't you relax and watch a little TV, or take a short nap."

"Thanks for the coffee, Mum. I think I will, just for a few minutes." But before I did, I called Uncle Jim to inform him of my whereabouts, and to talk to him about Dad's condition. Somehow, I expected him to be concerned, but I can hardly fault him for the tone of indifference on the other end of the line.

"Uncle Jim, it's me. I'm at Mum's. I've been at the hospital most of the day with Dad."

"We'll, I guess you do what you have to do. Joyce and I have been here all day waiting. We didn't know how long you'd be. Joyce will make you something to eat whenever you get back…"

"Thanks, Jim, but tell Auntie Joyce not to fuss. I'll get something later at the hospital, or just have something here with Mum. I'll be OK."

"Thanks, Jim, but it'll probably be late. I don't want Joyce to go to any bother. I'll just open it up when I get there. I left the blanket and pillow in the front foyer. Tell Joyce not to bother with a sheet. I'm OK."

"Whatever. Just give us a call when you're done. We'll get the bed ready for you. Tomorrow's your last day you know. It's sure been a short visit. Wish we had more time. There's never enough time. We'll leave the door unlocked as usual. Try not to make too much noise when you get here; don't want to wake up Joyce."

"OK Jim. See you later. Good night."

Night would come sooner than I had expected. Uncle Bill had paid Dad a short visit just after my departure. I had been resting for only a few short minutes when my cell-phone rang. I jerked to a sitting position and answered.

"Peter? This is your Uncle Bill. You'd better come right up to the hospital. Your Dad is failing."

"I'm on my way, Uncle Bill."

Mum had been napping just around the corner. She had not been sleeping. When my phone rang, she had bolted up too and was in the living room like a shot.

"That was Uncle Bill, Mum. He's with Dad right now. Dad is failing fast. I've got to go right now. I love you, Mum. Please keep praying."

"I'll be right here," she said. I'll be praying. Don't worry about coming back tonight. I know you're needed there. Please tell Bob I'm praying for him."

"I will, Mum. Thank for your love and prayers. I'll call you as soon as I know more. It'll be late. I'll probably go right to Jim's tonight." I gave Mum a hug and kiss and headed to the seventh-floor elevator and out to my 'reserved' space near the edge of the parking lot. The night was cold. The streetlights cast low dull shadows across to the ancient two-story brick apartments just a stone's-throw from the high-rise, not fifty yards down the abandoned alley where Dad's empty apartment sat. That would be Dad's last earthly home, within earshot from my mother's seventh-floor apartment window. He had been so close, but so very far. She had wanted to reach out, just to say hello, if only to convey her condolences, but it was so very far away. An eternity in time. Instead, Mom had opened her apartment window and was waving as I opened the van door.

"Be careful, Petah. Don't forget to call. I'm praying. Tell your father I'm..."

Uncle Bill and Aunt Earlene had called the immediate family. They would come as soon as they could. Dottie and her husband had stopped by to see Dad, but had left before I arrived. When I reached the hospital, I parked in the same spot and hurried up the cement walk to the glass doors. It was already getting late and frost had settled on the cast-iron railings. There had been little sun that day; the cold New England night sky was choked with dark low-lying clouds, engorged with massive mountains of snow.

I entered quickly and without protocol. From the hall desk, I could see the faithful nursing staff entering and exiting Dad's room. They flew like angels in the night bringing light and warmth. One of them still wore little green antennae. She squeezed my hand as I passed by.

"We love your Dad," she whispered. "We're so glad that you came to see him. He's resting. We've had to increase his dose of morphine for the past few hours. We thought it best to call you now. He hasn't much time. Go on in."

When I entered, Dad was still alive, but his breathing came hard, and he was unconscious. Uncle Bill had arrived earlier and was sitting next to the bed.

"I can't bear to see Bob like this," he said, near the point of tears. "Peter, what would we have done if you hadn't come? You made so many trips. You've been such a good son. Bob did his best you know. He and Dottie had many happy years…"

Uncle Bill still joked and flirted with the nurses when they came in. It was just his way of masking his fear and sense of helplessness. He and Dad hadn't always seen eye to eye in the past. Old scars never seem to fade. Old skeletons still seem to rattle and sneer from deep within the soul's closet. Some never see the light of day. But on that night, Uncle Bill was visibly sane and docile, like a little boy in a helpless situation. He couldn't bear the heavy, incoherent breathing coming from the bed, the long intervening periods of deathly silence, and the pale yellow hue on Dad's wizened face. He slowly moved to the corner near the door and sat it silence, his eyes flushed and wide with fear.

Moments later, Uncle Louie and Aunt Bobbi came in. Aunt Bobbi is a down-to-earth country girl with a sweet smile and tender disposition which she still bore well into her eightieth year. Uncle Louie was a soft-spoken farm boy who had never made much fuss over spirituality or the finer points of Christian faith, but who was one of the only remaining 'old-guard' in the family. He said very little, but loved Dad and was there to visit nearly every day. Works without faith, you might say. Then again, genuine faith is not something that is always visible. Faith, at least among New England folk, is not something that walks at the front of the parade, but it's there working behind the scenes to be sure that the parade comes off as planned, smoothly but not with excessive fanfare, rain or shine. That's what the folks sitting at the curb expect. There *will* be a parade, 'come hell or high water!'

I wasn't sure that Dad could hear anything at all, but I picked up his big black Bible with the electrical-tape binding and read several chapters while Uncle Bill listened from the corner, and Uncle Louie and Aunt Bobbi looked on. Dad's favorite nurses came in briefly from time to time to administer more morphine. Within the hour, their visits stopped and we were left alone standing around Dad's bed. For some reason, Dad's other three brothers had been indisposed and hadn't been able to visit that night.

Dad was lying on his back with the sheets pulled up close to his neck for warmth. His breathing was extremely rough now. I stroked his hair and spoke words of consolation. I started quoting some of Dad's and my favorite verses from memory. I think that I may have sung a short stanza from one of his beloved hymns, but the memory is unclear.

With the exception of Uncle Bill, who couldn't bring himself to approach the bed and witness Dad's last moments, the three of us stood closely to the bed and held hands. I was standing at his right side. I placed my right hand on his erratic, heaving chest, and my left hand on his brow. I began to pray and weep, ever so silently. In an instant, Dad took one last deep, tortured breath and expired, coughing up fluid from his lungs. Without a second thought, I took the white towel near his head and wiped his open mouth. He was gone. He had passed over to the other side, leaving the cold lifeless shell of a corpse behind. The fight was over at last. The last battle had been fought and won. He was safely home. I kissed his cold brow one last time and covered his face with the sheet. When I finally turned to look toward the door, Uncle Bill was sitting in the corner, weeping uncontrollably like a child. We all hugged and comforted each other as best we could. The nurses and other staff came in shortly after to prepare the body and to express condolences. The young Christian woman whom Dad had befriended in recent days stopped me on the way out to thank me for being there.

"Your Dad was a wonderful man," she told me. "We all loved him. We were praying for him. Thank you for coming." The Irish nurse, the redhead, was the last to stop me by the front desk.

"We try not to get too attached to our patients," she reiterated, "but your Dad was a special man. We'll miss him. We're so glad you were able to come to be with him."

I thanked them both, as well as the doctors, whom I had then met only for the first time. The maintenance engineer who had befriended Dad met me somewhere in between.

"Your Dad was a good man. We were good friends."

I left the hospital for the last time. It was after 9 p.m. The air was quiet and solemn as I walked slowly, as if in a dream, down the icy cement walkway and steps to the parking lot below. The van was waiting faithfully there, alone in the dim light. I reached for my cell phone before starting the engine.

"Mum, this is Peter. Dad is gone." There was an eternal silence on the other end.

"I'm sorry, Peter. Are you alright? I've been praying for you. You'd better get to Uncle Jim's. He's been worrying and wondering about you. Joyce had been expecting you for supper hours ago. You'd better call Jim. I'll be OK. Call me in the morning.

"Mum, I'm sorry. I'm sorry for you."

"Well, she replied, trying to be strong and hold back the tears, we weren't together all those years. He was with Dottie. He was happy. I'm glad that he had those years after…"

"Mum, you had eight happy years together. You were man and wife for eight happy years," I replied, wanting to bring what comfort I could. But I knew that in some strange way, a bit of Mum and the small remnant of happiness that she may have felt had died with Dad too. "You were a good wife, Mum, and you had a good few years. They produced me didn't they?!"

"You've been a good son, Peter. You were good to your Dad. It was so good that were able to be with him…"

"I wanted to be with him, Mum. He was my father. I wanted to honor him and be with him...well, while we still had time."

It was getting cold in the van. And it was getting late. I dialed Uncle Jim's number and waited...

"Jim, it's me..."

"Where have you been? Joyce and I have been waiting for you all night. Joyce made supper for you..."

"Uncle Jim, I'm sorry. I thought I told you that I wouldn't need to eat; that I would get something here at the hospital, or eat with Mum..."

"Whatever. You'd better call your Mom. She'll be worried too."

"I just called her, Jim. She's OK. Uncle Jim, Dad's gone. He just passed away. I'll be along in a moment. I'm sorry if I caused you and Joyce any trouble...Please tell Auntie Joyce that I'm sorry..."

"Oh, well, I' m sorry. I guess you did everything you could, even if your Dad didn't...well, whatever. We'll be waiting here whenever you come. If you want, Joyce will get something together for you to eat. Drive slowly. It's slippery on that back road. Take your time. We'll be here."

I had not told Uncle Jim about Dad's recent efforts to help the family, quite in spite of the meager resources he had at his disposal. Our daughter, Esther's wedding was to take place in just one week. Just a few weeks before his death, Dad had inquired as to the wedding expenses. Esther and her *fiancé,* Steve, had planned a simple reception in a beautifully renovated, customized barn near our home. But as frugal as they both were, the cost was considerable. When I mentioned this detail to Dad, he made a snap decision on the phone.

"I want to help Esther!"

I was shocked. Dad had never been either inclined or able to help anyone in his family before. He had asked me about details and costs. Friends and volunteers had offered to decorate and do the cake. My son-in-law, Matthew is a deejay, and volunteered to contribute time, equipment and his own inimitable energy and talent. All things considered, the cost, though it had been duly budgeted, was nearly a thousand dollars more than any of us could afford.

"I've got a little money left over from Social Security. I'm going to give it to Esther for her wedding!" Let me know the amount. I'll contact Dottie and have her get the money from my account. I'm letting her handle my account. She was like a daughter to Dottie and me…"

"I know, Dad, thank you. That's very generous. Esther will be thrilled."

The check, made out to Esther Colman, had arrived the next week, just days before my final visit. That money had been just about all Dad had left in his account after Dottie Samara's death the November before. The rest, as I would later discover, would be used to cover the modest meal for the immediate family at Blake's restaurant on Manchester's west side, the same restaurant were Dad and I had eaten a few years earlier. We would eat in a small banquet room not far from a small table in the adjoining

250

room where my Dad had confessed to his son that he had been a 'prodigal father.' The father had returned and the son had been waiting with open arms. It was that return that we would commemorate in that small room. It would be a celebration of love lost and rediscovered, a celebration of reconciliation. But Dad would not be present for that final meal. We had already had our last meal together of ham and cheese on white bread, and pistachio pudding in a plastic cup. It was Dad's favorite.

"Thanks, Uncle Jim. I'll be right there."

Jim's bark was worse that his bite. He just had a tough time accepting my spending endless days with a father who had neglected a son, his grandchildren and great-grandchildren for most of their lives. He was probably right. Had Robert Colman not been my father, there would not have been any justification for my behavior on his behalf. But he was. I had done all that I could. I had no regrets. I bore no grudge. No bitterness. I was the child who had become a father to the man. And I was content.

Chapter Eighteen

'Things the Eye Has Not Seen'

(1 Corinthians 2:9)

The sole of the foot teaches all things.

(Bambara proverb)

The sole of the foot is the least conspicuous part of the body, yet it bears the weight of the whole; it is first to absorb the pain of injury. In an African context, where young African children run barefoot, and workers sometime walk and work barefoot in the fields, there is always the danger of thorns, snakebites or similar dangers. Yet, the foot bears the pain and burden without complaint.

What burden of pain my parents' damaged relationship and consequent rupture caused them to endure, I shall never fully know. I am not even certain that I will ever really understand the ways in which my own life has been affected as a result. Though I am keenly aware that I have, in addition to my own peculiar weaknesses and flaws, inherited a curious blend of assorted idiosyncrasies from both parents, I am loath to attribute blame. In an imperfect world, the sovereignty of divine intervention notwithstanding, one is ultimately responsible for his or her own successes or failures. Though the fathers (and mothers) may have eaten sour grapes, and the children find their mouths embittered with the taste, they are not bound to keep those same grapes in their proverbial mouths forever, but may chose to cultivate a sweeter generation of grapes for themselves and their children.

Years ago while living in West Africa, I heard the story of two men. One was young and robust, boasting great physical strength, but lacking experience. The second man was aged. The strength in his tired, weary body had long since abandoned him. They both shared the same desire to take a long journey. The young man was quite eager to go, but the direction and destination were unknown to him. His elderly counterpart had made the trip many times in his youth, but was now too weak to walk the distance. One day the old man suggested that since he knew the way, but lacked the strength to travel, the young man should carry him on his back while he showed him the way. Having agreed to the proposition, the two men set out on their journey and eventually arrived at their destination, the one, having lacked the strength, was refreshed, having been carried, and the other, relieved to have had such a wise guide.

On one particular day during those same years, I had been traveling a very remote, unpaved road between African towns. While stopped at a police check-point, I was approached by a young soldier carrying an AK-47, which was standard issue in that part of the world at that time. The young man was traveling in same direction as I, and requested a ride. I thought it wise to accept. We rode the distance together. During our conversation, I happened to mention the same story of the two men, and made some remark about the importance of younger men needing the wisdom of their elders to avoid the common pitfalls that they may be prone to encounter or endure. During our journey, we happened to pass through his village of birth. Just on the outskirts of that village there was a deep ravine. He took the opportunity to recount the following story:

"Do you see that deep ravine?" he said, pointing to a rugged escarpment near the side of the village. "Once when I was a small boy," he continued, "I was playing at the bottom of that ravine with some of my friends. It was the end of the dry season, and the clouds were black with rain. Suddenly, we heard a terrible rumbling noise. The sandy ground beneath our bare feet rumbled. We thought that it was the sound of thunder. Suddenly, my father came running and screaming down the side of that ravine and scooped us up in his arms, carrying us safely to the other side. When we turned our heads, a massive wall of water and rocks came thundering by right where we had been playing. We were young and did not recognize the sound of the flood. We cannot survive without the wisdom of our elders."

Cultural differences and circumstances aside, there is a strange similarity here to my own situation, though with just a slight ironic twist. My father and I could very well have exchanged roles in this scenario had Dad been present when, as a young boy, I had found myself alone and unaware of impending dangers. As a father myself, with children and grandchildren, and now approaching the late fall, or early winter, of my earthly existence, I'm not sure that I possess or have exercised the kind of cumulative wisdom sufficient to spare my own children and peers the perils they may face in the current ideological and spiritual floods which seek to destroy an entire generation. Neither am I certain that my own father, in spite of his reputation for strength, heroism and spiritual resolve, possessed sufficient courage and wisdom to have completed the journey he had undertaken as a young man and husband. Perhaps he was afraid. Perhaps it was just fear of the unknown, fear of replicating the errors of his predecessors, that caused him to hesitate. Perhaps that's why, one day, he exited the trenches, stood on the edge of the ravine, scanned the dark horizon, and walked slowly away.

In the days just prior to my father's death, it was the son who found himself responding to a father's cries for help and understanding. It was a son who ran to the edge of the steep ravine to watch a weakened warrior struggling against forces that were far too overwhelming, groping for some kind of emotional foothold, some semblance of purpose, some sense of understanding and comfort from the son whom, for all practical purposes, he had chosen to ignore. In his weakened condition, he hadn't the strength to survive the ordeal. So I went to him, not with the intention to rescue him or to restore him to his former self, to his former strength, but to simply seek reconciliation and to restore a measure of lost love. No son can claim to be entirely innocent in such a relationship. All relationships, and their consequent actions, may be traced to higher or deeper origins. For both my father and me, that higher source of strength and spiritual vitality, our 'dwelling place through all generations,' had been God Himself. But at the end of this particular parable, the prodigal father who had chosen *not* to remain at home, now found himself to be alone and helpless, waiting for the son who had always been there, and who was waiting and longing to receive his lost father with arms outstretched.

***

The night of Dad's death, when I returned to Uncle Jim's and Auntie Joyce's small cottage on the hill overlooking old Grenier Field, the lights were still on. As I stepped through the sliding door into the dining room, a room that hadn't changed for fifty years, a room that I had grown to love, Auntie Joyce greeted me with an innocent, but unfeeling complaint.

"We've been waiting all night for you. We had supper all ready for you…"

I walked slowly past the Aunt whom I love, and walked to the far side of the small living room area where Uncle Jim was sitting in his favorite armchair.

"Geeze, Pete, where've you been all day? We've been waiting for you. Joyce had supper ready..."

I have never doubted my love and affection for Uncle Jim, nor shall I ever do so. He is the father I never had. He is the man who has unselfishly given of himself for others, and more particularly, for me, nearly my entire life. He is the one who was always there to help and to encourage. He was the one who called; the one who came; the one who brought me with him everywhere he went. For all practical purposes, I had become, and shall always be, like his adopted son. But on this night, quite in spite of the affection I held for him, I found myself unable to endure his indifference.

"Uncle Jim," I responded softly, but with a strained tone of frustration and impatience, "my father just died. I have been with him all day. He just died in my arms. I felt his last breath. I felt the agonizing rumble of fluid in his diseased lungs; I wiped his mouth and covered his face for the last time. I'm sorry if I missed supper..."

Uncle Jim sat motionless in his chair, unable to respond. The meaningless drone and senseless static of the television filled the room. Life goes on. I don't know what Uncle Jim felt or thought at that precise moment in time, but there was not the slightest hint of remorse or sympathy in his look. To be fair, it was obvious that he had had his share of issues to deal with in recent days. He and Joyce had been the victims of a near-fatal accident a couple years back. Their neighbor had broken into their home on several occasions and helped himself to some of Jim's hard-earned possessions, including his father's, my grandfather's rifles and some coins, not to mention the forty-or-so cases of irreplaceable collectable antique bottles he had stolen from Jim's trailer. The legal proceedings had taken over two years, with little or no reimbursement. It seemed that someone was just waiting for Jim to drop the case, or die, whichever came first. But he had done neither. In the meantime, Jim and Joyce have helped the same gentleman's daughters who came frequently to knock on their door in the middle of the night, fleeing homeless and penniless from their father's abusive behavior. Nice neighbor. Nice father. So in the sunset of their lives, when they should be enjoying some measure of peace and comfort, they are having to work harder than ever just to survive. How could I expect my uncle to be sympathetic? How could he possibly understand? Or perhaps, in another way, he understood too well. But before he could bring himself to say anything at all, Auntie Joyce, who is of old traditional English stock, had glided into the living room and was standing quietly by my side. Without warning, and quite contrary to anything that I had ever witnessed in her characteristically reserved behavior, she suddenly embraced me weeping quite uncontrollably. There were large watery tears in her stolid English eyes.

"I'm so sorry I was angry with you," she sobbed, as she embraced my neck with uncontrolled dignity. "I'm so sorry," she repeated, "It must have been so difficult to see your Dad like that...to see him die. Please forgive me for what I said. *I love you.*"

Uncle Jim sat there in a mild state of shock. He was paralyzed, his eyes peering straight ahead in disbelief. Then he looked up and uttered a strained, near-silent phrase:

"In sixty years of marriage, she has never told me *once* that she loved me."

Now *I* was the one who found himself once again in the role of counselor and consoler. I hardly knew how to respond. I was caught in a strange, unstable vortex of emotion. I'm certain that Joyce had not heard his earnest, but 'off-the-cuff' comment. Her hearing had become much worse in recent days. Mutual miscommunication, aggravated by a host of physical ailments, was at the root of much of the frustration both of them had to endure in the sunset of their lives. When they went swimming together, Joyce could hardly stand, but they went into the water hand-and hand like two little children suffering from infatuation. Jim kept his composure, while Auntie Joyce retreated to the kitchen to make two cups of English tea. She reappeared a few minutes later with hot tea and honey and a plate of assorted cookies and chocolates. We had a small snack and got ready for bed. When the lights went out, Uncle Jim returned to the living room where I was just about ready to jump into bed. I was exhausted.

"I'm sorry," he offered sheepishly. "It's been so damn hard. I know that you needed to see your father. I may not have seen eye to eye with him on most things, but he *was* your father. I know that you did everything you could. I expected that you'd do what was right, and you did. You've been a good son. You must be pretty tired. Get some sleep. I'll see you in the morning and we'll go from there. Did you call your mother? She'll be worried. Well, good night. We won't be up too early."

That was it. No sense crying over spilt milk. Life goes on. It was Jim's way of offering a modest apology without giving up too much ground. But his own love and concern was never a question. It was his turn now to be a child to the father of the man. He was only trying to be a son to a younger father returning home. The sun was setting fast on his life. He was loath to speak of death, but he was afraid. And I was afraid to bear the thought of losing another father.

Uncle Jim wasn't one to express affection or to put words to his emotions, unless he was expressing disgust for the injustice or impropriety of others, and the impracticality of their actions. *"Why do people always have to use the word 'love?'"* he used to complain. *"Isn't it enough just to know it without having to say it every time?"*

"Good night, Jim. Sleep well. I am praying for you and Auntie Joyce every day. We love you, though I know you don't like to hear it…" *I just couldn't resist saying those words, though I knew that they made him uncomfortable. He would later admit to me in a rare moment of transparency that though he was confident of Joyce's love, it was "nice to hear it once and a while."* I'll see you in the morning."

"OK, dear"

Uncle Jim could be surprisingly affectionate when he wanted to be.

***

The father whom I recognized and loved, but never really knew, was gone. I called my wife, Judith, from Manchester. She called the children. They had all been praying for me, as had my students at Carmel Catholic High School. They had been coming to my homeroom and stopping me in the corridors to assure me of their prayers. Some of them were the same students who had delivered a beautiful basket of violets to my room a few months earlier when Dottie Samara Colman had died. No doubt, they had believed that she was my biological mother. The gesture had brought me to tears. But during these last months of my father's life, countless friends and colleagues, along with many members of our church family, were all praying for both my Dad and me. We were never alone. I never felt a sense of hopelessness or a loss of faith. But I did experience a tinge of confusion and deep emotion having to spend the most intimate moments of my life with my Dad near and around his deathbed. What Morrie Schwartz said, as reported by the author Mitch Albom in his remarkable story *Tuesdays with Morrie,* is the absolute truth: "When you know how to die, then you know how to live."

Strangely enough, in another watershed conversation with my Uncle Jim about a year ago, just about the time I was trying to explain my feelings at my Dad's passing, another poignant aphorism came to mind, one particularly appropriate in my own situation: "Death ends a life, but not a relationship." The context in which I quoted that priceless phrase was a phone conversation. My Uncle, whom I love as a father, had commented that once an individual is dead, he or she is also, for all practical purposes, forgotten. End of the road. I told Uncle Jim that night in no uncertain emotional terms that I couldn't have disagreed more. Relationships were meant to be eternal, which is why we must do everything within in our power to restore and heal them when they are damaged and suffering, or even seem beyond resuscitation. In the case of a life-threatening rift and seemingly irreconcilable rupture, one must strive to effect genuine reconciliation.

In the parable of the prodigal son, the father was dying for the lack of a son's love, while the son was dying due to his senseless rejection of a father's love and the pursuit of self-gratification and a misguided sense of independence. Of course, the opposite is often true as well. A son may just as easily die for the lack of a *father*'s love and a father's misguided sense of self-centered independence and self-indulgence. In either case, the demise or death of a relationship comes through the kind of ignorance and pride that simply refuses to either offer or receive another's love, or perhaps both. Of course, on a rare and painfully inexplicable occasion, both may be separated by tragic circumstances well beyond their power to control or change.

***

Before returning to Chicago, Uncle Jim offered to accompany me to the funeral home where we had agreed to meet the Director to discuss Dad's burial, and to make arrangements for the funeral service. Dad had requested to be cremated. It was the most practical and least expensive option. Uncle Jim and I found the plain white building on the upper north end of Manchester. It was an old nineteenth-century mansion with the characteristic thick gray-granite foundation. It had been tastefully renovated on the inside; delightfully abandoned to mask any semblance of joyful, domestic occupation, but quite suited for a more formal function, namely, the tastefully morbid display of the deceased in a comfortably vacuous setting. Periodic, unexpected, but timely visits from cosmetically-enhanced corpses in ornate coffins were all that gave the stolid structure any life at all.

When we arrived, the building was empty, which was generally a good sign for the potential clientéle. We tried every door. No one was home. We lingered outside like laborers in a bread line, waiting for the Director to arrive. It was by appointment only. I was reminded of the day some years ago when I passed an old cemetery in

Vermont. There had been a sign at the opening in the stonewall that read "Entrance Only."

Our unscheduled wait gave Uncle Jim time to discuss the practical merits of cremation as opposed to a conventional casket.

"Seems like a sensible way to go," he commented. "I can't see spending all that money on an expensive casket if they're just going to put it in the ground and forget about it."

Just then, the Director, a middle-aged, well-dressed gentleman, pulled up in an expensive gray sports car, parked unceremoniously in front of the building, apologized for being late, and unlocked the front door with a small *skeleton* key. I couldn't help wondering how many families had lived in that house. How many meals, I wondered, had been lovingly prepared in the kitchen? How many crying infants and laughing children's voices had reverberated against those brightly papered walls? How many Sunday sunrises had kissed its crisp painted siding? How many days had successive generations of Moms and Dads and their smiling children, and perhaps the grandparents, awoken at the crack of dawn to smell freshly-baked biscuits or smoked bacon and eggs, dressed for Sunday service, and returned home for a family feast and a quiet day of rest and recreation?

But now there was nothing but emptiness. One had to die, and pay to be buried, in order to be granted access. Of course, it was the family that was expected to pay.

We were escorted into a large living room, the old family *parlor* where, ironically, before the existence of the funeral home, such services used to be held and bodies displayed. The *parlor*, as the French word suggests, was the place where family members and friends came to console one another and to sit and talk. A lost art. As the three of us sat together in the ornate, but empty room, it occurred to me that perhaps the reinstitution of the old tradition wasn't so bad after all. The only elements missing the day we visited were the family members and the comforting conversation which customarily took place there. Progress.

Once the papers were explained and signed, we were informed that the cremation process would take about a week. The body had to be taken elsewhere, north to the capital, Concord, to be precise. The procedure and protocol required to transport the body and return the ashes were scrupulously regulated by law.

After the preliminaries were cared for, we had a casual conversation in the very room where Dad's body would have lain had he chosen a conventional service. It is nothing but a strange twist of irony that the only surviving son and an uncle who had become, for all practical purposes, a surrogate father, should share a lively, casual and congenial conversation in such a setting with a total stranger who was to become my father's stand-in escort and executive to conduct him ceremoniously to the grave and beyond. Uncle Jim had seized the occasion to book the next flight, should the occasion arise. He was warmly received and assured of every convenience. *"Here's my card."*

"As a World War II veteran, your Dad has the right to a military contingent at the funeral service. Is that something that you would like?" the Director asked with the utmost of consideration. I was delighted. I hadn't thought of this detail. This would certainly lend a sense of dignity and integrity to the service. It was to be a small service with just immediate family members and close friends present. Dad would have approved. He would have been proud. It was more than appropriate.

"Thank you! Yes, yes, that would be wonderful." I responded, still in a mild state of shock from the previous day's events.

"All you will need to do is send me your Dad's discharge papers and any other pertinent information from the local VFW Chapter here in Manchester. I'll be happy to take care of all the details. Don't worry."

"You are very kind," I answered. *All I could think about at that moment was the ride back to Uncle Jim's house, and a good night's sleep before my flight back home early the next morning.* I was relieved that I wouldn't have to care for any such details. I had already agreed with Dad, at his own request, to officiate at the service when the time came. All I had to do was prepare something appropriate for the brief ceremony at the morgue and thereafter at the gravesite the following week. I would be returning soon enough. But for now, all I could think about was returning home. Dad was already there.

***

Esther and Steve's wedding went beautifully. They had worked together for months to plan the simplest, but prettiest ceremony and reception as possible. Families from southern Illinois, Ohio and New England flew in for the occasion. Jim and Joyce and my Mom flew in from Manchester. They had a wonderful time. Uncle Jim took every opportunity to express his concern about the apparent exorbitant expense, though every effort had been exhausted to cut corners without sacrificing anything that would be critical for the enjoyment of all. The ceremony was simple, but very moving. The reception at the newly renovated barn was festooned with beautiful fresh red roses and white decorative lights. A dear friend who was a professional cake decorator had volunteered to do it all as her gift to the couple. She even threw in a special desert table complete with a chocolate fountain and chocolate-covered strawberries. The music was lively and joyful. My son-in-law, Matt, who is a professional deejay, orchestrated the music and dancing in his own uninhibited, inimical style. Both the father of the bride and Uncle Jim were in the spotlight with Esther, whose breath-taking beauty was accentuated by her laser-like, sapphire-blue eyes. Auntie Joyce brought down the house dancing the jitter-bug with Matt until he was too tired to continue. Joyce is eighty-six. At the end of the day, bride and groom drove off in a sable, spit-shined Hummer splashed with white roses and wide smiles. An unforgettable occasion. It couldn't have come at a better time.

The excitement of marrying our youngest daughter and fourth child brought a sense of joyous closure, and just a tinge of sadness, to that phase of our nearly thirty-four happy years of marriage. The last of our little birds had left the nest. We've been circling the old nest ever since wondering whether we will ever land, and just what we'll do when we get there; tidy up the old nest? Or find a new one? We're no longer giving flying lessons; we now spend our days just keeping the old runway functional and the hangar well stocked for an occasional repair or maintenance check for routine visits from friendly aircraft. From time to time, just to break the monotony, we take a trip ourselves just to get a fresh perspective on a familiar landscape, then it's back to earth and taxi to a safe landing.

Esther's wedding gave me just the happy reprieve that I would need as I prepared to return for my father's funeral the following week. I would need every ounce of strength and stamina for the challenge ahead.

Chapter Nineteen

'Inglorious Miltons'

Robert E. Colman Manchester – Robert E.
Colman, 81, died March 18, 2005, at the Veterans
Affairs Medical Center. He was born in
Manchester on July 20, 1923, to Sumner C. Chase
and Nellie B. (Moy) Colman.

So began the small column in the Manchester Union
Leader. *"Where the Spirit of the Lord is, there is Liberty!"*
was its legendary motto, etched in the top left corner of
nearly every page. This was a curious motto for a
conservative New England paper with a rabid right-wing
Editor-in chief, the infamous William B. Loeb, who lived
in colonial Ipswich and was known to carry a hand gun for
protection from his sworn enemies.

Mom had mailed me the short obituary. The terse,
inconspicuous column was not uncommon, as obituaries
go; except that this tiny, tombstone-shaped splash of ink
had waited eighty-one years to find a final resting place.
This was the only Dad I would never know. The entry's
size and succinct style, also not uncommon, seemed to
render it woefully insufficient. Did anyone realize that my
Dad had been a hero at Guadalcanal? Did anyone know that
he had been decorated twice as a combat hero? Did anyone
remember those years as a police officer, during which time
he had nearly lost his life twice. Could anyone remember
the hard work and heroic feats expended to make a

comfortable home for his new bride and only son in the Dunbarton wilderness? Was anyone aware of the long, tedious grind at Granite State Optical, the tortuous heat of the knitting machine mill, and the General Electric plant in Hookset? What about those years as a volunteer at the Veterans Hospital (that's what it used to be called), and in more recent years, Dad's genial stint as everyone's beloved greeter at a Cain & Janosz Funeral Home, the same home that would now be in charge of his *own* burial arrangements? It would be his home-coming, but no one from the family would be at the door to welcome him this time. And what about the little wooden shoe-shine kit he had made as a student at Central High School, the kit with the shoe-shaped foot on the top and the deep, narrow, dark-stained box for brushes and small circular cans of polish? Or the little table Dad made...?

I don't suppose there's enough room in the local paper to include a man's personal history. But certainly that's all recorded in another book, somewhere? Or maybe there is a transparent record of every sound and every sigh, or every fear and joy, of every failure and disappointment, trapped somewhere in the semi-clear, semi-clouded thickness at the bottom of that old bedroom window-pane, warmed by the heat of each day's sun, waiting to be freed from anonymity, yearning to be released and returned home. Just maybe.

***

When I returned for Dad's funeral the next weekend, I packed a small suitcase, one pair of dress shoes, and the one dark suit which had somehow shrunk over the past ten years. It still looked good enough, and still reflected an air of old-school professionalism, but somehow the jacket now preferred to remain unbuttoned, just for comfort; and the pants no longer insisted upon the necessity of a belt, though a good belt is just what was now required to protect the entire waist assembly from walking off the job for good!

The short flight was pleasant enough. As we approached the Manchester airport, I couldn't help but think of a conversation I had had with a very kind gentleman on the same flight several months earlier when my father had first been diagnosed with cancer. The gentleman's name, if I recall, was Mr. Steven Bachelor. This was a curious incident, indeed, since I recall having encountered, quite ironically, during many weeks of research on the Colman family history, the name of a certain Rev. Stephen Bachelor, the infamous, but relatively unknown "Unforgiven Puritan" of Hampton, New Hampshire. The Rev. Bachelor and Thomas Colman, both of whom had been among the early settlers of Newberry, Massachusetts, had traveled together to the northern-most territories of the colonies, settling in *Winnacunnet*, which would later be called Hampton. The Rev. Bachelor had been the willing victim of a series of unfortunate, miscreant misunderstandings with the Anglican Church of England, and had been compelled to seek greener pastures in the New World. He was later denounced while pastor of the historic Church of Hampton, begrudgingly confessing to having coveted a neighbor's wife, whom he had observed (not too unlike David's promiscuous observation of Bathsheba), and admired as 'chaste,' and who had nearly become the victim of his unholy intentions. But the object of his secret affections had become aware of his sinister, surreptitious desires, and had reported him to the elders of the congregation. At first, as the story goes, the good Rev. Bachelor refused to confess to his nefarious intent, but later, according to the official record, was unable to contain the poisonous truth, and forthwith, "during the Lord's

269

Table," confessed the truth of his willingness to commit the grievous misdeed, according to the record, "had the woman consented."

I shared few, if any, of these shameful details with Mr. Bachelor during our conversation. After all, how could I be certain that the infamous clergyman of Hampton was not the patriarch of Mr. Bachelor's own family, and thus the contemptible progenitor of his own history? Had it been true, and this gentleman another Oedipus fleeing his home in Corinth, en route to Thebes to evade the horrible prophecy that would eventually be his unspeakable undoing, I would certainly not want to be the unfortunate messenger blamed for bearing, or in any way accompanying the bad news. "Out of sight, out of mind."

***

Family tensions had subsided considerably since my last visit. Uncle Jim was a little more sedate. He understood that this brief trip would be consumed with the details of the funeral. I stayed with Jim and Joyce as usual. They extended me every kindness and consideration. Uncle Jim did ask just once, however, why I needed to spend so much time with my Dad's side of the family. Wasn't it enough that I had come all the way out to New Hampshire to do the funeral? Was I expected to spend every waking moment with the family too?

"I'm going to see Mum first thing in the morning, Jim, and then I have to stop in to see Uncle Arthur. He and Aunt Mary are making all the arrangements for the cars and flowers. They've printed instructions for everyone, and directions to the cemetery. I have to check with them about the ceremony. I need to know if they have any special instructions or requests; anything else they may expect me to do, in addition to the service itself."

"Do you have your message ready? Do you know what you're going to say? " asked Jim. Uncle Jim always seemed to be as concerned about the content of my message as I was. He always wanted to be sure that I would do well. This is curious, indeed, since he had rarely ever heard me preach, and he was not one to attend church on a regular basis. But he had heard me preach a few times over the years, and was always ready to offer a few honest, wholesome, generally constructive words of criticism.

On those rare occasions when Jim did attend a service, usually during one of our year-long 'furloughs' from service in Africa, I was not uncomfortable (though rarely eager) asking whether he had approved of the message, though it was just as rarely necessary to ask. He was always the first to offer kind, but clear-cut criticism.

"Could have been a bit shorter, and a bit more to the point. Seemed like you took a few detours. I wasn't able to follow all of it. Seems like you could have gotten there and back again sooner. Otherwise, it wasn't too bad. I don't mean to find fault…"

"Thanks, Jim. I do appreciate your advice. I'll work on it."

Though I never told him in so many words, what Uncle Jim thought about my preaching mattered more to me than he will ever know. Certainly, I was concerned to be faithful to the truth, as I understood it. But I also wanted to be faithful to Jim, to make him proud. He was like a father to me. I didn't want to lose him or his good opinion; or to give him any reason to be disappointed. Losing one father was hard enough.

"You might want to keep it just a bit abridged this time around. You understand. People will be grieving. They are pretty washed out. Just try to offer some words of comfort; well, say whatever else you think is important. I'm sure that you'll do a good job. You always do. Call us when it's over. We'll decide what to do with the rest of the day then, until you have to return." Jim was never short on advice.

"Thanks, Uncle Jim. I'm ready. Thanks for the good advice. I knew that he was concerned that I do well. He also understood that officiating at my own father's funeral would be difficult. *I couldn't help but wonder how I had managed during all those years of ministry, of countless funerals and weddings...without Uncle Jim's sound advice.* But he was right. He wanted to be sure that I had the strength to do this one. This one would be different, to be sure. This was my father.

It would be a simple ceremony. Essentially the same kind of ceremony, in the same small mausoleum, in a remote corner of the Pine Grove Cemetery, not far from where we had buried Dad's wife, Dottie Samara Colman, just five months earlier. I could still see Dad sitting there in the wheelchair in the front row with the big Cheshire cat smile and the tear-filled eyes. Uncle Louie and Aunt Bobbi were standing by Dad's side; all his brothers were sitting in the front row, on the hard make-shift bench. Uncle Frank was his same old stoic self, barely a change of expression, though his eyes were flooded with emotion and his silence deafening. Even Uncle Bill had managed to quiet down and keep his knees covered; though he had been boisterous at the door, the final moment of reality and reckoning had silenced him as if death had gripped him by the throat. Uncle Artie was crying freely, but trying to maintain some semblance of dignity. And poor Uncle Richie, without teeth and dressed in tight-fitting slacks, tennis shoes, and a second-hand jacket about three sizes too short, sat in utter silence and composure, like an angel. But he had been shell-shocked; what could anyone expect?

While we waited for the rest of the family, I stood statuesque by the small table. Minutes later, the funeral director appeared with Dad's incinerated remains in a small white cardboard box. The Director unceremoniously walked to the front of the mausoleum and placed the tiny box with Dad's ashes on the foot-square table. Dad had forfeited his front-row seat, but he would be the center of attention, one last time, on this cold New England winter morning.

As I took my place behind the table, the family went silent. There I was with Bible and hymnbook in hand, ready to pay tribute to my hero. As I stood silently and reverently, I could see and hear the sound of the wintry New England winds swirling outside, struggling to get in and envelop the small assembly in their cold arms. Instead, they moved on and circled, as if celebrating their immortality, the cold gray grave-markers frozen solid in the lifeless, frigid landscape. Dad was ready to join them and take his place next to his wife of forty-four years. The young woman referred to earlier as Dad and Dottie's 'adopted' daughter, stood speechless and solemn next to Dad on the other side, her big brown eyes filling with tears.

***

"Peter, do you think I will be able to attend the funeral service at Pine Grove?" Mom asked shortly after Dad's death. I had to think carefully about my response. I didn't want to offend my mother. She was eighty years old. She had only been married to Dad for eight years; and that had been fifty years ago! What should I tell her? Right or

273

wrong, something deep down inside me didn't want to deprive her of being present at the burial and final earthly 'remembrance' of the only happiness, the only husband she would ever know in this life. Who could possibly object to such a request? Why should she be deprived of one last moment with Dad? Hadn't fifty years of loneliness, pain and penury been sufficient payment for whatever mistakes had been made; whatever sins committed? How could I refuse to be sympathetic at such a time as this?

"I don't see why not, Mum," I had responded. "I don't see why it should be a problem. *I felt certain that Dad wouldn't have objected in his present condition...*

She seemed consoled, but an uneasy feeling lingered in my soul. She had had virtually no contact with Dad's side of the family all those years. It was obvious that my uncles harbored a certain resentment for my mother. It was also obvious to me that I would never understand all the reasons why. They had simply avoided my mother since the divorce. Had she done something so unspeakably wrong as to merit their disdain? Or, had they just accepted without question whatever version of the story my Dad had related to them over the years? I will never know. Perhaps that is best.

I stayed with Mom in her small apartment one evening during the weekend of Dad's funeral, but on the very night before that difficult day, I slept at Uncle Jim's and Aunt Joyce's house. My mother had suggested that I stay there with them. There was a bit more space. It would be more restful. Mom was always thinking of me; always doing whatever would be in my best interest, usually at her own emotional expense. These had been fifty long, lonely years for her. But it was early that evening that the unexpected happened. We were in the living room watching television when the phone rang. Aunt Joyce answered.

"Hello? Yes, Peter is here."

"It's for you, Peter. It's Frank Colman. It's your Uncle Frank."

Why would Uncle Frank call me here? And why would he call me tonight, at this hour? My heart skipped a beat. I was in a slight state of emotional paralysis. I had spent most of the day praying and collecting my thoughts in preparation for the service the next morning at the Pine Grove Cemetery morgue. Uncle Frank was the second oldest of five brothers, the next in line behind my Dad. He had never called me in his life. It could be anything but a coincidence.

"Peter, this is your uncle Frank."

There was little emotion in his voice. It was his nature not to mince words; to cut to the chase.

"Hello, Uncle Frank. Are you alright? Is everything OK?"

"Sure, everything is fine. But, Peter...well. I'm just calling to tell you something. We heard that you had invited your mother to the funeral tomorrow..."

There was an awkward pause on both sides of the line. I had no idea that anyone even knew that Mom had been mentioned in my conversation with Dad, though I wasn't entirely surprised that he had shared our conversation with Frank, who was the second son and perhaps the closest when it came to family matters. I

275

remember having promised my mother that I would tell Dad that she was thinking of him and praying for him, but only if the moment were right, knowing full well that there would never be such a moment. It was while I was on the phone with Frank that I remembered having created such a moment.

"Dad, Mom wanted me to tell you that she is thinking of you and praying for you."

I wanted to believe that it would mean something to Dad; that somehow he could allow a moment of forgiveness and forget the past. But, as always, his reaction was polite, but indifferent. I dared not say much else. Had my mother been present, Dad would have felt extremely uncomfortable. There was no reason to invite her presence now by forcing a conversation, let alone mentioning her request to visit Dad in the hospital. I had already made it clear to Mom that a visit would be inappropriate under the circumstances. But when I did mention Mom, and conveyed her greetings to Dad, his response was classic Bob Colman.

"The past is the past. We all make mistakes, Peter. What's done is done. It's all under the blood." *Problem is, some of us have to go on living,* I thought.

I don't recall that he ever asked me to return the greeting. It had been sixty years, almost to the day. The young woman he had knelt with in the apartment that day back in 1946, his young bride-to-be; the young woman whom he would lead in a 'sinner's prayer,' as an unspoken requisite to marriage; the same woman who dispensed with lipstick to earn his kisses; the woman who had given birth to his only child…and there would be no parting word.

That was the way Dad wanted it; and that was the way it would be. Forever. End of story

"We heard that she might come to the ceremony," Uncle Frank continued. "Well, we (the four brothers) have discussed this; we don't think this would be good. We don't think that Bob would have approved. We don't want your mother to be present. Tell her, Peter, that the family is not in agreement with this. We don't feel that she should come. It will just make people uncomfortable."

I remember having a silent gut reaction to this request to exclude my mother from the public ceremony. *What about Mom? Did anyone ever give a second thought about how she felt having been handed divorce papers and having had to live the better part of her life penniless and without companionship? Did anyone ever consider her feelings? Having been deprived of a husband in life, would she now be deprived of his memory in death?* These were my thoughts, though in all honesty, Mom's presence, given the circumstances and the prevailing bitterness toward her, could have been nothing but awkward for her and for me.

Suddenly, I was that young boy again, sitting in my father's car, trying desperately to figure out which of my parents to believe. Whom should I believe or trust? To whom do I owe trust, loyalty or love? I was being pulled in two directions further away from the parents whom I loved. Even in death, I had to be the arbiter in their relationship; the one who had to mediate. I could not afford to fail to act unlovingly and insensitively toward my own mother. But something inside me told me that I had to respect my father's and his family's wishes as well. I wanted to rebel and take a stand in my mother's favor. Let the family deal with it. Can anyone deny her this final wish? I was between a rock and a hard place. But seconds later, the answer came. I would explain the situation to Mom. She would understand. I would be spared the pain and the potential confrontation and embarrassment.

"Mom, this is Peter. How are you? *She suspected that something was amiss by the quiet, nervous tone of my voice.* "Mom, I'm so sorry, but I've given it some thought and I don't think that it would be appropriate for you to be at the funeral tomorrow; it might make some of the folks on Dad's side of the family uncomfortable..." *I couldn't bring myself to tell Mom about Uncle Frank's phone call, or the fact that my uncles had most likely discussed the issue with my Dad in his last hours.*

"Peter, I was so looking forward to coming. Your Dad and I *were* married, you know. We *did* have eight happy years together..." Our marriage *did* produce a fine son."

"I know, Mum. I know that this is difficult for you. I 'm sorry, but I think it would be best if I went alone. Please, Mum, try to understand." *Here I was again, appealing to my mother, at her own emotional expense, and in my father's behalf. What it was that kept me from asserting myself in Mom's favor at that moment, I do not know. Perhaps the absence of a father early on in life had deprived me of sufficient courage? Perhaps I was just trying to do the right thing by everyone, or perhaps I was just a coward?*

"I will take you to the gravesite after the funeral. We will have a few moments there, together; a few moments to pray together and to remember Dad, our own private ceremony, OK Mum?"

278

"Ok, Peter. I understand. I don't want to create an uncomfortable situation for you. I know that this is going to be hard for you. I don't want to do anything…"

"Thanks Mum. Please pray for me tonight. Pray that I hold up."

"I have been praying for you, Peter, day and night, and for Judy and all the children, too. This must be hard for them with you away from home and having to do all of this alone. I'll stay here and pray. Please call me when the ceremony is done."

"I'll stop by after the funeral and the meal with Dad's family, Mum. We'll go out for dinner, OK?"

"Ok, Peter, but I have plenty of food right here in the fridge…just call me."

"Good night, Mum. I love you. Thank you for understanding. I'll see you tomorrow. I'll drive you to the cemetery later in the afternoon, OK?"

"Good night, Petah." Her voice was on the edge of quiet; she was near the point of tears. I couldn't bring myself to tell her that it had no doubt been my own Dad, the man whom she had never stopped loving. I suspect that it had been Dad's request that she not be present. Did he despise her that much? Was the pain of memory that deep? Was there no place for the kind of forgiveness that he had imposed upon others? Having done so little for either me or my mother in life, could he deprive us of this last request now?

Chapter Twenty

Retrospect

When a cow has no tail, it is God who shoos the flies away.

(Bambara proverb)

Whatever his reasons; whatever the circumstances and buried feelings that compelled him to feel the way he did toward my mother, I could not tell her that it had been Dad's request. I'm not sure that I had even understood myself, at the time. Knowing of that final rejection would have extinguished any last small flicker of love and happiness that may have still existed under the cold, hurtful heap of ashes that had once warmed a troubled young woman's loneliness and emptiness. That fire had long-since expired. If there was still the tiniest flame still burning in her wounded, grieving spirit, the smallest flame of hope that someone still loved her, that someone still cared, then the very least that I could do, that I must do, as her only son, was to protect that fragile flame from going out for good.

The intervening years after Dad's departure had been sadly, painfully silent. Of course, there was the occasional, but always-awkward visit. All I recall is having been happy just to see Dad. Though he always parked a few houses away, I remember running to the car, while mom strained to see from the third-floor window of our apartment. I looked forward to seeing that big smile under

Dad's gray dress hat. But just as soon as I got seated in the car, after a firm grip on my arm or that wide Cheshire-cat smile, there would always be some sort of comment about mom, something that made me feel trapped and uncomfortable. Sour grapes. And then there was the painful memory of the visit with relatives at the quaint, but spacious campgrounds on the hills overlooking the lakes in Brattleboro, Vermont. I loved being with my grandma Nellie, but I was young and was not used to being separated from my mother. So I cried and complained until Dad had been constrained to bring me back home, never to return again. Maybe it's just as hard for a little boy to forget as it is for a hardened Marine to forgive.

As I stood remembering, one of the only bright spots in an otherwise lonely vigil had been the endless drum-sets (which I cannot recall ever having learned to play) and the cowboy suit at Christmas, complete with black gun belt and twin 'pearl-handled' cap-pistols, and 'real' chaps and spurs! Neither Roy Rogers nor Hopalong Cassidy ever looked so good. I didn't have a horse to go with the outfit, but I had my faithful Daisy air-rifle and genuine Davy Crocket coon-skin hat and a life-size bright red fire-truck complete with foot-pedals, a shiny bell and twin wooden ladders attached to the sides. What more could an eight-year boy ever want or need?

These were the kinds of memories I could have wished to have shared with a captive audience during this final moment spent with my father, but time and circumstance prevailed. What I did manage to recount were the most enduring moments of all, moments that would come nearly fifty years later as I sat with Dad in the solitude of his hospital room as we shared a half of a ham and cheese sandwich (on white bread) and a small plastic cup of pre-packaged green pistachio pudding.

Dad's Post was VFW 8401. The flat magnetic badge on his brown veterans' cap read "Robert Colman, Advocate, Post 8401, Bedford, New Hampshire – Veterans of Foreign Wars." He also wore a bright red "U.S. Marines cap with a gold W.W. 2 insignia, and his paratrooper wings dead-center above the visor. I was never called up in my college days, during the Viet Nam conflict, but I had often thought of serving as a medic or a chaplain. After Dad's death, I wore his red cap for several weeks in honor of his bravery and memory. I also wore his gold-plated wrist watch with the flexible band, and Dad's wedding band on the opposite hand as my own. If I couldn't have a father during those forty-four years, at least I would wear his ring. I have since taken it off. The watch stopped running about a month after the funeral. These, and a few pictures are all I have left of my hero.

***

When the morning of the last day finally arrived, I awoke just after dawn, made up the couch, took a shower and shaved, and sat at the breakfast nook in the warmth of the overhead mosaic lamp.

Where had time gone? How many revolutions of the earth had passed? How many cold New England winters had left their frigid signature on the granite landscape? How many times had those tall pines on the back hill cracked and groaned in the wind? There I sat, alone, in the same blue-board breakfast nook that had not changed in fifty years. How had this little cottage stayed in that same quiet spot without spinning off into space, or collapsing under the weight of high winds and world calamities? But there it sat, without complaint or comment. And there I sat, as well, as if I had been welded to the same spot for fifty years, holding my breath, contemplating the passage of time, preparing for the next moment.

In those quiet moments before Jim and Joyce awoke, I perused the Bible passages which I intended to read to the family, and reviewed my personal notes and comments.

I also carried the copy of an aged red Christian hymnal which contained my father's favorite songs, many of which he had sung in song services years before while his tiny son stood in the back pew waving his little arms. In fact, this was the same hymnal that I had used at Dottie Samara Colman's funeral. And I prayed one last time.

"Lord, give me strength today. Help me to be strong. Please give me just the right words to say. Help me say what is honorable to Dad's memory. Help me to be sensitive to the family, to give comfort. Please, let Your light and love shine through me. Make me a blessing, *and help me not to choke...*"

When Uncle Jim and Auntie Joyce finally awoke and shuffled in and out of the bathroom and toward the kitchen, their comments were kind, but brief.

"Oh, Peter, you're up already? So early? We didn't hear you...have you been here all alone? Have you been here long?"

While Auntie Joyce made simple conversation to compensate for the harmless abnormality of seeing someone else occupy the nook at such an extraordinary hour, Jim sauntered in, without his teeth and glasses, still in his briefs, the thin white wisps of hair on his head scrambling to find some kind of order...

"Geeze, Pete, you up already? Didn't know that you were going to get up so early. Do you want some breakfast?" Joyce already had the water boiling for her morning tea, and was preparing small dishes of fresh fruit, cheese, and toast and cold cereal.

"Do you want coffee, Peter?" Aunt Joyce kept fresh ground coffee on hand just for me. She prepared two or three cups in an old tin coffee-maker with thin stem and tin lid with the tiny raised glass with the pinnacle-shaped percolator.

"Sure, Auntie Joyce. Thank you. Please don't go to a lot of trouble."

"Oh, gosh, it's no trouble. I don't make a big breakfast..." Aunt Joyce always said that, and then proceeded to lay out a half-dozen dishes of assorted tidbits: at least three varieties of cheese, mixed fruit (including blueberries, strawberries and sliced bananas), toast, English muffins (of course), several brands of cereal, and two or three kinds of home-made jams (raspberry and marmalade were standard fare). Fresh butter, milk and honey were always present to sweeten the touch. It was just a small breakfast. She didn't have time to prepare much else. A small lunch would fill the dining-room table.

"Thank you, Aunt Joyce."

"Well, do you know what you're going to say today? Is everything prepared?

"Yes, Jim. I've been preparing and praying for days. A greater preacher than I by the name of Dwight L. Moody, I believe, once said: 'If you want me to speak for two hours, I'll get up right now. If you want me to speak for five minutes, give me at least a week to prepare.' Any fool can get up and shoot off his mouth. The last thing I want to do, Jim, is to waste precious time spinning lengthy sermons and theological treatises at a time like this. I've been praying and asking God for wisdom to say just the right thing in just the right way. No more, and no less."

"Good. You always seem to know what to say. Just remember that the people there will need to hear words of comfort." Uncle Jim always gave good sound, honest advice. And I always listened, though with just a tinge of skepticism. I was always sensitive to Uncle Jim's criticism, and resented it just a bit, to be completely honest.

"I don't know what I would have done without your advice during all those years in ministry in Africa…" That was always the ace. That was my defense.

"Don't know how you made it," was his simple, but playful reply. The truth is that I cannot conceive having 'made it' as a young boy without the loving, caring, unpretentious and unrelenting stoic affection that Uncle Jim never failed to send my way. Ironically, for a man who never made any overt, pretentious claims about a personal faith in God, he had been very much like God Himself, a father to the fatherless. And I loved him for it. *"Death ends a life, but not a relationship."* (Morrie Schwartz)

After a light breakfast, I traveled alone down Harvey Road toward old Brown Avenue and on to the Pine Grove Cemetery. The cold black cast-iron fence was glazed with clear ice. The ageless landscape was reminiscent of something akin to Poe's House of Usher. The granite pillars at the entrance to the sleepy cemetery stood motionless, expressionless, in the cold silence, like tireless sentinels watching patiently as the living filed nervously by under the shadows of their speechless, auspicious frowns. Here, for more than a century, in this remote garden of withered pines, they had surveyed their weary parishioners passing through the temple doors and move reluctantly through green corridors, each stopping, lingering, and then coming to rest in the cold comfort of their assigned granite pews. From there, each one, in irresistible succession, subdued by their weary toil, closed their tired eyes and listened to the solemn church bell toll the end of a final day of cherished pilgrimage. As I drove quietly through those narrow corridors in the pre-dawn fog, withered stones bowed in macabre homage at the prospect of a fellow mortal and wind-swept warrior who would soon swell their placid ranks.

The small gray marble mausoleum sat quietly, sedately, in the far corner of the grove, like a faithful caretaker reflecting on the passage of years; its face was respectful and serene, smiling rarely, if ever, in the solemn discharge of his duties. The few parking spaces near the entrance to the cemetery were empty. The office was closed, and appeared to be abandoned. Wasn't there work for the living here among the dead? Was there no one standing watch, protecting their restful charge from intrusion? The only sound was an occasional rustle of dry leaves and a maverick wisp of wind that had dared a quick, perilous run across the sacred sanctuary.

Reverently, I parked Uncle Jim's black conversion van in the farthest space from the entrance, uttered another silent prayer for good measure, and approached the glass doors at the mouth of the marble tomb that was the mausoleum. They were locked. Having returned slowly to the van and the still-warm solitude of its beneficent frame, I reread the several passages of Scripture I had planned to use that morning in the service. Just then, I heard the benign breath of tires on sandy pavement as Uncle Frank and Uncle Richie drove up in Frank's old sedan. Uncle

Frank looked so much like Dad that he could have passed for his twin. He pulled up slowly into the closest space near the entrance, cut the engine, pulled the manual brake, and rolled down the window. Uncle Frank's upper torso, in the same manner as my Dad, filled the entire driver's seat, his massive stomach resting firmly on the lower part of the steering wheel. He strained to turn his head, as if it were tied by some invisible cord to the opposite door, and peered through the open window with big brown eyes and that same shameless, but curiously sedate grin.

"Good maw'nin," he intoned. "You got here urly enough, Petah, I guess. Nobody here yet, I s'pose. Didn't they unlock the dowahs? Well, I guess we'yah here, right? I'll go look for the cayah-takah. Be right back."

In the meantime, Uncle Richie, who had been sitting in the back seat, staring and listening to our brief conversation with a glazed, distant look, suddenly exited from the back seat with a start as if he had been raised from his seaman's bunk with the blast of ship's reveille. He stood near the car and snapped to attention, greeting me with that same broad, toothless Colman smile. His form was almost comedic, but betrayed a depth of thought and emotion that was simply incapable of sane expression. He wore a tight threadbare jacket, open too wide in the front and pulled back under the arms. The sleeves were too short, revealing a stained long-sleeved shirt without buttons. He wore a faded, wrinkled, second-hand tie; the makeshift knot stood out in twisted elegance like a farm boy in an over-sized, borrowed suit, standing awkwardly at the edge of the dance floor. His pants were ill-fitting and short, and seemed to have disowned his colored socks and worn tennis shoes. But he possessed the smile and composure of a recluse genius about to receive the Nobel Peace Prize.

288

"Hi Petah,"

That was all he cared to say that morning. He knew. He understood. Behind the years of tortured memories, pain and penury, lay buried the youthful energy and simplicity of a beautiful man whose youth and intelligence had taken a cruel blow. But he was there. He stood proud. Behind the sad façade was a proud and grateful man whose soul was only visible to the closed and compassionate eye.

Uncle Frank seemed surprised, but delighted that I had been the first to arrive. The sobriety in both his and Uncle Richie's faces seemed to be tempered with a tinge of relief. It had been a long ordeal. The family was tired and anxious for some sense of closure, but even closure could not relieve the pain and uneasiness embedded in their stoic New England brows. They were eager to get the day behind them. The longer we stood there together in the cold of the dark gray morning, the more obvious it became that the cemetery's eerie silence and sterile demeanor was not one which either of them were eager to embrace. Quiet, unseen voices seemed to beckon them to join their company; silent stares seemed to permeate the air's stillness. Their day would come soon enough. Today they were just spectators. They wouldn't dance today. They had come to pay their feeble, but heart-felt respects, to lend their humble support, to give their final salute to a fallen comrade and friend. Protocol would have to take a back seat. Nothing could dissuade or deter a Colman from anything he or she had determined to do. Even death itself would have to wait in the wings until the ceremony was over and the Colman brothers had had their say in memory of their beloved brother. This was family time, and it was sacred. Death would have to wait out in the cold until the ceremony was over. Even then, he would need permission before he could interrupt again.

One by one, a few more cars arrived: the two other brothers, Bill and Artie and their wives, aunts and cousins (including my long-lost cousin, Marion, or Marylou, as I had always known her as a child back in Pinardville). I hadn't seen Marylou since we had played together in their old house by the Merrimack River. We had been eight years old. It had been fifty years earlier. Somehow, she looked older than I had remembered...She wasn't the smiling, lovable, endearing, huggable eight-year-old I had expected. How had she allowed herself to age so? How in the world had her brown curly hair gotten so gray? Was I the only child who hadn't changed? Must I now be father to my cousin too? We hugged and embraced as if we had been with each other just a week before. It was a brief, but sweet reunion. Time is kind, but unapologetic.

By now, the caretaker had arrived from somewhere in the mute solitude of the granite hive of maintenance and administrative structures clustered on the small mound in the center of the cemetery grounds. As he approached the glass entrance, I could see the faceless, tireless church beadle in Hawthorne's *Scarlet Letter* trudging toward Hester Prynne's ignominious dungeon door, quite oblivious to the wild rosebush beneath his feet, his sole duty: to escort his angelic, enigmatic charge toward a shameless gallows.

The caretaker unceremoniously, but routinely greeted his guests, and unlocked the glass doors of the mausoleum, exposing a vacuous hall and high marble walls. He moved slowly, but purposefully in the direction of the bare front sanctuary wall, unlocked a small utility closet hidden in the texture of the vertical marble slabs, and proceeded to remove the same small wooden table that we had used in precisely the same spot four months earlier. He covered the table with the same plain white cloth. No frills.

When he had completed his tasks and quietly disappeared once again into the cold sanctuary of the cemetery landscape, I took it upon myself to commandeer a finely finished rectangular maple table that had been inconspicuously standing watch in one of the adjacent hallways. I placed the table in the middle of the empty enclave and carefully placed a few of Dad's Marine photos and his old black Bible on the now-sacred altar. The table, for its part, could not have imagined that it would ever had played such a prominent role in Dad's funeral on that cold March morning. There was no visible protest, in any case.

By now, twenty or thirty members of the family entourage had filtered respectfully into the mouth of the sacred cave. The funeral director had also arrived in the intervening moments just before the scheduled start of service, carrying a tiny white cardboard casket. He looked like a confident beau delivering a corsage to his beloved date. But the flower in the little white box was the ashen remains of the only earthly father I would never really know, but the father whom I, somehow, had come to deeply love. How could such a man be reduced to this?

Thou turnest man to destruction; and sayest, 'Return, ye children of men...Thou carriest them away as with a flood; they are as a sleep: in the morning they are like grass which growth up. In the morning it flourisheth, and growth up; in the evening it is cut down, and withereth...The days of our years are threescore years and ten; and if by reason of strength they be fourscore years, yet is their strength labour and sorrow; for it is soon cut off, and we fly away.

(Psalm 90:3-10)

291

The words seemed etched in gold on the plain, faceless box sitting weightlessly on the table. Then, just minutes before the simple ceremony was to commence, there was a gentle disturbance outside. Someone opened the glass doors momentarily, and a sudden gust of winter wind managed to slip through. Silently, it swirled and circled among the somber guests, its sweet lament echoing off the stone chapel walls. Before it could finish its mesmerizing song, as if in a dream, two young marines in full uniform, bright blue and red with smart white caps, appeared at the chapel door. To my utter delight, the funeral director had honored a son's last request and pulled gently on bureaucratic strings to arrange a color-guard. I was relieved. Elated. Dad would finally receive the respect and the meager measure of recognition that he had long deserved.

But there was a momentary problem, a moment of confusion. Just as quickly as they had arrived, they left again. Heads turned. Someone ran for the trusty caretaker again, arousing him from ceremonious slumber. The two young marine recruits had somehow locked their bugle in their vehicle, along with the keys! Seconds later, the caretaker came to the rescue. With some sort of improvised device, he managed to rescue the two battle-hardened warriors from the jaws of defeat, delivering both them and their vehicle from certain shame.

In the meantime, once the more-seasoned of our company had been seated on whatever benches and folding chairs we had been able to requisition, I stepped behind the tiny table, behind my Dad's box of ashes, and waited in silence for the restless, but respectful parishioners to quiet.

Time stood still. Decades of Christian ministry and public speaking, in any of three or more languages, and I was speechless.

Chapter Twenty-One

A Time to Weep

To every thing there is a season, and a time to every purpose under heaven: A time to be born, and a time to die...A time to weep, and a time to laugh; and a time to mourn...

(Ecclesiastes 3:1-4)

There I stood behind the small white box containing Dad's meager ashen remains, the humble remnant of one solitary life. My beloved, though to some extent estranged, New England family stood in solemn, strained sobriety in the cold, silent bowels of the miniature enclave that was the Pine Grove Cemetery Mausoleum.

***

"Dear family and friends, we are gathered here today to honor the life and memory of our beloved father, brother and friend, Robert Everett Colman. Most of you have known my Dad longer than I myself, and can share many memories, but as his son, I am here today to share the little I know, some of which you may have never heard before..."

As I stood silently before the small assembly, the details of those distant years came freshly to the surface. I was a boy again. I found myself once again at the foot of that legendary tree, watching the dramatic ascent of my strong hero rescuing the kitten stranded in the treetop adjacent to the second-story window in the old Dunbarton homestead. I relived my close encounter with the black-widow spider and his crushing defeat in the tall fruit-jar, and of the miraculous deliverance of the marauding skunk from the pernicious grip of a mayonnaise jar. I recalled Dad's construction of the chicken-coop, and fast-forwarded to those midnight trips to the old barn to watch the foraging herds of deer. In my mind, Dad was rolling me up in my 'Indian blanket' to protect me from the cold, empty upstairs bedroom, as the north winds whistling relentlessly against the frozen, slanted pane of my bedroom window. And then, among the final frames in the short reel that was my childhood, I was standing with Mom and Dad in the bright gray chapel at Camp Hebron, watching a five-year-old son glance upward for his parents' approval before going to an old-fashioned altar, the first steps in his journey toward Christ. And then, in no time at all, Dad and I were painting the living-room wall of our 'new' apartment on Manchester street bright red, right over the existing wallpaper! And then, just as quickly, Dad was gone from my young life; he had turned and walked away, without even saying goodbye. Just that quickly, he was gone, almost forever.

As I stood there that day behind the small table, I told Dad's story as I had understood it, and those events that I knew to be most important to him. It began on that day long ago when a young Marine on the island of Choiseul (Fr. 'only choice'), under the cross-fire of Japanese guns, dad surrendered his heart to God. Then there was the unforgettable race for cover on the island's sandy shore when Dad, who hadn't had the time to tie one of his boots, had broken his foot while on the run, and had been evacuated back to Camp Pendleton, thus surviving further combat and possible death at Iwo Jima. There were other, less heroic circumstances that did not bear repeating, and which I would only come to know after Dad's burial.

Some things are better left to the past, forgotten and buried forever. Some things are better left for God's attention and consideration alone.

Sharing my childhood memories with Dad came easier. Those were the vivid boyhood memories of our early 'frontier' days on the Dunbarton farm: dad's sharp-shooting skills from the shed roof, and the skunk's fortuitous escape from a menacing mayonnaise jar; the image of a rugged hunts-man returning from the wilderness, smiling and dragging, a 250-pound, ten-point buck over the stonewall across from the kitchen window. Then I described the image of Mom and Dad standing side-by-side in the old gray wooden chapel (with long, lean gray pews) at Camp Hebron Bible Camp, nodding approvingly as their tiny five-year-old son stepped from the pew and walked the 'sawdust trail' to an altar of prayer. In fact, this one frame was what was to become the only surviving memory of a child's mother and father actually being together, happily, in one place. Then there was the indelible episode of tiny 'Jack' watching admirably as his invincible father stormed the aged, withered beanstalk in search of a frightened baby kitten. *It had never occurred to me before that the same little creature may have also been looking longingly and hopefully from its fragile look-out's nest in the top of that old tree at the frightened gaze of a tiny boy far below; another little creature standing helplessly at the base of that tree, watching and waiting desperately while his giant of a dad climbed perilously, precariously closer to its tremulous perch, only, after his father's heroic intervention, to be rescued and returned to the comfort and security of a little lad's grateful hands.*

Did anyone ever think to interview that little kitten? Is there a tiny, unwritten record of that little creature's harrowing rescue from the frightful heights (or depths) of virtual anonymity? Just a thought.

But the eulogy had to be curtailed, if only for one eternal moment in a vast, immeasurable sea of silence. I stood transfixed, as memories flooded the hidden recesses of my mind. Time stood still. The tiny, stone-faced gathering was motionless, like a weathered stand of withering oaks in a cold, lonely wasteland.

Stony silence, but for the whispering winds that encircled the gray building in their cold embrace. Slowly, I found the words. I called the family to attention and thanked them for coming to be with their beloved brother and friend one last time. He had taken his final journey home, and they had come that day to wish him a safe and pain-free passage.

Yea, Though I walk through the valley of the shadow of death, I will fear no evil: for thou art with me; thy rod and thy staff they comfort me. Thou preparest a table before me in the presence of mine enemies: thou anointest my head with oil; my cup runneth over. Surely goodness and mercy shall follow me all the days of my life: and I will dwell in the house of the Lord for ever.

The small delegation stood serenely, but statuesque. Waiting. Wondering. What would an estranged New England son say in the small, somber, singular moment which Providence had bequeathed in the eternal passage of time? There he stood, an only son, poised to eulogize the only earthly father he would ever, or never, know, addressing a familiar but frail body of souls, refugees in time, the meager microcosm of human beings who were the remnant of the Colman clan. There they stood, in expressionless silence, weakened warriors of a rugged past. They stood statuesque, in utter respect, like living stones, like moving marble head-stones, their faces engraved with the pains and paltry promises of a tranquil, yet tortuous past, fragile reflections of their sleeping granite ancestors, like sober spectators, standing quietly in the sacred cemetery precinct encircling the morgue.

Another young woman and her husband stood near the spot where my Dad had sat during the ceremony for his wife four months earlier. The funeral director stood respectfully near the front entrance, so as not to interfere with the short service. He had arranged every detail single-handedly, and would be paid a modest fee for his services, but the short family service was one portion of the proceedings from which he politely declined participation. The two young Marines stood in sharp attention to the far side, awaiting the exact moment for their practiced intervention. I was still bursting with muted pride at the very thought of a Marine color guard. Their sudden, unexpected appearance just before the service wasn't quite what one would call a tempest in a teacup, but their presence lent dignity and character to an otherwise somber and lack-luster ceremony.

After a short, spontaneous opening prayer, I shared some of Dad's and my favorite verses, all from the King James translation of the Bible which he loved and read daily:

Lord, thou hast been our dwelling place in all generations...He that dwelleth in the secret place of the Most High shall abide under the shadow of the Almighty...

(Psalm 90)

For God so loved the world, that he gave his only begotten Son, that whosoever believeth in Him should not perish, but have everlasting life.

(John 3:16)

And we know that all things work together for good to them that love God, to them who are the called according to his purpose.

(Romans 8:28)

For to me to live is Christ, and to die is gain...I can do all things through Christ, which strengthens me.

(Philippians 1:21; 4:13)

Therefore if any man be in Christ, he is a new creature: old things are passed away; behold, all things are become new.

(2 Corinthians 5:17)

For I am not ashamed of the gospel of Christ: for it is the power of God unto salvation to everyone that believeth; to the Jew first, and also to the Greek.

(Romans 1:16)

These were among the small selection of verses which I shared with the family, verses Dad had cherished and shared with others during his lifetime. How a man with such a passion for God, and an equally unquenchable intolerance for any form of ungodliness in others, could justify a life of virtual separation from his only son is a mystery. But his own tortured journey, and whatever hardship he may have inadvertently caused me along the way, does little or nothing to discredit the truth of the faith in God, which we had come to share as father and son.

300

I had spent the previous days perusing a number of Dad's favorite hymns from an old Alliance hymnal, the same kind of hymnal he would have used during his early years as Sunday School Superintendent at the Christian and Missionary Alliance Church at the corner of Merrimack and Hall streets in my native city of Manchester. The first hymn I shared with the tiny assembly had also become my own favorite in recent years:

Great is Thy faithfulness, O God my Father, there is no shadow of turning with Thee; Thou changest not, Thy compassions they fail not; as Thou hast been Thou forever wilt be...Pardon for sin and a peace that endureth, Thy own dear presence to cheer and to guide, strength for today and bright hope for tomorrow—blessings all mine, with ten thousand beside!

I had chosen several others, with titles like "*I Will Sing the Wondrous Story*," "*T'was a Glad Day when Jesus Found Me*," "*It Is Well with My Soul*," and others, but, the time being short, I settled on another old favorite: "And Can It Be That I Should Gain," a lesser-known hymn written by 18th-century English evangelist Charles Wesley (1707-1788). No other hymn expresses in simple profundity the unlikelihood of an uncelebrated father and son sharing a time-tested faith. As our family stood in stunned silence, I quietly read three of the five verses of that timeless hymn:

And can it be that I should gain an interest in the Savior's blood? Died he for me, who caused His pain, for me, who Him to death pursued? Amazing love! How can it be that Thou, my God, shouldst die for me? He left His Father's throne above, so free, so infinite His grace: emptied Himself of all but love, and bled for Adam's helpless race. 'Tis mercy all, immense and free! For, O my God, it found out me. No condemnation now I dread; Jesus, and all in Him, is mine! Alive in Him, my living Head, and clothed in righteousness divine, Bold I approach th'eternal throne, and claim the crown though Christ, my own.

There was one final song that had come to mind, a song that cannot be found in the conventional hymnbook. That particular song, a song, which both of my parents had known and loved, I had recalled from memory, and had chosen to sing. So standing alone in that morbid, but hope-filled granite mortuary, I attempted the verses I knew, praying that my emotions would not crumble, or my fragile tear-ducts rupture:

"I traveled down a lonesome road, and no one seemed to care; the burden on my weary back had bowed me to despair. I of't complained to Jesus how folks were treating me; and then I heard Him say so tenderly: 'My feet were oh so weary upon the Calvr'y road; my cross became so heavy, I fell beneath the load. Be faithful weary pilgrim; the morning I can see. Just take your cross and follow close to me...'" (Anon)

Just before I was to offer a brief homily in Dad's memory, I invited family members or friends who wished, to briefly share memories or comments. Uncle Bill was the first to speak. For just a fleeting second, I panicked. I feared that Uncle Bill, in his inimical, uninhibited way, would try to shatter the solemnity by dropping his false teeth or lifting his pant-legs to flash his skinny white legs and peerless artificial knees. But the man who had sobbed in the corner, unable to watch or to approach the bed while his brother had breathed his last, was all but serious and

302

sober. Bill the comedian had long since exited the building. Dear Uncle Bill, not to be denied the first word, stood white-faced and wide-eyed.

"Bob was a good brother and friend, the best brother a man could have. He was always there to help and give counsel. It was Bob who took care of Mom during her last years. He was a source of strength for us all."

The tribute continued, with utter sincerity and the simplicity of childhood innocence. But then, Uncle Bill came back to planet earth.

"When Bob found out that he had cancer, and tried to get a room at the V.A.; he was told that there was nothing available. Imagine that? Nothing available for a veteran Marine paratrooper and decorated war hero who fought at Guadalcanal, and a former Goffstown and Manchester police officer who nearly lost his life protecting the population? There was no way I was going to accept that! So I marched right up to the V.A Hospital and told them doctors in no uncertain terms what kind of a man Bob Colman was. The next day they called Bob to tell him that there was a room available on the first floor right near the front desk. There was no way in hell that I was going to see my brother pushed around like that, not as long as Uncle Bill is in the neighborhood..." Bill cut a wide swath. The nurses remember him too.

After Uncle Bill's well-intentioned tribute, Uncle Louie made a few simple remarks, as did Dad's other brothers, Frank and Arthur. Uncle Artie had been the closest to Dad in recent years, and loved him dearly. But a few short phrases into his brief, heart-felt eulogy, Uncle Artie's eyes reddened and swelled with tears, and he fell silent. I'm not certain whether anyone else spoke, though I seem to recall that a young woman, a woman also named Dottie, made a brief remark, something to the effect that "Bob and Dottie were like my own parents. They loved me like their own daughter." Uncle Richie stood with a simple, toothless smile. "Bob was a good man," was all he could manage.

I was aware that any 'message' I intended to deliver should be brief and heartfelt. I was burdened to share an element of deep faith and conviction which had sustained both my father and me throughout the years, but particularly during our final days together. But while I do believe that the experience of grieving for a deceased loved one or friend affords human beings a unique occasion to reflect upon the issues of personal faith in God and the ultimate destiny of one's eternal soul, I have little tolerance for free-lancing opportunists who seize such occasions, and, in a mercenary manner, prey upon people's emotions to coerce them to turn God-ward. Jesus Himself failed to seize such an opportunity to sermonize when visiting the tomb of his diseased friend, Lazarus. John records that "Jesus wept." Representatives from the orthodox Jewish community who were also present did not fail to capture the significance of Jesus' response: "Look how much he loved him," was their comment. Then, rather than eulogize his good friend, or to express profound sentiment or offer a riveting, spell-binding discourse to the gaping crowd, Jesus simply resorted to the extraordinary by raising Lazarus from the dead. (John 11:17-44) A memorable ceremony, indeed.

"Dad was my hero. He was a man of faith, and a man of prayer; a man who led a difficult life. His life was a rocky road with twists and turns, and unforeseeable potholes. But Dad was also a man who kept the faith and

304

finished the race, an allusion to the Apostle Paul's remarks to his young understudy, Timothy:

> *I have fought the good fight, I have finished the race, and I have kept the faith. Now there is in store for me the crown of righteousness which the Lord, the righteous judge, will award to me on that day—and not only to me, but also to all who have longed for his appearing.*
>
> (2 Timothy 4:7)

I then briefly shared the story of Dad's conversion experience while in the Marine Corps, though I am sure that most of those listening had heard it before. What they had not heard, however, was that minor detail about the boot that he had failed to lace, and the broken foot, on that fateful day on the bullet-ridden, blood-soaked shores of Guadalcanal. It was that small detail that Dad had shared with me in the V.A. hospital room during our last days together before his death.

Chapter Twenty-Two

No Shadow of Turning

He (God) is not a man like me that I might answer him...if only there were someone to arbitrate between us, to lay his hand upon us both, someone to remove God's rod from me, so that his terror would frighten me no more.

(Job 9:32-34)

An eulogy is not the time and place to address personal flaws and failures. Judgment belongs to God alone. But the irony of my father's and my relationship is difficult to ignore. The 'Parable of the Lost Son,' recorded only in Luke's gospel (Luke 15: 11-32), is the passionate account of a loving, forgiving father who embraces a rebellious, reprobate son who had malevolently squandered his promised inheritance to satiate his unbridled lusts. Finding himself utterly desolate, and facing starvation, the repentant son returns to his father's waiting arms, and is received and rewarded, without as much as a mention of his sins, much to the consternation of his older brother. There is no mystery as to Jesus' intent in telling this story. The Gentiles, or non-Jewish peoples, had no inherent claim upon the Kingdom of heaven, as strangers to God's holy covenant, and even less expectation as recipients of His favor and acceptance. Their Hebrew colleagues took great pride in their strong religious history and heritage as Yahweh's chosen race. Now the tables were slightly turned, or at least repositioned. The heart of Jesus's message and ministry is that God loves all men, and seeks desperately to restore all peoples to faith and fellowship with Himself. And while God's commitment to Israel is firm and just, He is equally disposed to receiving and forgiving all peoples, irrespective of race or spiritual condition. At least this is my understanding of the parable. And this accounts for the surprising, but understandable reaction of the older brother who couldn't help but resent his father's wholesale acceptance of his unworthy and criminal sibling.

The force of this simple story cannot be ignored. There are few relationships so critical, so spiritually profound, so potentially life-transforming, or troublesome, than that of a mother or father and his or her child. In this case, the uncommon depth of love that the father had for his son, and his rebellious son's ultimate restoration, is echoed in his father's words: "My son was dead, but now is alive; he was lost, but now is found." Was the son lost to the father, or the father to the son? The obvious answer is yes. The blessing, or the curse, is reciprocal. Prodigal sons are more susceptible to blame than are their fathers, particularly in near-eastern cultures. But in such situations, fathers must bear some, if not a major portion of the blame.

My reflections upon this story brought me inevitably back to a conversation with my Dad some years earlier during breakfast at a small diner on Manchester's west side. That was only one of two occasions when my father and I had gone out to eat. On the second occasion, I had invited both my Dad and his wife to dinner to celebrate Dad's birthday. That was the only time in our lives that Dottie had accepted to accompany my father and me anywhere. But on the aforementioned occasion, we had a very illuminating, but brief exchange. In the course of the conversation, I had mentioned that the story of the lost son.

I do not recall how or why the particular story had come to mind. But at that point in the conversation, Dad made the comment that this was his 'favorite story.' I recall having felt a tiny, imperceptible shutter. Was this going to be another one of Dad's sermons? Was I going to become the unwilling victim of another subtle spiritual assault? Was Dad holding a grudge? Was he poised to remind me of my sins, or seize the occasion to assert his own innocent claim to martyrdom, at either my mother's or my expense? I hesitated only for a moment before asking the obvious question:

"Dad, do you think that I have been a prodigal son?"

"No, Peter," he responded calmly. "I have been a prodigal father."

I had never heard, nor would I ever hear again, my father admit to anything of the kind. I had always nourished the suspicion that Dad had been the primary factor in my parents' divorce; I never had any reason to believe otherwise. But for whatever reason, at this particular moment, Dad had chosen to return to me, his waiting son. I was confused, and somewhat consoled. I had no reason not to welcome him back. That was the last time we would go out together, and the last time we would share a meal together, until we shared that last half of a ham and cheese sandwich and small plastic container of pistachio pudding, the day before Dad died. He had no appetite for the sandwich, but had reveled in the few tasty teaspoons of sweet green pudding. They would be his last on earth.

So I briefly summarized the story of the parable of the lost son, as a tribute to my Dad and his love for God. It was his story, and it was mine. In doing so, I believe that I was also honoring his wishes to share with his family the message of redemption and reconciliation that was so very precious to us both.

Cast your bread upon the waters, for after many days you will find it again.

(Ecclesiastes 11:1f.)

Whatever Solomon meant by these enigmatic words, it is clear that the smallest sacrifice of what is essential for one's survival helps to prepare for what is unforeseeable, and can only spell blessing for the participant.

I had cast my bread, my meager portion. I had appealed earnestly with my grieving family to return home; to reach out to a loving father, a father inclined to receive his children, to forgive them, with a loving heart and with open arms. And then I rested my case. I knew that I had walked a thin line. I wanted to be earnest without being offensive. I was exhausted and nearly to the point of tears. All of the events or recent weeks were weighing upon me. All of my conversations with my father, and the agony of those final days, and his death, were fresh in my mind. I offered a personal prayer of thanks for Dad, and comfort for his brothers and the small remnant of the Colman clan present that day. Then I slowly retreated from behind the table, and stood quietly to the side with my back to the cold marble slab wall.

It was then that the Marine contingent, in full uniform with brass buttons, swords, and a modest display of insignias, went into action. One young white Marine had positioned himself discretely near the rear entrance of the mortuary. After a brief moment of silence, he played taps on the bugle, which he had gratefully retrieved from the locked van just a short time earlier. The clear, bold, mesmerizing notes penetrated the cold stillness of the room like a sweet, but blinding burst of sunshine in a darkened cave. I stood motionless. The hair rose slightly on the back of my neck, and I began to tremble, clinging to the cold wall for support. When the purity of the final notes had subsided, the bugler's companion, a young black Marine, in bright blue and red uniform, with white gloves and hat, walked slowly to the front table where Dad's ashes lay quietly, but reverently, in their small white cardboard tomb. With finesse and practiced protocol, this young soldier gently, but assiduously removed the folded American flag from its resting place near Dad's remains. Then, without warning, he turned resolutely toward me, walking with dignity and poise, until he stood just inches away. He dropped to one knee in front of me and recited a few phrases in Dad's honor...something about his distinguished service as a United States Marine. *Dad was climbing that tree again...but this time he would not be coming down ... he was climbing higher...*

Then, to my utter amazement, he stood up, looked straight into my eyes, and handed me the flag, reciting a similar tribute and thanking me for my father's life and service. Little did this young Marine know that now *he* had become a father to *this* man. He then bowed, turned and walked away to join his comrade near the front door.

It seemed for just a moment that I was all alone in the room. I was standing off to the side of a surreal event, holding one of the only priceless remnants that I would ever possess of my earthly father. I was speechless and overwhelmed with emotion. The muscles in my throat were tied in a hard knot, and eyes were big with silent tears of joyous sadness and subdued pride.

311

"Lord, you have been our dwelling place throughout all generations...You turn men back to dust, saying, 'Return to dust, O sons of men...'"

***

After Dad's funeral, my uncle Bill made it quite clear that as Dad's only son, I should be the one to go through Dad's effects and 'take whatever I felt was important.' After all, he was my Dad. That day had been so emotional that I had forgotten to remove Dad's wedding ring and wristwatch. Dad was cremated. When I returned for the ceremony, I discovered that the young woman with whom I had played as a child...the woman who was also known affectionately as Dorothy, or Dottie, the woman who had come to be loved by Dad and Dottie as their own adopted daughter...had remembered to retrieve both Dad's wedding ring and watch. I asked for them. When we met at the morgue for the final service, she very warmly and graciously handed them to me in a small plastic zip-lock bag.

"I have been holding them for you," she said. "I thought you would want them. After all, he's your father." *Is he your father, too? I was tempted to ask. But it was not the moment. Surely, someone would have told me by now, if it were true, I reasoned.*

It never occurred to me at the moment that perhaps she believed that my father was also her Dad, and my step-mother her mother...that she was equally deserving of the token, the souvenir, of their relationship. That perhaps it was her father's ring as well, in which case she was entitled to it as well as I. If there were a hint of truth in that, her relinquishing those items could be conceived to be a very gracious act. But I dismissed the thought, and slipped the small zip-lock bag in my inner vest pocket. Dad would have wanted me to have them.

Later that day, I slid Dad's wedding band on my ring finger, next to my own. It seemed odd, but entirely appropriate at the time. Imagine, a total of seventy-nine years…forty-four years as a father without a son, and thirty-five years as a son without a father. But the ring was all I had to remember a father whom it would have been too easy to forget. It was the only way I could share those years. I slipped on the watch too. It was gold-plated, with a bright face and a flexible band – Dad always wore a flexible band, but it wasn't expensive. It stopped a few days after I returned to Chicago. Too much time had been lost. After about a week, it occurred to me that the ring was too conspicuous. My wife asked my why I was wearing it, although I suspect that she knew; she did not object to my wearing it, though years of neglect by my father had not compelled her to respect him, or even feel sorry for him.

What possible justification could he have had for 'protecting' his son and five grandchildren by ignoring them and keeping a quiet distance from them? There was no possible justification at all. There was no acceptable excuse. Not in her mind.

But keeping and wearing Dad's ring was my only tangible way of remembering, of absorbing the grief, and, perhaps, of even bearing a small token of guilt, supposing, of course, that there had been even the smallest invisible trace of guilt or regret in the otherwise near-perfect circle of gold.

I still keep the large, well-worn gold wedding band hanging on a modest brass hook above my desk, between two old windows, and under an oval framed baby-picture of my Dad. The glass panes serve to filter my grief, allowing the light of each new day to enter, and stale hues of lingering doubt and debilitating darkness to exit. Hanging there silent and unencumbered, like the memories it embodies, it still retains its original shape and value.

The framed photo, too, bears the weight of a living symbol. My late grandmother, Nellie Moy Colman Dwire, gave me the picture some years ago. The old photo could have been taken yesterday. The strong little arms and legs, and high 'Buster-Brown'–like leather shoes…the perfect round face with large brown eyes, generous, but perfect ears…and the hair, well-groomed and gathered to a small handsome peak at the top of his head. He was a miniature Marine, the picture-perfect miniature of the model father-to-be, and almost the photocopy of another strong son whose black-and-white baby photo his mother had given to him twenty-seven years later.

'The child is the father of the man' *The enigmatic lines from Wordsworth.*

Dottie's presence that day at the morgue, for all practical purposes, appeared to be quite ordinary. After all, hadn't she been Dad and Dottie's 'adopted daughter,' as they were fond of saying? Everyone present at Dad's funeral seemed to know and accept that she had been a very intimate part of their lives. She had brought roses for every one that day. Why hadn't I thought of that? It was a nice gesture. But as I looked into her tearful eyes during the ceremony, I couldn't help but wonder what she was thinking. She was happily married to a fine man and good husband, and had been for many years. They had a child of their own. But today, that day, as she stood silently with the surviving members of the Colman clan, like a wild flower among a proud stand of perennials, grieving the loss of a beloved brother and friend, she had the appearance of a young bride, disguised as a wedding coordinator, who had relinquished her entitlement of lifetime of filial bliss to another.

To me.

But this was one sacrifice I was more than willing to accept. I had been the beneficiary of little else. I simply expressed my condolences, as one would to a family member, and proceeded to the business at hand, the burial of my father.

***

Besides the undisclosed quantity of ashes concealed in a tiny white cardboard box on the small wooden table in front of me, they were the only personable *remains* I had of my father ('remains' was one of Ben Franklin's preferred terms for his deceased relatives 'effects'). After the funeral, I returned to Dad's apartment. Dottie and her husband were already there, discretely sorting through Dad's papers and attempting to organize and distribute his effects ('remains' would not have been the appropriate term here). Dad had designated Dottie, out of respect for Dottie Samara Colman, the *executrice* of his meager estate, including a small amount of money that he had saved from Social Security. With their permission and blessing, I proceeded to the back bedroom where I managed to salvage Dad's large black, weathered Bible with the gold-print thumb-dividers, and his wallet, where I found his stamped aluminum *Veterans of Foreign Wars: 'Life Member'* card and his driver's license. There were also two pictures: one of his wife, Dotty Samara Colman, and one of the younger Dottie as well. There was also a folded, faded one-dollar bill in the billfold and a quarter in the change pocket. It's always smart to keep a spare dollar tucked away, and a quarter for

315

a phone call. Or at least it used to be the case. But not any more. Dad would not be needing any money now for his journey.

Chapter Twenty- Three

From Death to New Life

When the service had ended, and the funeral director had discretely retrieved the non-descript white box containing what remained of Dad's DNA, my uncles and the others embraced me and we exchanged words of comfort, as is customary. There were the usual 'beautiful service' comments as we proceeded slowly from the morgue to the waiting caravan of vehicles for the short trip to the gravesite. It was snowing. The twisting, pock-marked pavement was narrow. Had it been during the darkness of night, I would have fully expected the headless horseman of legendary Tarrytown to appear from between the ancient tombstones in the labyrinth of irregular contours of hills and gnarly trees that comprised the cemetery.

The air was gray and cold. The landscape resembled the infamous 'corpse out'leant' in Hardy's *Darkling Thrush*. But that day, the 'coppice gate' was swinging freely on its withered hinges, and the tiny thrush's voice had been stilled by the frozen blanket of winter snow. The small, silent caravan moved slowly through the frozen path of snow and ice like a mechanical march of little black penguins wobbling over polar ice, their eyes thick with blinding snow, but their strong hearts and stalwart forms filled with hidden fire, keeping pace with the length of days and interminable destiny.

There was no gravestone as yet. It had been ordered, but would take at least another week to arrive. There was only a small square hole in the frozen turf where Dottie Samara Colman's ashes had already been laid. Dad and his wife would be buried together. It was only fitting that they should after forty-four years of marriage. But the realization was bitter-sweet. Mom had been denied love and companionship in life, and she would be denied Dad's presence, or at least the symbolism of peaceful proximity, in death as well. Neither had she been allowed to attend the service. Perhaps it was best. What's done is done. It makes no sense to try to unravel the knot, or deny the reality of events that are, for all practical purposes, irreversible. Perhaps irrevocable. But I felt a twinge of sadness as I approached the site where Dad's earthly remains would find their final resting place. Some months later, in the late spring-early summer, I would return to the cemetery with Mom to at least allow her the courtesy and comfort of seeing the gravesite and acknowledging the loss of a husband and the fragile thread of happiness and intimacy that they had once known, and a semblance of serenity and security that had produced an only son, a son who had now become as a father to his own mother.

The ground surrounding the gravesite was cold and damp, as the caravan disgorged its weary passengers. But there was a growing sense of collective comfort and relief as the family gathered around the solemn site. The committal service would be necessarily brief.

"Friends, we gather here to commit to this resting place the body of our beloved father and brother whose spirit is already with the Lord. While this spot on earth will hold the form of one whose memory we shall always treasure, we look not here in sorrow as those who have no hope. We believe that to be absent from the body is to be present with the Lord, and that to die is gain. We therefore commit the remains of Robert Everett Colman's body to the ground in the renewed and fresh hope of the soon coming of Christ, at whose appearing the dead in Christ shall rise and we which are alive and remain, shall be caught up together with them to meet the Lord in the air. And thus shall we ever be with the Lord. Wherefore, we comfort one another with these words."

With the aid of the same tiny black Pastor's Manual, I read a few short verses from Scripture and added some final personal remarks, focusing again upon that critical passage in John's gospel which records Jesus' conversation with Mary and Martha following the death of their brother, Lazarus.

"Lord," Martha said to Jesus, "if you had been here, my brother would not have died...Jesus said to her, "Your brother will rise again." Martha answered, "I know he will rise again in the resurrection at the last day. Jesus said to her, "I am the resurrection and the life. He who believes in me will live, even though he dies. And whoever lives and believes in me will never die. Do you believe this?" "Yes, Lord," she told him, "I believe that you are the Christ, the Son of God, who was to come into the world."

(John 11: 21-27)

"Forasmuch as it hath pleased Almighty God in His great mercy to take unto Himself the soul of our dear brother and father and friend here departed: we therefore commit his body to the ground; earth to earth, ashes to ashes, dust to dust; in the sure and certain hope of the resurrection to life eternal through our Lord Jesus Christ; who shall change our corruptible body, that it may be like

319

unto His glorious body, according to the working of His mighty power whereby He is able to subdue all things unto Himself. Amen."

The committal service was over. Dad's ashes would soon join Dottie's in that small parcel of earth, under the only tiny tree in that section of the Pine Grove Cemetery. A bronze military plaque would later be added, to be placed in the ground in front of the stone, complete with permanent metal military jackets to sheath miniature cloth flags. Dad had smiled his broad Cheshire-Cat smile and said 'I love you.' Now he was a living memory under a cold slab of granite, engraved with the name 'Colman,' the only real, visible vestige of solidarity that we would ever again share. A rose may be a rose by any other name, but that stone, and that name, is the only place on earth that bears any direct personal relation to this New England son. Like the infamous and enigmatic Ethan Fromm of New England lore, that particular 'granite out-cropping' is a mere pinpoint of a wealth of vibrant, hidden history lying beneath the quiet surface. It is a place which still feels the frozen stillness of winter, warmth of summer sun, and the vibrancy and caress and comfort of spring breezes and the company of fresh flowers and life-sustaining color.

After the final prayer, and one final glance at the small dark opening in the frozen earth, the small remnant of survivors hurried into the warmth of the waiting vehicles and exited the cemetery. But before leaving, the funeral director took me aside.

"Mr. Colman, you did a fine job today. You paid a wonderful tribute to your Dad. He was a very special person. You know that he had spent the past several years helping me at the funeral home as a volunteer. Your Dad had a very special way of bringing comfort. He was always cordial; he always showed up in a suit and tie with a big smile; he was a real strengthening presence at the door. People always looked forward to seeing him. He always seemed to know what to say. Neither Bob nor I could have chosen a better person to have done what you have done today, or shared what you have shared today. Your presence here has truly been, well, shall I say, 'providential.' I have attended many such services in my many years here, but this has been one of the best, one of the most moving. Did you notice how the people lingered? They didn't seem to want to leave. They seem to have taken comfort from your every word. By the way, did you know that my own wife is buried in one of the same chambers in the morgue, just a few feet from where you stood to deliver your Dad's eulogy? I was standing there next to her while you spoke. She would have enjoyed listening to you, as I did. I have taken much of what you shared to heart. Thank you. Please don't be concerned about your father's burial. I will care for every detail. We will place your Dad's ashes in a small cylinder. They will be covered immediately. The stone will be placed over the spot very shortly. You are welcomed to return anytime. Please feel free to contact me for any reason."

"Thank you, sir, for your kind words. God has really sustained me through these days, as you know. My last days with Dad were difficult, but extraordinary. 'Good grief,' you might say. It was a reunion of sorts, and a real season of deep reconciliation. You are aware of my story, I believe. Dad and I had been separated since he left home in 1956. I was eight years old at the time. But those early years when Mom and Dad were still together yield precious memories. One of these days, when I feel inspired, I am going to write the entire story, or at least as much as I can possibly commit to print. Those ageless 'granite outcroppings,' you can imagine, still conceal an unfathomable wealth of mystery, some of which may never be unearthed.

Well, I've been at this business a long time," responded the director. I always try to keep an objective, professional air about such matters, but let me break protocol and tell you something today. Look around you at these weathered gravestones. Each one bears a name. Each one represents a long personal history. Like you said, in a very real sense, these are not just mute markers; these are 'living stones.' I believe that is the term you used. There are real people buried here. This is a virtual village of 'granite out-croppings' here. In my own opinion, there has to be more. The story isn't over. There will be reconciliation and redemption, for some, on the other side. What you said this morning has a ring of truth. Believe me, I know. I have seen too much of death not to believe in life."

"There are details, of course, that I will never know," I continued, "but isn't that always the case? Perhaps that is best. I suppose that there is nothing hidden that shall not some day be revealed. But our family history, culminating in Dad's own life, and our fractured relationship, is too rich to ignore. One day soon I shall recreate the unforgettable story of one New England son and his quest for reconciliation with an estranged father. Perhaps you are familiar with the poetry of the great Romanticist, William Wordsworth? In recent days, one of his shorter, but more elusive poems has been lingering near the front door of my mind:

> *My heart leaps us when I behold*
> *A rainbow in the sky:*
> *So was it when my life began,*
> *So is it now I am a man,*
> *So be it when I shall grow old*

Or let me die!
The child is father of the man:
And I could wish my days to be
Bound each to each by natural piety."

"Mr. Colman, I cannot tell you what a pleasure and inspiration it is for me to have known you and your Dad. You are very much like him, you realize, a chip off the old block, you might say, no disrespect intended. Please, here's my card. Please don't hesitate to call if I can ever be of service..."

I smiled. *How would I call if I should ever be in need of his services?* It reminded me of a day some years earlier on a trip back to New England. My wife and I had passed a very old cemetery, when I happened to notice an old worn sign on the stone gate that read *Entrance Only.*

"Thank you, you have been a wonderful help to both Dad and me. I am very grateful, in particular, for your having pulled some strings to arrange for the Marine color guard. I was delightfully surprised and deeply moved. It was perfect."

****

After the committal service, and a sedate, collective sigh of relief, the non-descript little caravan of cars exited the cemetery grounds and proceeded down South Willow to the Queen City bridge and Blake's restaurant, a small, friendly establishment on Manchester's west side. The 'back room' there had been prepared to receive the Colman clan. The tables had been placed side-by-side, and extra chairs brought in to accommodate the crowd of about twenty-five souls. There was little room to walk, but the environment was warm and friendly, just as Dad would have liked it. The soft pallor of sadness had since lifted,

323

and there was a subtle sense of levity, even laughter, presided over by Uncle Bill who was still trying desperately to drown his own grief with a chorus of comedic remarks and obnoxious expressions. Sure enough, upon entering the tiny room, Bill opened his eyes wide, hugged all the ladies, and said, "Did you miss me?" He then dropped his over-sized dentures for the doting crowd. I could see Dad's semi-embarrassed smile and suppressed laughter. "That's your Uncle Bill," he would have said.

The meal was nothing fancy, but it was adequate: fried chicken, boiled vegetables (carrots, if I recall), heaps of mashed potatoes and thick gravy, mounds of hot dinner rolls and slabs of fresh melted butter. It wasn't the Ritz, but it was sumptuous and plentiful. The servers were young and efficient, and took Uncle Bill's flirting and disingenuous outbursts in gracious stride. I fully expected him to slap one of the girls on the backside, but he knew better. Aunt Earlene, in her quiet, loving way, kept him on a short, flexible, invisible leash. She would have thrashed him later, and confined him to the shed, or taken away his allowance.

Just before the meal had been served, Dottie approached me discretely and informed me that the expenses for the dinner would be covered by a small amount of money that remained in Dad's savings account. Otherwise, I had no knowledge of Dad's meager financial resources. As far as I had known, he had effectively depleted his account when he had sent a generous sum to help cover the cost of our daughter, Esther's, wedding reception back home in Illinois a few weeks earlier. Dad had also given me a very modest sum during the months just prior to his death to help defray travel expenses.

After Dad's death that night at the Veterans Affairs Medical Center (formerly known as the Veterans' Administration Hospital), I had retrieved the old worn Black Bible (bound with black electrical tape) that he had been using. The Bible had belonged to his father, my grandfather, the late Sumner Chase. I also retrieved Dad's Veterans of Foreign Wars cap, bearing a variety of military pins, along with a pair of miniature paratrooper wings from World War II, and his black, weathered wallet.

***

The day before I left Manchester, Uncle Bill and Aunt Earlene invited me out to dinner at a small steak house in Bedford, across the street from what used to be the Bedford Roller Skating Rink, the same kind of rink that Mom and I frequented back under the pines at what was once Pine Island Park. But few who live there now even remember the excitement and innocent revelry associated with such magical haunts.

When Uncle Bill started to flirt with, and insult the female server, I hardly knew where to look, though I am not entirely innocent of such harmless behavior myself.

"Hey, how yah do'in, sweetheart? You sure looked a lot younger and lighter the last time I saw yah!" belched Bill.

Allowing for a slight pause and for the unpleasant discharge of Uncle Bill's salacious comments to dispel, and without the slightest change of expression, or any evidence of offense, the woman looked calmly at Aunt Earlene.

"Where did you find this piece of trash?"

"In the dumpster outside," Aunt Earlene responded with just a twinge of shame and a slight smile.

"Maybe you should throw him back in while there's still time, though I doubt that they would take him. They're pretty particular about the garbage they collect these days."

Uncle Bill didn't seem offended either. He was loving it.

"You're a lot older and uglier than the last time you dragged your tired ass in here. I thought you'd be dead by now, or at least in a suitable coma..."

I couldn't believe what I was hearing. I've been known to push the limit before, but this was way out of line. And then, just as abruptly as it had started, it ended. They all started laughing, including Aunt Earlene. I was the only one who was duped and poker-faced. The joke was on me. Come to find out, they indulged in this little exchange every time they came there. It was rehearsed and expected.

"How you doing, Bill? It's been a while. What's the matter? You been on the lamb?"

"You look more beautiful than ever," Uncle Bill returned. If it wasn't for Earlene, I would have married you a long time ago."

"In your dreams. Now, what'll it be?"

"We want your best steaks, all around. And believe it or not, you can give me the tab this time! Oh, this is my nephew from Chicago. *And with a slight strain in his voice and a faint discoloration of red in his blanched face...*My brother, Bob, just passed away. Peter came to do the funeral, and what a funeral it was. Bob was a great guy, the greatest big brother a guy could ever have. So, the meal is on me tonight, no holds barred."

The woman expressed her condolences. It was probably the only serious moment that she and Uncle Bill had ever known. She later returned with drinks and food. But then, quiet surprisingly, Uncle Bill (whom I hadn't seen in more than thirty years) leaned on his bony elbows and looked straight into my eyes.

"Peter, when I die, I want my funeral to be just like Bob's."

That had been Uncle Bill's way of acknowledging the importance of what he had experienced, though he rarely, if ever, even intimated that of the seriousness of issues relating to personal faith. But for some reason that night, he had appeared vulnerable.

"I have faith, you know, Peter. I know I'm always fooling around, but I do believe. Heaven knows that I'm far from perfect, but what you said today was, well, pretty serious. I don't take it lightly. When the time comes for me to go, I want you to be there; I want it to be just like it was with Bob."

That was Uncle Bill's way of paying a compliment *and* going on record of admitting that he was a flawed human being in need of love and forgiveness too.

"I understand, Uncle Bill. I'm thankful that I was able to be here for Dad and the family. I feel honored and humbled. Dad and I had some pretty unique moments together. He told me things he had never shared before, things about himself and the war. I asked him some pretty pointed questions, and he answered me as best he could. And he told me he loved me.

"Bob was a good brother, Peter. But he wasn't perfect, you know, not as perfect as everyone seemed to think." And then with just a slight hesitation, and lowering his voice, Bill leaned toward me across the small table. Your Dad had a tryst with some girl after the war, while he was in California. He felt terrible afterward. He spent the whole night on a hill overlooking the ocean, crying."

Somehow, this news surprised, but did not shock me. Dad had never admitted to any such thing. Nor do I believe that he ever shared that shameful incident with anyone else after returning home. But I am sure that he made his peace with God, and had been forgiven. He never told me about it. Perhaps he was too proud, or was trying to spare me the pain, or he was afraid that I would think less of him. It would have been good if he had told me, I suppose. At least, as a young man growing up without a father to discipline and instruct me, and to guide me through those awkward adolescent years, I would have known what to expect. Or perhaps not. Perhaps the knowledge of my father's weakness and failure as a courageous young Marine, and new convert to boot, would have created fear and a failure of confidence. Or as Chaucer wrote in the *Prologue* to his *Canterbury Tales*, "If gold rusts, what will iron do?"

In any case, that was so much water under the bridge, as they say. That was along time ago, in a land far away. And Dad was gone. Sins committed and forgiven should be left buried in the past and forgotten. I suspected that there were many such sins, on both sides, and in every generation. Each of us has sufficient sins and regrets of our own to be castigating and condemning others for theirs.

Sure, Dad was not perfect, but he was forgiven, and he deserved to be allowed to rest in peace.

***

I was exhausted. I returned to Uncle Jim's that last night tired, but relieved. I had done all I could as a son. The moments I had spent with Dad were precious. Priceless. I wasn't sure that I would ever be able to explain to my family exactly what I had experienced and felt, but I would try. It would be even more difficult to explain anything to Uncle Jim, though I am sure that he understood more than he would ever care to admit.

New England soil is very difficult to cultivate. It is a rocky, resistant soil. It is even more difficult to prepare the terrain, to remove the ever-present rocks, and to plant and sustain a viable yield. Wild high-bush blueberries, as do various species of wild-flowers and mushrooms, do well in some regions. Small crops of corn and potatoes, and other low-yield vegetables do well, but require good fertilizer and constant care. Strawberries do well in time, but tend to be small. Like the native soil, New Englanders possess deep veins of rich sub-surface values and beliefs, most of which have been cultivated from generations of hardship and stubborn determination. They are weary and suspect of foreign prodigies and new-fangled products. They are pragmatists at heart. As a rule, they have no tolerance for superficial talk, but are honest and respectful of hard work and time-tested truths. It wouldn't be easy to try to talk to Uncle Jim about the funeral. No one would want a lesson in philosophy, or a sermon. Jim would just want to know whether I had gotten the job done, and gotten it done well.

Jim was sitting quietly in his recliner in the living room when I came through the door that night. He didn't

329

move or speak. I put my books on the table and hung my jacket on the back of one of the dining room chairs. An assortment of well-cleaned, labeled antique bottles was spread out on the table. Jim was a professional collector and *connoisseur* of anything and everything resembling an antique bottle or fruit jar, as was his apprentice nephew. I said hello, and quietly began to pack my suitcase on the floor near the television.

"Well, how did it go?" he asked.

"It went well, Uncle Jim. Real well. The whole family was there. We held the service in the same building as we did when I came for Dottie's funeral last November. The service was brief, but very moving. And there was a Marine color guard. I wasn't expecting that. It was very emotional, but God gave me strength. We had a small committal service and went to Blake's on the west side for dinner. I guess Dad had just enough money left to cover the cost of the meal. *Now that I think of it, it wouldn't have mattered. We could have all paid for our own in such situations.* I'm tired, but relieved."

"Well, that's good. You did well. At least the ordeal is over. You won't have to be traveling back and forth now. Your Aunt Joyce and I have been waiting all day. We didn't know if you would be having supper. Joyce had prepared something and put it in the oven if you're hungry…"

"Thanks, Uncle Jim, but I'm fine. Thanks for waiting up for me. And thanks for letting me stay with you. This has been a great help. I always enjoy coming here to be with you."

In the meantime, Aunt Joyce had come in from the back bedroom where she had been watching television. When she saw me, she broke into un-English-like tears of emotion and hugged me.

"Oh, Peter, did everything go OK? Are you alright? You must be exhausted and hungry. I've got some food in the oven..."

"No, thank you, Aunt Joyce, I'm fine. I ate after the funeral, just a couple of hours ago."

"I made some hot tea. Would you like a cup of hot tea?"

"Yes, that would be fine, Aunt Joyce."

Moments later, Aunt Joyce came back into the living room with an English porcelain teacup brimming with freshly boiled orange pekoe tea with honey and a dish of assorted cookies and candies, all on a tray table, followed by a small dish of large, fresh seedless red grapes and other pieces of fruit.

"Thank you, Aunt Joyce. This all looks so good."

"Well," asked Uncle Jim, "How did your sermon go? You kept it brief, I hope."

"Brief enough," I responded, without going into too much detail. "I talked a bit about Dad's experience in the military, and a few memories from childhood. I shared some of Dad's favorite stories and verses from the Bible, and added a few of my own. I tried to bring comfort to the family too. That's what's important."

"Yup, there's not much you can say when a person is gone that hasn't been said already. I still can't understand how you could talk so much about religion. I don't understand how anyone could come home from the war talking about God as much as your father did, and then get up and leave you and your mother, but I guess there's an explanation for that too. Whatever. I'm sure you did what you could. You certainly did more for your father than he ever did for you...Glad you're back. You'd better get to sleep. I'll help you with the cot. Don't worry about the alarm. I'll be up early. I don't need one. I'll get you up. Your flight leaves at 6:15. We'll need to leave here by 4:30 or so. It will only take us seven minutes or so. Hey, you've had a rough day. Say goodnight to Joyce. She won't be up when you leave. Get some sleep. I'll see you bright and early."

It wouldn't sound like it, if one didn't know my Uncle Jim, but behind the brittle veneer of every word was a generous heart of concern.

"Dad wasn't perfect Jim, and neither am I."

"That makes three of us," he responded.

"There are some things that I will never know," I continued; some things that I will never be able to figure out. Perhaps it's better that way. But we do the best we can do given the circumstances we have.

"I guess you're right," he said, as he slowly lifted his withered, but yet agile frame from the soft recliner. "I'll see you in the morning, Pete. Sleep well."

Jim was like a father to me. I loved him dearly. Though his hide was thick and tough, his bark was far

332

worse than his bite. I could tell that he, too, was relieved. And he was proud.

***

The return flight home from Manchester was blissfully charged, as if a sweet burden had been lifted. I felt as if I were in weightless suspension. I was in mid-flight, traveling hundreds of miles per hour over faceless landscapes, but my tired feet were firmly planted on the floor. I was going home. I would be in my familiar classroom by 6:15 the next morning. Everything, and nothing, would ever be quite the same again. My students would be asking me about my trip, and about my Dad. I would share what I could, but little more. I would have to save the detail for the book, and for another day. Back to the real world. Or was that the one I had just left behind? In any case, it would be good to be 'back home,' to be back with my wife of thirty-five years, back to the old 'farmstead' in the northern wooded Chicago suburbs. Chicago was a beautiful metropolis by night, or by day. O'Hare International Airport was second to none with respect to its sheer magnitude and multitudinous maze of traffic. But, I thought to myself, as we circled for the final descent: *'Not everything that glitters is gold.' Not even O'Hare could hold a proverbial candle to that ubiquitous red beacon on the hill behind Uncle Jim and Aunt Joyce's cottage overlooking old Grenier Field.*

Postscript

*Every mother in the natural world bears her own
young, but it is the* word *that bears its own
mother...*

(Mande proverb)

Sometimes the very effort of self-exploration and
self-expression yields a rich trove of hidden insight and
inspiration. In some cultures, the exercise of oral
expression is a very real and revelatory component in the
on-going drama of human relationships, individual and
collective. The 'word' cannot be separated from reality.
The more one probes and seeks to give expression to the
spectrum of human experience, the clearer one sees, and
the closer one approaches the source.

When the patriarch of the Colman family left the
shores of South-Hampton, England, in April of 1635, he
was thirty-three years of age. What his relationship with his
father was in his hometown of Wiltshire cannot be known.
Whether he ever saw his birth-father again after arriving in
the New World is a matter of speculation. He was a man of
industry, a respected husbandman by trade. Yet for some
reason known only to him, Thomas failed to discharge his
duties. The livestock entrusted to his care were confiscated,
and the resources in his trust redistributed to their owners.
It is assumed that he left the fledgling colony on the shores
of the Parker River (Newbury) in relative ignominy, and in
an impoverished state.

There is a thread of ambiguity running through Thomas Colman's tainted legacy. The once-honorific (howbeit humble) pilgrim husbandman and entrepreneur appears to have been banished from his new home. To remain would have been self-deprecating, and perhaps humiliating. Thomas was too proud a man to allow a minor misunderstanding to restrict his freedoms and quench his independent spirit. He sometime thereafter forged a potentially fruitful, but infelicitous partnership with the infamous Rev. Bachiler, who, in turn, managed to forge a less-than-commendable record of controversy with the ecclesiastical authorities in England. It seems certain, from a careful scrutiny of the record, that the noxious root which catapulted the good Reverend Bachiler to acquire the dubious title of the 'unforgiven Puritan' of Winnacunnet (later known as Hampton, on the shores of New Hampshire) was, in fact, his inordinate attraction to, and insatiable affection for such young women in his community who happened to drift too close to the treacherous shores of his carnal appetites. Why Thomas would choose to keep company with a man of such notorious and dubious character remains a mystery. Perhaps misery loves company, as the saying goes. Neither is it surprising to learn that both Colman and Bachiler, though mentioned in some early documents as having been included among the founding settlers of ancient Winnacunnet, are curiously totally absent in others. One can only assume that the reputations of neither man were sufficient to commend them to the community's list of upright citizens. The fact that Thomas Colman was later influential in bringing accusations of witchcraft against the unfortunate soul known as Eunice 'Goody' Cole, also of Hampton, would seem to be a discredit to any semblance of dignity, propriety, or personal moral integrity he may have been tempted to claim. Another case of the pot calling the kettle black. In any case, superstition prevailed over reason, and over righteousness, and the poor woman was found to be guilty, lost her modest estate, along with her estranged husband (who tried in vain to intervene in her behalf), and spent the rest of her lonely life in a Boston prison.

Thomas's illustrious career culminated in his having removed from Hampton and migrated to the small island off the New England coast that would later be known as Nantucket, where he obtained the posthumous distinction of 'first settler.' It was there that the patriarch of the Colman family died and was buried. Why he went there is unknown. Why he stayed is equally uncertain. Whether he had ever returned to his native England is unlikely.

There were certain exceptions to the ignoble Colman legacy. The most outstanding was a certain Dudley Colman (1745-1797) who had served with honor in one of General Washington's legendary regiments during the Revolutionary War. Dudley was a graduate of Harvard.

***

In retrospect, and in stark contrast to his forgotten predecessor and namesake, my great-great-grandfather of Auburn, New Hampshire, also named Thomas, was, like the majority of his robust offspring, known to be an honest, hard-working man. After the Civil War, the Colmans, who had settled on the shores of the Massebesic, lived close to the land, without notoriety or celebrity status, which, had it been offered them, they would have politely eschewed. They worked the farm and the mill, raised strong liters of children, feared God, and behaved the best they knew how toward their neighbors, as the Good Book instructed.

There was one exception to the tainted, but nonetheless honest Colman legacy in the turbulent current of recent generations. My grandfather, Sumner Chase

Colman, and his bride, Nellie Moy, also of Auburn, had, like my own father and mother enjoyed a few early years of marital bliss, before parting ways, due, apparently to my grandmother's infidelity. Her own four sisters also married hard-working men of Auburn, and led relatively happy, peaceful lives. But Nellie's own father had eaten sour grapes, and the children's teeth had been set on edge. The sins of the fathers seemed to have been visited upon the children. Nellie's congenial, but reprobate sire, old 'grandpa Moy, of Auburn, had also been raised 'down on the farm,' but he had the incurable habit of molesting his neighbor's pretty daughter's and wives. He was a notorious womanizer. His raucous wanderings from the confines of the Moy farm were only curtailed when, after having been banished by his good wife for a period of six tortuous months, he was put on punitive probation, and finally allowed to return, having been forced by his beneficent bride of forty-plus years to renew his vows of marital fidelity under punishment of death by neglect and/or starvation. The maverick thread of infidelity and unscrupulous moral behavior was sufficiently deleterious to compromise the entire rugged fabric of an otherwise strong and salubrious Colman history.

The story of my own father, Robert E. Colman, has already been told. His story, too, reveals a curious, almost contradictory vein in an otherwise unproductive and superficial family substrata. While his experience was laced with imperfection and an inordinate series of impurities, which, to be sure, are far from uncommon in the history of the race, there exists, nonetheless, in this same vein, the obvious presence of uncommon redeeming forces. It would seem that I, too, as the only surviving son, though not without imperfections, to be sure, have been the fortunate exception to the rule in the on-going drama.

The story is still being written.

Somehow, the separation of forty-four years from my father was incapable of severing that fragile thread of affection, admiration and pride by which I had managed to remain irrevocably attached to the infamous Colman legacy. Indeed, it may very well be that, due to pervasive benevolent forces well beyond the purview of my own flawed condition, I have become a significant healing link in a fragile, redemptive chain. In this regard, I can claim nothing that I would presume to describe as meritorious. I had inherited a godly, though far from sinless heritage. I had been the beneficiary of a loving, though equally imperfect, God-fearing, grass-roots New England family, including a loving mother and her stubborn, but selfless brother, my affectionate uncle James Rogers, also of Manchester. Like the proverbial leper seen dancing in the middle of a crowd, a leper who could have only been present due to a surfeit of friends, so I, too, without any reasonable 'claim to fame,' or inherent goodness, have been found to be dancing.

Not all is evident. But some things are undeniable. Not all circumstances and situations are explicable, like the wind, whose presence and direction is discernable, but whose source and sovereign influence defy any reasonable explanation. In my particular case, the winds, though sometimes contrary and unpredictable, were nonetheless favorable: A nineteen-year-old Marine has a dramatic conversion experience under fire on a remote island in the Pacific. That experience reordered his universe forever. And though one dare not presume to second-guess Fate, it is no mystery that the same young paratrooper would have been elsewhere in that same universe, or nowhere at all, had he not failed to tie his one boot, again, while in danger of his very life. That small mishap, or oversight, took him effectively out of harm's way and back home again to relative safety. And although whatever forces conspired to spare his life to that point proved to be less than efficacious *vis-à-vis* his Christian vow to protect the indissoluble bond of conjugal love to which he had committed himself before a sacred altar, he *did* keep the faith over the long haul; and he *did* manage to somehow, at least in the beginning, and with the help of his young bride, inculcate in their only son, small, but viable seeds of that same rock-hard faith. His failure to be a faithful father to his son did not preclude his son's efforts, however imperfect, to be a faithful son. And forty-four years later, while the so-called 'prodigal father' lay on his death-bed, the son returned home and embraced him with open arms.

***

In the late summer of 2007, I returned to the old Colman homestead at 1 Morse Road in Dunbarton, New Hampshire. Its present occupants, a gracious, aging, but robust couple, welcomed me in. When I grasped the old steel shed-door latch, the same latch that I had once pushed open as a child of three years, it was like shaking the firm hand of an old friend. The wide oak boards, which comprised the country kitchen (now remodeled) still creaked softly as if to whisper welcome to a lost son. The old staircase leading to the upstairs bedroom with the same slanted window, had a fresh coat of paint, but they were the same fourteen stairs where I had played and dreamt as a child. The small carved numbers over the original 'Portsmouth Door,' of the Colman house, read 1822. The house was built by a certain David Eliot, (circa 1820). I have often wondered whether this same New England patriot was related to the 17th-century Puritan missionary to the Algonquin Indians. As the Eliot lineage is legendary in the early history of the New England colonies, some distant connection is more than plausible.

But there is one final detail. There was at least one clergyman in the long New England history of the Colman clan, Rev. Henry Colman (1785-1849). In a twist of irony and providence, my own father, Robert Everett Colman, had also aspired to become a preacher and missionary, to which a few scattered sermon notes and scribbled references in his old black Bible attest. But his dream was not to materialize. Quite contrary to all circumstances which would have naturally discouraged such a venture, his only son was to become a student and graduate of the former Missionary Training Institute at Nyack, New York, an institution which had the modest distinction of being the first such Bible college in the nation founded exclusively for the training and deployment of Christian missionaries to remote lands across the globe. Not coincidentally, Bob Colman, who, by the unfortunate dislocation of events in his marriage, was absent during the formative and most fruitful years of his son's pilgrimage as a pastor and missionary of the Christian gospel, found himself to be in critical need of his son's comforting presence in the final days of his earthly sojourn. His only son, Peter, having been ordained as a minister of the Christian gospel, and having served fourteen years as a missionary in West Africa, was now teaching high school English in a northwestern Chicago suburb when the phone rang. It was my Uncle Bill:

"Peter, you'd better come right away. Your Dad is not well. We don't think he's going to survive the week."

I booked the first flight to Manchester and started to write his story.

My story.

"Mr. Bachelor, did you say? My name is Peter. Peter Colman."

The liquid, opalescent glass at the base of the aging windowpane has gathered to even greater breadth and thickness, ever so minutely, in recent years. Though understandably fragile, the glass is increasingly clear. It still bears the warmth and breathes the freshness of each new day. It still stays firm and braces with imperceptible courage and a clear sense of duty and gratefulness the onslaught of winter winds and the relentless force of the changing seasons. That same old window stands watchful vigil in the upstairs bedroom of the old Dunbarton house. The tree is gone, but the child is grown. The child who watched his hero climb on withered limbs toward heaven, and back again, is now a man.

The father of the man.